TWO SUMMERS

TWO SUMMERS

Nixon and Trump by Greyhound Bus

Tim Albert

Elbow Publishing

Also by this author

Mostly We Had it Good: a baby boomer's journey

Medical Journalism: the writer's guide

Winning the Publication Game (4 editions)

An A-Z of Medical Writing

Write Effectively: a quick course for busy health professionals

To my travel companions Geoffrey and Morris.
And to Barbara of course

Contents

THE BIT IN THE MIDDLE

BACK EAST

Preface

Just over a year ago I was struggling to write a brief introduction to this book. At the time I thought we were in the middle of a global pandemic; I didn't realise we were barely at the start. Also at the time I was trying to reconcile my long-standing affection for America – and Americans – with some of the things I had seen and the attitudes I had discovered over the previous summer. Particularly disturbing was the intractable political divide, presided over by Trump whose re-election most people told me was looking inevitable. With a few misgivings, I concluded my Preface then on a hopeful note: that the kindness shown to me by so many Americans would somehow see the country through.

What a difference a year makes. In the United States we have seen a pandemic slewing out of control, a re-ignition of racial conflict and hatred, a bitterly contested presidential race, and a stolen election or foiled insurrection depending on one's tribal allegiance. As I write, the drama continues as America's once vaunted democratic structures are mired in bitter stalemates (and plenty of litigation). My confidence that the generosity of American people will find a way through is wearing thin.

What is clear now is how extraordinarily lucky I was in the year I chose for my adventure. That American summer of 2019 will be remembered as a time when we could connect with other human beings without a second thought (and not through a mask); it will also be remembered, with hindsight, as a time when the roots of the current upheavals were hiding in plain view. It was a privilege to have travelled through such interesting times – and to have done so by bus. I hope you will enjoy coming with me on my journey.

Tim Albert
Leatherhead, June 2021

Acknowledgements

As you will discover, I was not in the best shape to undertake this trip, and I owe a huge debt of gratitude to those who supported me. Marguerite Pease deserves a special mention for asking the question that set the idea of this trip rolling around my head. In the months that followed, several people helped to get me physically and mentally fit enough to sit on a bus for up to twelve hours a day: Dr James Steinhardt, Nicole Walker, Philip Silk, Andrew Harris, Sue Buckland and Lisa McEwan. Several others added support and advice, notably Michael O'Donnell, Jane Smith, Mary Banks, Tim Duggan, Nick Bamford, Dudley Buchanan, Jackie Connor and Martha Irvine.

Caroline and Robert McCowen lent me their treasured copy of the 1969 BUNAC handbook, and Annie and Ben Donovan-Aitken and Nick and Nicola Hurman chased down and bought for me a 1968 (first edition) Michelin guide to New York. Julian Mildren patiently nursed my technological skills and equipment into the 21st century, and thanks to the systems he had set up was able to be at my electronic elbow throughout my journey.

The success of the trip itself owes much to those who offered me lodgings, meals, information and conversation. Not all are identified fully in the text, and it would be wrong to blow their cover by listing them here. For the record, those who are mentioned, often with job descriptions, are mostly those who spoke to me in an official capacity, usually by appointment. To all and equally I offer my heartfelt thanks.

Many people kindly nursed me through the final stages. Those who read full drafts were Sarah Peskin, Ric Papineau, Esther Ripley, Deborah Takiff Smith, Jon Ford, Nick Stobbs, Christine Gowing, Alex Williamson and Michael Hampson; their views were enormously helpful. Others fact-checked specific items, and (as usual) saved me from making some embarrassing errors. I am sure mistakes still lurk, so please let me know if you spot them and I will correct them at the next opportunity.

Thanks to Caroline Petherick for the editing, Sally Ellis for the typesetting, Su Jones and Paddy McEntaggart for the cover design and map, and Llia Apostolou for guiding me through the e-marketing. I am especially grateful to Elizabeth Gowing and Rob Wilton of Elbow Publishing who, for a second time, have not just backed one of my books but also provided sound publishing advice, invaluable and detailed textual comments and (most importantly) large portions of encouragement.

All the above will agree that the I owe the biggest thanks of all to my wife Barbara who, when she agreed to marry me in 1980, was blissfully unaware of her additional future roles as counsellor, nurse, financial controller, critic, proofreader, morale booster, proofreader again, link with reality, provider of useful relatives – and of course sometime fellow traveller. It goes without saying that without her constant support this book would not have happened.

Notes on language

This is a book about America written by an Englishman, and therefore raises some tricky issues of spelling and terminology. I have written unashamedly in British English, and while I have tried to limit the use of British expressions, I have not exorcised them altogether. The two styles of spelling were particularly troublesome, however, and I ended up using American spellings in proper names (Pasadena Senior Citizens Center) and elsewhere British spellings (the centre).

Since 1969 one or two words that were used routinely (such as 'negro') have quite rightly been rejected as offensive. However, when I have used those words in my original diary I feel it would be dishonest to change them now, and they appear here, occasionally, for historical accuracy.

The Golden Jubilee Greyhound Bus Tour, 2019

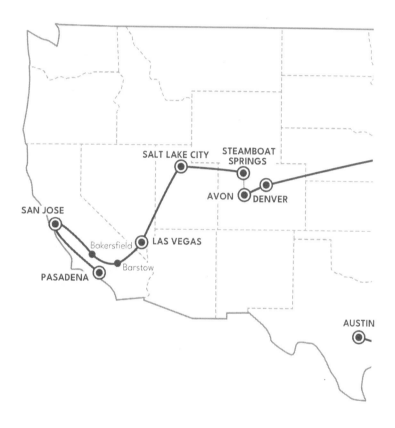

EAST

1. The idea that didn't go away

I was with my dental hygienist, Marguerite, when the idea crept up on me. It was May 2018, and as I was settling myself down onto the chair she lobbed me a deceptively gentle question:

'Are you planning any overseas trips for the near future?'

'Maybe America next year,' I replied. 'For a golden wedding party.'

She made approving noises, tipped me back and started to give my teeth the full pressure-washer treatment. I countered the tedium by counting the years back to when the golden couple had wed. That took me to 1969 – a year that for me holds enormous significance.

It was the year I'd had my Trip of a Lifetime. As a 22-year-old social sciences student, I spent my summer in the United States. For two months I travelled – and slept – on Greyhound buses, clocking up 12,000 miles. For the third month I stayed at a YMCA in California, working as an intern on the local paper. I came away with a set of cuttings that oiled my way onto one of the few journalism courses in Britain, which in turn set me up for a lifetime of writing, then teaching about writing. This experience changed my life …

As Marguerite continued her buffing I continued to reminisce. We baby boomers had been brought up watching American shows on our early black and white TVs. We'd followed the Lone Ranger as he and Tonto threaded their horses among giant cactuses and through massive mountains. We'd roared with delight at the social gaffes of the Hillbillies, a simple family from the Ozarks who found oil on their land and moved to Beverley Hills. We'd marvelled when lawyer Perry Mason finally found the crucial piece of evidence that would save his client from the electric chair.

Travelling to America, I'd imagined, would take me into a world of long cars and towering buildings, gorgeous vistas, beautiful girls with glossy hair and gleaming teeth, and fast-talking gun-toting cops. (I glossed over the possibility of robbers.)

I started to plan a trip for summer 1969. The planning took me over a year, during which time the Olympics were rocked by Black Power salutes,

Apollo 8 circled the moon, and violence broke out at the Democratic Party convention in Chicago. President Nixon succeeded President Johnson.

When I finally got to the USA, I sailed off Long Island at sunset, gazed at the Grand Canyon and Niagara Falls at sunrise, rode a horse in Texas, marvelled at the wasteful opulence of the Houston Astrodome, swam in two oceans, and saw my first ever shopping centre in Washington DC. I tasted food the like of which I had never tasted before, and marvelled at the quantities. I returned with a love of America and Americans (and, reader, a decade later I married one).

Still in my dental chair I started to wonder how the memories were so fresh – and put it down to the fact that, for one of the few times in my life I'd kept a diary. And I have it still: 30,000 words in an elaborate style, over one and half spiral-bound exercise books. On top of that I still have six boxes of 35 mm colour slides ...

It was at that moment when a dangerous notion slammed into my brain: why not mark the golden jubilee by going back and doing it again?

My unique collection of contemporary records would give me plenty of material for a book. As I travelled the country again, I could compare Nixon's America with that of Trump's. I could also compare how travel in general – and bus travel in particular – have changed. And look at the possibility that I too have changed.

It was a perfect storm of an idea, the kind that makes you say: 'Shit! I can't possibly *not* do that.'

I left Marguerite with a smile on my face. It was of course an unusually sparkling smile.

The smile quickly faded. Within days I was asking myself whether trying to repeat the trip of a lifetime was the plan of an ageing fool.

In 1969 'I sailed off Long Island at sunset, gazed at the Grand Canyon at sunrise...

I was now 72, not 22. My 1969 diary has as its hero a young man bounding with energy, needing little sleep, showing little fear (even of heights), and snatching meals (unhealthy ones at that) whenever he can. Apart from a smattering of morning headaches (clearly caused by drinking and chatting the previous night), my only reported medical problem came directly from riding the buses and was what I described in my diary (fairly often, it must be said) as a 'sore arse'.

Not surprisingly, half a century of life has left its mark. I have got used to comfortable beds, regular food, the companionship of marriage, door-to-door travel in comfortable cars and on occasions (particularly work-related) flying in the more comfortable sections of a plane. My bones are definitely not as pliable as they were, my muscles less strong and my eyesight not as acute. Five years after my trip I developed a nasty disease – ulcerative colitis – which is now less troublesome than in recent years, but still means that access to toilets looms larger in my life than it would for most people. About ten years ago I developed a severe allergy to wasp stings and started carrying Epipens.

As I have changed, so too has modern travel. Back In 1969 I bought a single pass for all my journeys, and I used coin-guzzling long-distance phone calls and a network of *postes restantes* to make all my in-country arrangements. I took photos with a Pentax camera and had to wait until I got back home before they were developed. I wrote my diary with a ball point pen and borrowed typewriters on which to write my letters home.

These skills were now hopelessly outdated. The tasks I would need to do – writing, storing, researching, reading, booking hotels, finding bus routes, hailing Ubers, taking photographs, tweeting, liaising with Airbnb hosts, writing home, checking on the weather, keeping up with the news on two continents – are now all done electronically. As someone who still used a mobile phone for conversation only, I had a lot of catching up to do, in terms of both equipment and skills.

The final question was whether America would still be a good place to visit. During the first few weeks after my epiphany, Harvey Weinstein had been accused of rape, 70 former US attorneys had protested at the separation of migrant children at the border, and Starbucks had closed all its branches for a day for staff racial sensitivity training. Three mass shootings – in a school, an arts centre and a newspaper – had left 16 people dead.

Viewed from England, public discourse in America seemed increasingly bitter. My American friends and relatives didn't help: 'I must say, you are brave to visit while we are under the tyranny of Cheeto head,' wrote one. 'Crazy Times,' wrote another. 'All the players and the details make my head spin.' And a third: 'Still no joy in Mudville as the world races to recapture its pre-World War One nationalistic/populist/nativist/fascistic fervour.'

Still the mantra kept going around my head: 'I can't possibly *not* do that'. I started some gentle planning. I bought some meditation tapes, hired a personal trainer and enrolled on a Pilates class.

I hit upon an important linguistic distinction: I would not *repeat* the trip – I would *revisit* it. I would be away for 60 nights, in two distinct phases. I had to take the bus; that was a given. But unlike last time I would not sleep on board, but stay in proper beds. I even persuaded my wife Barbara to do some of the trip with me, though I found she was curiously reluctant to travel on the buses.

I started to pore over my 1969 diary. I tracked down a couple of people who figured in it, and I noted down my opinions, adventures and even some restaurants that, according to Google, might still be open. One day, going through my papers, I found an unexpected bonus – a full set of letters home that my mother had painstakingly photocopied.

I started to flesh out a route: like last time I would go from New York down to Florida and across to Texas – and then, in the second leg, go from California across the country back to New York. I would hit most of the main cities I had visited then, but I would also make sure I went to smaller places less visited.

Then followed a wobble: some six months into the planning my health

Proud owner of two blow-up companions. Will they be needed on the buses?

teetered. My back seized up three times (once when helping Barbara up after she tripped over a pothole), and then my right shoulder locked. I started to feel nauseous and lost my appetite, with my weight suddenly dropping about a stone, which sucked me into a merry-go-round of mainly unpleasant medical tests. The doctors found nothing wrong, though made it clear that this was not the same as saying nothing *was* wrong.

The mantra – 'I have to do this' – kept recurring, and I persevered.

I practised madly with my new tablet (a Microsoft Go I called Geoffrey) and my new mobile phone (a Motorola I called Morris). I gave up on any thought of using my new Olympia digital voice recorder (Olive of course) and bought six pocket-size spiral notebooks from W H Smith instead. In what I thought was a masterpiece of anticipation, I purchased off the web two rubber blow-up companions – a neck cushion and a circular ring to sit on during longer bus trips – though I thought it best for these items to travel incognito.

One week before departure I paid an emergency visit to my dentist, not for another polish but for a troublesome tooth to be extracted. With two days to go I visited our local emergency centre after the bite of an unspecified insect started to swell alarmingly. As my good and implacably honest friend Jackie said to me: 'Let's face it. The really interesting thing about your trip is whether you're going to make it.'

2. Getting there – this time sober

Tuesday 1 July 1969

4.30 pm. Through gates at Heathrow. 5.20 called. 5.50 up.

8.30: Food. Stomach cramp. By this time everyone on flight is slewed, so what the hell if we crash! A feeling of timelessness …

9.30: Emerge from lavatory. See Greenland through the clouds (and the odd iceberg). Fantastic. Shock hostess by refusing a brandy. Notice sun is higher than when we left. Snack.

8.15 US time: coming down. Lots of water and hills. Circling – the houses, with their swimming pools, are so methodically arranged. I see my first four-leaf clover [motorway junction] – *from my 1969 diary*.

Monday 1 July 2019

3.00 pm US time: Barbara and I have been flying for some hours over the same desolate seascape that I noted in my 1969 diary. Now we are starting our descent over the same hills and houses and motorway junctions towards New York JFK. I have not drunk too much nor has my stomach cramped, though my neck and feet are feeling stiff. I am not as excited as I was back then; I would describe my mood as watchful. After all, it has been 50 years.

Last time I was young and it was a carnival: I travelled on a charter flight organised by BUNAC – the British Universities North America Club. It had branches in most British universities and it supplied information, travel and an invaluable handbook based on 3,000 information slips provided by members who had travelled the previous year. (I have been loaned a surviving copy for 1969, and now, swathed in bubble wrap, it is safely – I hope – in my bag in the hold.)

We were a homogeneous group then: young students for most of whom (myself included) this was their first long-haul flight. We were excited, but also a little scared. We wandered up and down the aisles, and congregated

'See Greenland through the clouds (and the odd iceberg). Fantastic' - my first transatlantic flight, 1969.

by the lavatories at the back to compare travel plans (with a little boasting wherever possible) and to pledge to meet up in improbable places.

The airline food was much better than our normal student fare, and was served to us with a full set of proper cutlery and an elegant menu written in French. To our amazement we were plied with free drinks – too many for me as it turned out. 'It was like a plane filled with the Students' Union,' recalls my friend Dudley, who also flew with BUNAC that year. (And it was a friend of hers who this year loaned me the BUNAC handbook.)

A half-century later the flight seems dull. We have become more blasé about air travel. Many of the passengers are in tight family groups (the summer holiday season has begun) and rarely chat to others at the back of the plane. We are enduring the flight, not enjoying it, though we assume those on the other side of the curtains are having a much better time than we are.

A young man sits across the aisle from me, wearing his earphones over his cap, munching steadily through bags of crisps he has brought onto the plane. For the full eight hours he gives me not even a suspicion of eye contact. Is this a foretaste of what's to come when I get to the buses?

The food isn't a patch on what I remember, and I have a running battle with the packaging, the first sign that my ageing body may find it hard to cope. My arthritic hands make me call for help to prise open the water bottle top. I get access to my pretzels only after I have smashed the package open with my fist. The jam for the scone spurts out of its little container onto my white polo shirt.

There is one improvement on last time: our progress through the formalities when we land. Last time I wrote: 'It took a long time to convince the immigration authorities that we were neither TB patients nor Communists – and that we had no fruit or x-rays.' This time we are through in half an hour, largely because the bulk of the processing is done by robots, to which we are directed by harassed staff with loud voices.

Once the robot has scrutinised my passport and taken a most unflattering picture, I am directed to an official. He asks why I plan to stay longer than my US-born wife, and when I tell him that I am about to relive my youthful bus trip he breaks out into the kind of smile normally reserved for children.

'Road tripping eh? You wouldn't catch me riding in anything other than my own car,' he says. 'Good luck.' He hands me my passport. I am in.

In 1969 our arrival in New York was well orchestrated by BUNAC, who as part of the deal provided travel from the airport plus a two-night stay in a hotel, where they organised lectures on finding work, race relations and 'the American personality'.

I wrote home:

> After a short drive, which left us [the bus-full of British students] full of admiration for the coach driver, we arrived at the Hotel McAlpin, within spitting distance of the Empire State Building. A few of us took a short walk around the block, despite temperatures of 85. Stopped at a coffee bar over the road and had an iced coffee (25c). Barman and cash register right out of a movie. Saw first cops, yellow cabs and steam coming out of the road. I knew I was no longer in GB.

Half a century later we have no coach to meet us, not even a shuttle bus. We take the Air Train to Jamaica; it is free to get on but costs $5 each to get off. We then take the Long Island Rail Road to Penn Station, a 20-minute journey. Barbara tells me we are passing through Queens. There are some tall glass-fronted blocks of offices and apartments, but generally the roads, shops, homes, yards and offices look much as I think I had left them 50 years ago. Graffiti lines the route, and the wide roads beyond are clogged with cars at a standstill. It's not an impressive welcome, but I suspect most railway lines into city centres give those kinds of views.

Penn Station is just a few blocks from the McAlpin hotel, where I stayed before. At the time it was fading (we slept four to a room), but when it was built in 1912 it had been the largest hotel in the world. At its peak it had

'I may not have been impressed by the Empire State Building in 1969. I am now.'

2,500 guests and 1,500 staff, the fashionable Marine Grill, and designated floors for males, females and night workers.

The hotel closed in 1976 and the building now houses 700 apartments. So I have booked at the Stewart Hotel nearby. It also has an early 20th century feel to it, with ornate bronze-relief elevator doors, and a massive lobby with a massive sofa looking rather like the maquette of a brutalist housing estate. We are given a larger room than we expected: it has a small kitchen which I immediately annex for my office.

We meet friends, Wolf and Rita, for dinner. Wolf is in real estate and believes that Trump will be re-elected: 'There's too much money riding on him for anything else to happen.' But he is despondent: 'He's chasing away foreign money – Russian, Chinese. Residential sales of homes over $4 million have dropped 10–15 per cent.'

We have artichokes and share a pizza at Macy's, then go across a few blocks to a Cuban-Chinese fusion restaurant. We try crispy pigs' ears; Rita has a rice dish and asks them to hold the Spam.

Barbara and I walk back. I may not have been impressed by the Empire State Building in 1969, but I am now. Artfully lit, it dominates the area, an icon.

Its surroundings don't do it justice, though: they are urban seedy, with tourists, late night shoppers at Gap and H&M, pretzel vendors, litter, and a pair of police officers queuing for a hot dog. There are also quite a few people settling down to sleep on the streets, one or two stripped to the waist in the heat, and one already asleep in full view inside an empty shop. Barbara says quietly that she has just seen a syringe lying on the pavement.

That night there is constant noise from the traffic below. I feel a little queasy, my shoulder aches, the farewell bite from the insect in my garden itches underneath its bandage, and the air conditioning is starting to do a number on my sinuses.

But my Golden Jubilee Greyhound Bus Tour is under way.

3. New York: memory lanes

Tuesday 2 July

My most immediate task is to get an American phone number. We go to a T-Mobile store, where two helpful staff members fix me up with a US SIM card for a month. Since my phone only has a slot for one card I give mine to Barbara, whose phone has two. It is an act that will have consequences.

But now I'm ready to explore New York – and could there be a better place to start a tour of America? And I have no less than three guides to steer me around the city today: Barbara, who lived here from 1968 until 1980 (when she came to England to marry me); a recently bought paper edition of the *Michelin Green Guide*; and the 1968 edition of what was then called just the *Michelin Guide*.

On my first trip I'd splashed out on the latter. It was the first edition and much admired as I walked the streets – and even once as I rode up in a lift. I parted with it many years ago, but for this trip four cousins have clubbed together to buy me another.

In 1969 the city blew me away: the height and range of the buildings, the sheer number of people and the energy and the noise they generated – and emporia of all kinds piled high with seductive products, many of which I was seeing for the first time. (In my diary I'd mused that it must be hard for a country to promote materialism and pack people off to a major war at the same time; in retrospect they didn't manage it for long.)

Now we have chosen to start with the city's most famous shopping street. 'One is never tired of strolling on Fifth Avenue,' says the 1969 guide. 'The striking views of the principal skyscrapers, the frequently-changing shop window displays, and the elegance and beauty of New York women contribute to make it one of the most fascinating walks in the city.' Will this still be true?

Half a century on, any comments on New York women would (quite rightly) be considered offensive. But I can comment on other changes, notably the opulent shop windows which, as we quickly notice, are fewer. Turning onto Fifth Avenue we come face to face with a listed building that used to be Altman's department store. It opened in 1906 and closed in 1969 and was, says Barbara, a grand establishment. The flags hanging outside today proclaim it as the Graduate Center for City University of New York.

Just over the road was where Ohrbachs used to be. It was at the other end of the shopping spectrum – 'a centre for bargains, where bejewelled matrons flock for copies of Paris styles', according to my 1968 guide. It closed in 1987 and a huge office block has soared in its place. We go in and talk to the lift operators: it is now occupied by 'business corporations', says one. His colleague talks of another building nearby that has been sold to a Chinese business.

'What will they do to it?' I ask. 'Modernise or vandalise?'

'Your generation *would* say that,' he replies.

A little further on we reach what used to be Lord & Taylor – 'Well out of my league,' says Barbara. It closed six months ago and is surrounded by hoardings, one with a Notice of Asbestos Abatement stuck on it. The clean-up is scheduled to take just under a year, it says.

We pass many more stores, but they are specialists such as Zara and Banana Republic. The British-owned Top Shop is there, but lies empty and forlorn.

We have a change in pace: at the public library – a 1911 Beaux Arts masterpiece according to the modern *Green Guide* – we go up some steps into a forecourt where we find a small table with the sign 'Public Poet'. Behind it sits Garrett Buhl Robinson, in brown shorts with a purple shirt

and a jaunty straw hat, along with copies of his books. He offers to declaim for us and seems surprised when we say yes. He duly declaims.

After his performance he says that he has been living in a hostel. I ask if he makes money. 'I am a poet,' he says, which kills that line of enquiry.

I buy one of his books, called *The Nobody*, which contains poems, prose and some rather good photographs of New York. 'To Tim and Barbara', he writes in a flamboyant hand. 'Everybody is a somebody because life is a miracle.' It costs me $20 – and there's no discount for a fellow writer.

I look at his writings later. They offer an alternative view to the razzmatazz of Fifth Avenue:

> We may call out for others
>
> But our desperate cries
>
> Are lost in the commotion
>
> Of traffic rushing by.

(from 'World of Strangers', in *The Nobody*, Garrett Buhl Robinson, G B Robinson, 2018)

Behind the library is Bryant Park. My 1968 *Michelin Guide* called it an 'oasis of coolness in overheated Manhattan'. A few weeks after I had flown home, it was the scene of a major Vietnam War protest. Later it became a centre for homeless people and drug dealing.

Now, tidied up, it buzzes again – 'one of the loveliest outdoor spots in the city' says the contemporary *Green Guide*. It is lunchtime and the space is packed with office workers and their take-out packages; there is even a Compost Concierge whose job it is to make sure that these are disposed of responsibly. Off to one side, 20 or so people sit and listen to a talk about de Quincy in a small area designated the Reading Room. A notice tells me that a knitting group is due to convene at 1.30.

Barbara and I continue our walk up Fifth Avenue. We look for signs of the Olivetti store, listed in my 1969 guide as exhibiting typewriters and adding machines against a background of Italian marble: 'You can try your hand at typing on a machine mounted on a post on the sidewalk,' it says.

We see no typewriter, though we are not surprised. I find an elderly doorman (well, he's my age) who tells me he also came to New York in 1969. He has no recollection of a typewriter shop even being here. Thus technologies flower and fade.

We continue up towards Central Park and the site of the former Bonwit Teller flagship store: 'sophisticated women's clothes and original accessories', according to the 1968 guide. 'A wonderful Art Deco store,' says Barbara.

I must have passed it in 1969 and would have looked up to see the highly rated panels depicting 'nearly nude' women dancing. But now the building has been replaced and the panels, which had been promised to the Metropolitan Museum, torn down and destroyed by the developer, apparently because of the expense of removing them and (flying in the face of art experts) their 'lack of artistic merit'.

The developer was one Donald Trump. The site is where Trump Tower, his flagship building, now stands. Its website shows him looking young and knowingly handsome, standing over an architect's model in which the tower seems to mirror his stance. The text tells us that the building is a 'world famous testament of Mr Trump's grand vision and ability to achieve tremendous success with everything he touches'.

We start stepping round police cars and concrete blocks, and know we are getting near. Across the road, behind a barrier, a small group of people offers pro-Trump posters and memorabilia. I am not sure whether they are partisans or pedlars, but from this side of the road they seem good-natured enough. Barbara is not keen to cross the road to look. A bus plastered with flags and 'Re-elect Trump' posters glides by; it attracts little notice.

It seems a little low key. As we hover outside the door, I decide to ask the uniformed doorman, a large, powerful African American in white waistcoat and blue tails, if I can go in.

'Of course,' he says, looking down (quite a long way down) his nose.

I feel I need to explain. 'I am a foreigner,' I say.

'I am sorry for you,' he replies. I see no trace of a smile.

The inside of Trump Tower looks like any other mall or shopping centre, apart from the security detail, conspicuous in their oxymoronic jackets with SECRET SERVICE written in large letters. The only other apparent link to the current president is that today's menu at the eponymous Trump Bar features Trump Burgers.

We go next door – and, it seems, back a couple of decades – into the hushed, cool, spacious showroom at Tiffany's. It is generously staffed with salesmen and security guards, charming and courteous, dressed in smart suits. Peeping out of the men's breast pockets, seemingly at regulation height, is a handkerchief in the company's familiar light blue. (The colour, I learn later, is known popularly as 'robin's egg blue'.)

I am more impressed than I was in 1969. 'Rather like Sainsbury's with jewels and a very slow metal-doored lift,' I wrote then. I added that as nobody seemed willing to serve me, I left. I returned a couple of hours later, though, and ended up buying a present for my parents: a silver-plate propelling pencil in the trademark blue bag.

Barbara and I go in to see how expensive it would be to buy another one. The rather grand sales lady pulls out a drawer – the pencils are all very fancy, including one with a serpent-entwined rod, which she confirms is for the medical market. She is a lady of mature years, and I share with her my 1968 *Michelin Guide*. She likes it so much she forgets she should be selling, and together we go through the 1968 map of Fifth Avenue that Barbara and I have been following.

The sales lady reminisces about the stores that have gone. 'That's where I bought my wedding dress.' She points to the map. 'And there is where I bought my knives and forks.'

We both have so much fun that I forget to ask the price of pencils.

Finally Barbara and I leave the world of beaming servers and gleaming jewellery. Fifth Avenue is still busy, but I can't help feeling that the glamour has gone. Barbara agrees: 'It could be any old high street,' she says.

On this day in 1969 I wrote in my diary: 'Took first subway: no cops, not too dirty and to my surprise everyone was very helpful.' This evening I take the subway again, to the Upper East Side.

'Be safe wherever you go,' calls out the woman in the ticket office. I am not sure whether it is a salutation or a warning. Fellow passengers are also willing to help, though they have to unplug their earpieces to hear my question.

We are travelling to the Upper East Side to meet Paula and Robert, who were Barbara's colleagues when she worked in television in New York. We eat at a packed Italian restaurant and talk about travel. 'In our day we travelled for experience but now it's all about rest – and taking selfies,' says Robert.

We also talk about Trump and Brexit. 'The world for our children is going to be completely different,' he says.

Wednesday 3 July

Today's walk with our half-century span of guidebooks will take us through the Wall Street financial district, which seems to be abbreviated nowadays into FiDi (not to be confused with FIDI, which apparently means Fuck It Do It, which may be the area's guiding principle).

We take the subway again and emerge from Wall Street Station into what feels like a city under siege: chunks of concrete, strange obstacles made of a metal that I cannot identify – and a portable police station sitting empty on a trailer. The site is gloomy and unwelcoming, sinister even.

We look up and see we are at the foot of another Trump building and these are the security precautions introduced after 9/11. Lowering our gaze we read a plaque: '40 Wall Street: Built in 1929–30 as the Manhattan Company Building, this picturesque 927-foot-tall skyscraper, built for the Manhattan Bank in 1929 ... was acquired by the Trump Organization in 1995.'

We walk the short distance to the Stock Exchange. When I was first here it was open to the public, but since 9/11 tourists have not been allowed in. This hasn't stopped dozens of them milling around with their eyes craned upwards and a restless hand cradling a mobile phone. It was here in 1969 that I recorded with some glee that a smiling Japanese man had bowed before me and asked me to take his photo. No-one needs my photographic skills today, nor does anyone seem to smile much – other than a brief flash of teeth when they take their selfies. Travel seems to be a much more solitary business these days.

Trinity Church, which I'd described as 'black and handsome', is also closed, in this case for renovation. We walk down the street towards what my original *Michelin Guide* lists as the Cunard Building. A security man stands outside where we think it is, and I approach him with my ice-breaking map to confirm this. He does. It is now operated by Cipriani SA. I look it up later: it is a top-of-the market hospitality business whose fortunes originated with Harry's Bar in Venice and which for a short while ran the fancy Rainbow Room in the Rockefeller Center.

The doorman asks if we would like to see inside. Would we not? He shows us the huge domed ticketing hall, built in 1921 and a pseudo-cathedral dedicated to the brief heyday of transatlantic travel. He points to a curtain, and says that behind there in pre-war days was the area reserved for those booking first-class passages.

In a small library off to one side, a man is talking on his phone. Our guide says he is his boss.

'Will you get into trouble showing us around?' I ask.

He says not. 'I like showing people. This place deserves to be seen.'

Barbara and I proceed to what used to be Battery Park, now rebranded as The Battery. It is right at the foot of Manhattan ('The best tip on the island', says one slogan). Lines of restless tourists hug the shade and wait to be ferried to the Statue of Liberty. We are seeking more recent history, however, and continue towards an area nearby which my 1969 guide lists as being under construction.

The space is now occupied by a pack of skyscrapers. One of them, 17 State Street, has made it into my modern guidebook as a 'sleek mirrored office tower … like an ultra-tall quarter-slice of pie'. I talk to the concierge, a middle-aged African American who tells me that the building was finished in 1988 and is 42 storeys high. The occupants are 'private' but, when I press him, 'mainly computer-related or lawyers'.

'There was a seaman's mission on this spot,' he volunteers. 'I used to get

Clutching our guidebooks inside the Cunard Building—'a pseudo-cathedral dedicated to the brief heyday of trans-atlantic travel'.

people coming in and telling me that.' As I leave he calls out: 'Herman Melville was born just around the corner!'

We are nearly back at the subway station, and start looking for the Chase Manhattan Bank building, presided over for many years by David Rockefeller. The 1969 guidebook awarded it three stars, the same number given to the Empire State Building. It was described as a fine modern building where the floor buttons in the lifts worked on the heat of a finger. The general accounting department in the basement housed 'computers rented for $2,000,000 annually, which worked around the clock and process an average of 2 million checks a day, worth over $2,000,000,000'. (The noughts are theirs.)

The building is still there, but no Chase Manhattan sign. The concierge confirms that we are in the right place, but times have changed. The building was bought four and a half years ago by the huge Chinese conglomerate Fosun run by the billionaire founder and chairman Guo Guangchang who disappeared for a few days in 2015, reputedly 'assisting a government inquiry'. Fosun's interests include pharmaceuticals, finance, real estate, asset management, Club Med and Wolverhampton Wanderers.

The building is now called 28 Liberty Street; the land it stood on used to be Chase Plaza and is now just the Plaza, we are told. This doesn't seem to be entirely true: when we go there we see a smallish sign on the wall – Fosun Place. The new owners are quietly making their presence felt. We then look up and see a sign looming over us: Trump Tower: we are at the back of the building that we emerged from earlier this morning. Two oligarchical empires facing each other over the greensward.

At the recommendation of the concierge we go to a café across the road. It's a huge place, filled with queues whose destination and purpose is not always clear. It's also filled with too much choice: I counted 4 soups, 5 entrees, 6 types of pasta, 10 types of bread and rolls, 18 jars of dressing, and four sections of 14 little bowls with salad components.

I end up with soup and an egg sandwich so large that I can hardly open my mouth wide enough to eat it. I yearn for the days of bite-sized food and table service. When I go to wash my hands the sign promises 'motion activated paper towels'. The promise is false.

After lunch we cross a few blocks to what my 1969 guidebook lists as another construction site. Our mood changes. The building under construction during my previous visit became the World Trade Center, and was destroyed by terrorists in 2001. Part of it is now the site of a memorial dedicated to the event that traumatised America: 9/11.

At the heart of the site are two pools, around which hundreds of people ebb and flow. It somehow seems apart from the rest of the city; if there are traffic noises we don't notice them. Each pool follows the footprint of a collapsed building, and each has a sheet of water falling into a sunken pool which, lined with granite, seems bottomless. The sound of the falling water dominates. My guidebook tells us that the design was chosen from 5,200 submitted proposals and 'simultaneously suggests loss and regeneration'.

Around the pools are panels with cut-outs forming the names of the 2,983 people who perished in the attack; they are part of the symbolism of 'Reflecting Absence', the official name of the memorial. 'Visitors are invited to touch the memorial name panels', says a notice, and most of us do so, tentatively. Another sign tells us that on each victim's birthday a small white rose is placed by their names. Barbara sees two side by side: a rose apiece for twins Dana and Zoe. We go silent.

Staff are watchful and discreet. The place is filled with respect.

A volunteer points out to us the 'survivor tree', an ornamental pear, one of seven trees found still alive in the rubble. It was 8 feet high, badly burnt except for one branch. The city's parks department replanted and cosseted it, and then moved it onto this site at the end of 2010. It is now 30 feet tall and surrounded by admiring visitors; in its shadow a volunteer chats to a group of them and tells them that he too is a survivor.

We are sated: neither physically nor psychologically up for the hour-long queue in full sun for entry to the museum nor for the souvenirs on offer in the shop afterwards. Instead we walk away past the new buildings that are still springing up, including the spectacular and graceful One World Trade Center, nicknamed the Freedom Tower because it is 1,776 feet tall, recalling the year of the Declaration of Independence. We walk through Brookfield Place, a huge office and retail space looking out over the Hudson River. I overhear someone pointing out that the yacht 'over there' belongs to Leonardo di Caprio.

New York is back.

We take the subway to our hotel, collect our bags and walk the short distance to Penn Station, on our way to New Jersey. The approach is heaving with people going places for the Fourth of July holiday. A small group of people is handing out packages and leaflets, and though few travellers stop to take one, I do.

The gift is a bar of soap. The leaflet is headed: 'No kids in cages'.

Take a stand this July 4th

Right now in the United States of America:

· Refugees from violence and poverty are being held in prison camps

· Children are being separated from their parents, held in detention instead of being reunited with family members and forced to sleep on concrete floors in freezing cold cells without blankets, soap or toothbrushes

· People are being denied medical care and are dying in detention...

It puts me in mind of what our yellow cab driver was telling us last night as he drove us home from dinner. He comes from the West African state of Guinea and has been in the United States for 20 years. He says proudly that all his five children are American citizens. So what does he think about Trump and immigration?

'A country has got to have a border. But all this misery – this country is bigger than this. Everyone here has come from somewhere else, but some people have a bad attitude, and they got worse after Trump came to power.

'Migrants work hard here,' he adds.

4. New Jersey: where migrants settle

Thursday 4 July

Today is Independence Day. The big story in the morning news today is that President Trump is planning to hold a military parade in Washington. He was so impressed by the Bastille Day celebrations he attended in France last year that he decided to hold one of his own. According to the papers, he has whipped up bad feeling by inviting only Republicans to sit in the grandstand. The top military brass are sending their seconds-in-command, citing prior arrangements. But it appears that the President has been talked out of parading US hardware: only a couple of tanks are being sent in, and they won't be moving.

We are staying with Barbara's cousins Jim and Barbara in West Orange, a leafy part of New Jersey. On Wikipedia it has a surprisingly long list of Notable People, from music arranger Nat Adderley Jr (born 1955) to Abner Zwillman (1899–1959) a mobster found hanging dead in his home. But it seems a quiet place compared with New York, and we have slept well.

As I start my daily routines, I search my tablet Geoffrey Go for an important folder. I can't see it where it should be, so I search my files. I look on the cloud. I take out a memory stick. I take out another. I am about to ring Julian, my jovial computer coach back in England, when I happen to see the fugitive folder skulking in the shadow of another. It has taken 20 minutes out of my life.

The folder I was looking for contains my meditation tapes and on this showing I'm going to need them.

Back in 1969 I spent Independence Day at the Cedar Point Yacht Club at Westport, Connecticut. My first letter home started with what seems to my older self a nice turn of phrase: 'I am now writing in a small boat in a small bay off Long Island (Oyster Bay). There is not much movement in the water so if you can't read this it's the gin and not the swell.'

I'd had the good fortune to know, through my father, a New York lawyer,

Richard Goldwater, who had agreed to sponsor my trip. On my third day in America Richard and his wife Maria whisked me out of the city. We spent the holiday itself coming well down the field in a yacht race, for much of which I had been in a Dramamine-induced sleep. That night we rafted up to watch the traditional fireworks and on the way back I fell asleep again, this time because of the gin.

I had never been in a yacht club before and I was intrigued: 'full of bronzed, beefy, bourgeois Americans in ridiculous shorts', I wrote in my diary. I also noted (twice) the lack of black members.

I took a keen interest in the behaviour around me. I wrote:

> One interesting custom is the complimenting of the boats, on which they lavish much time and energy. Here 'Keeping up with the Joneses' seems to be related to how clean the boats are rather than their size. When a 'good' boat passes we say, 'She looks good'. The customary reply here is not 'So does yours' or 'Not bad, eh!' as I imagine they would do in England, but a drawled, smug, 'Thank you'.

At one gathering a doctor from another boat urged me to grasp the opportunities of 1969 – and become a doctor.

I became concerned at the number of disposable goods around, and wondered whether the American economy was becoming dependent on them. And I got my first taste of American politics: 'The news media are full of Vietnam, and sitting in a plush yacht club it is difficult to imagine that this is a country at war', I wrote. Later, describing a gathering with other boat owners: 'Richard argues that Nixon is a negative nothing'.

At the end of our stay we went to a Chinese restaurant, where the meal ended with two surprises. First, Richard and Maria asked for our leftover food to be put in a little box so we could eat it the next day. Then, I wrote, 'We are each served with an impregnated cloth to clean our hands'. What a strange place this America was turning out to be.

Later in the morning I leave with Barbara, Jim and another cousin to visit the Baron Hirsch Jewish Cemetery on Staten Island, where their great-grandmother is buried. In 1960, 87 headstones were smeared with incendiary words (some in German) and yellow paint. That and other incidents led President Dwight D Eisenhower (Republican) to declare that freedom and decency could be destroyed if Americans were to ignore the 'virus of bigotry' or permit it 'to spread one inch'. (*NYT* 13 Jan 1960)

The gravestones are in mixed condition. We find the one we are looking for, with the word MOTHER in large letters below her name, and the dates 1845–1908. She had come from Minsk in Belarus in 1898 with her two youngest daughters; her older children had already emigrated but her husband was too ill to travel and had been left behind. Her direct descendants include several professors, a labour mediator, a planning director for the National Park Service, the chairman of the board of New York University and a soldier who landed with the US 1st Army in Normandy and went on to take part in the liberation of Buchenwald Concentration Camp. Dangerous stuff, immigration!

We head down Route 1 towards the town of Elizabeth, NJ. I am told that McDonalds is still going strong, but the Roy Rogers restaurant has ridden off into the sunset. At the other end of the scale, also gone is the Ford Assembly Plant at Edison, a 100-acre site which turned out 6.9 million cars from 1948 to 2004 – Pintos, Mustangs, Falcons, Escorts and more. Now it's a shopping centre with Fuddruckers, a hamburger outlet I have never heard of, though it was founded in 1980 and has branches in many parts of the world, particularly the Middle East.

We drive on to Elizabeth, where we stop outside Barbara's childhood home. She lived here with her mother (an early single parent) and her grandparents, who had come from Russia in 1898 and 1902. Her grandfather was manager of a furniture warehouse owned by two brothers-in-law.

Barbara stays in the car and looks around. She had heard that someone had placed a plaster gnome in the garden but is pleased to see there is none. The house is the model of neatness in a suburbia of neatness. From the upper floor hang two flags – one American, one Portuguese. Several other houses on this street are flying the same two flags.

'These people are exactly at the same stage as our grandparents were,' says Jim, who works as a tourist guide at Ellis Island, the reception centre for millions of immigrants around the turn of the 20th century. 'This is the second stage. They came here, and they survived. Their first language was not English. But they started to build things up and buy nice homes in middle class areas, and they settled down.'

Jim's house is on a hill overlooking Manhattan and this evening he suggests that we go out into the field behind and watch the fireworks. When I hear that there will be bugs flying around I decide not to go. My farewell insect bite is still swollen under its sticking plaster, and I am conscious of the travels to come.

A country built on migration: the gravestone of Barbara's great-grandmother who migrated from Belarus to America in 1898.

Instead I install myself in front of the TV to watch Macy's Fourth of July Fireworks Spectacular on NBC. This has been an integral part of the celebrations since 1976 and takes place on and around Brooklyn Bridge. The televised proceedings start with a surprising homily: a distinguished, elderly, white gentleman (I miss the name) intones: 'By and large it was immigrants who made the bridge, and it was a bridge not a wall. Afterwards they celebrated with fireworks.'

The programme switches to younger presenters, who gush that tonight we will see 25,000 shells on the bridge alone. On our 56-inch screen the effect is spectacular. The fireworks flow down and off and out and up from the bridge, as well as from four barges, with the buildings of lower Manhattan as their backdrop. They dance in time to the music, an eclectic collection from *Casablanca* to *Star Wars* with some *Colonel Bogey* thrown in. The colours are sumptuous.

From time to time the cameras cut away to servicemen, such as a white-suited sailor and a soldier holding up his young daughter. It seems a little 1945.

By my calculations the show goes for 22 minutes without advertisements. When they do come, they are typically American: Coca-Cola, Toy Story 2, Bank of America (unless this is owned by Chinese interests) and Pringles (Kellogg's – definitely American). An advert for a Honda HRV Sport manages to creep in down the running order, as does a promised cure for sleeplessness.

Afterwards, and in our honour, we all watch the BBC News, in which Chris Buckler reports from Washington on what has turned out to be a fly-past and a speech that was genuinely presidential. 'This was much more measured than we are used to … a genuine attempt to say it's one country and that people should be celebrating on the Fourth of July,' says Buckler.

Is this a sign that the divisions I have been hearing about are starting to heal? It could be bad for the book – but good for America.

5. My first Greyhound: only it isn't

Friday 5 July

Barbara's relatives have been trying hard to disguise their feelings that my plan to travel around their country on buses is more than a little crazy. This, I soon figured out, is because the Greyhound brand has vastly different meanings on either side of the Atlantic.

In the UK its status is high. Its buses provided me, and a surprising number of my contemporaries and their children, with the means to travel through a country the like of which we hadn't seen before. The buses themselves weren't that comfortable, but they carried us to our adventures at a reasonable cost.

They also provided an amiable social scene. I met students from Britain and other European countries, and we formed and reformed ad hoc social groups to go and explore the world outside our bus stations. I met young people from the United States, many of them seething with discontent – about society, about their elders' incompetence, about the Vietnam War and the risk of being drafted. Oddballs (I put it much less politely five decades ago) flitted in and out, the odd whiff of pot wafted across the aisle, and racial compositions changed constantly. But I felt safe on the buses, and I was.

Americans, on the other hand, see the buses differently. They may have travelled on them when they were young and strapped for cash; their children may have travelled on them when they too were strapped for cash. But it was expedience, not adventure. Now, as soon as Americans can afford to drive or fly they do so. Those who are left to take the bus are predominantly the dispossessed: old people who don't drive, young people who haven't a car, immigrants, and those who want to keep a low profile and avoid airport security checks.

What's more, over the past half-century, Greyhound buses have made the US news with stories that have rarely reached us in the UK. The company has had to weather two vicious strikes (with strikers killed by buses), two bankruptcies, and (at the time of writing) eight fatal accidents, including one caused by a tyre blow-out on an articulated lorry as late as August 2018.

The company isn't even American any more: it was taken over in 2007 by FirstGroup, the Scottish transport company who run British buses and trains, including the strike-prone suburban trains that happen to be our main route up to London. But improvements have been made to the Greyhound buses and a casual, younger image is cultivated. The buses have leather seats with plenty of leg room, power points and washrooms, says the website. 'Times have changed and so have we,' boasts the Twitter page. 'Free WiFi on board. Oh yeah!' shouts the ticket app.

But bad news still follows them. A few weeks before my trip I made the mistake of googling Greyhound buses and immediately found two items of 'breaking news'. In one, a young woman facing assault on a bus managed to call the police and have the man arrested; in the other a driver who had crashed her bus was found to be drunk. I also came across a discussion on whether it was true that only criminals travelled by Greyhound: I did not linger in that conversation.

At about the same time cousin Jim sent me an article from the *New York Times* documenting how the buses were now the major route for migrants coming across the southern border, putting many of the bus stations in a state of siege. The next morning I awoke to hear on the BBC News that FirstGroup had put Greyhound up for sale. I consoled myself with the thought that anyone who puts a company up for sale is going to pay it close attention for the next few months.

Anyway, today I am about to find out what Greyhound bus travel is like in 2019. My first trip in 50 years will take me from Newark to Washington DC in just over four hours, I hope. Barbara has agreed to come with me for this journey. In Washington we will stay the weekend with her childhood friend Debbie, and then I will travel south towards Florida while she flies east back to London.

First I have to work out where the bus station is, since the address on the app is not the same as the one on my paper ticket printout. We try to phone Greyhound but I get put through to a call centre and they don't have that kind of information. In the end we plump for the address next to a railway station rather than one in the middle of a shopping mall. Luckily we have guessed right.

The Greyhound station is dark and crowded, with all the benches full – apart from two rows of seats occupied by two noisy couples who have used their copious luggage to mark out those two full rows for themselves. We look for our bus listed on the overhead screen, but can't find it. Alarmed, we stop a baggage man who looks at our tickets and tells us that we are looking at the Greyhound bus departures, but we are on a Bolt bus. This must be the bus equivalent of a code share, though this is the first we hear of it. My first Greyhound bus trip in half a century will have to wait.

When the Bolt bus arrives it looks clean and comfortable, with WiFi and foot rests which work. At 11.40, on schedule, to a babble of diverse languages, we leave. Our driver is Sabatha. An hour into the journey, the two ladies on the other side of the bus are still chatting away. The two couples who colonised a whole double row of chairs in the waiting room are continuing their boisterous conversation. A woman just behind me is fast asleep, wrapped in a shocking pink blanket. A young man just across the aisle cracks his fingers and returns to his screen.

I go to the little washroom at the back, not because I am desperate but because I feel it is in the spirit of journalistic endeavour. It's a grim experience. The cubicle is tiny and dark, though not too smelly. Underneath the seat is a red streak that I convince myself is disinfectant.

We draw into Baltimore and stop near what look like mounds of salt; I discover later that they are – piled up ready to keep the roads running next winter. My 1969 BUNAC guidebook said it was the sixth largest city in the USA, but now it is around the 30th mark. The big manufacturing industries have gone and the major employers are now hospitals and universities. From the bus I can see modern buildings for Johns Hopkins University, a massive stadium for the Baltimore Orioles baseball team, and a light railway. What I don't see, but am constantly being told, is that the city's murder rate is persistently one of the highest in the country.

Some passengers get off and we space ourselves out for the last leg. We pull into Washington DC bus station pretty much on time. In 1969 my report on this journey was: 'short sleep and arse ache'. So far I have had the first but not the second. This is encouraging.

We walk out onto the street to call an Uber. We can see no street signs or numbers, and end up standing outside a supermarket. Even so the driver finds it hard to locate us. He is a bright young Eritrean and his car is clean and cool. He came to the USA eight years ago and recently moved from San Francisco to study web design. Not surprisingly, he loves the country.

He believes that immigration should be controlled, but that it should be done better. 'The Democrats behaved just as cruelly for years and it's just politics.' He says that in Washington he has to keep his opinions to himself in case he gets into arguments.

6. Washington DC: the assaults on news

Saturday 6 July

Washington is a city where who you know is important, and in 1969 I was in luck. My sponsor, Richard Goldwater, had been involved in Democratic politics, and his wife Maria had worked for a Democratic congressman. They had arranged for me to stay with their friend Bill, a civil servant in his early thirties who worked and lived in the city. I could not have had a better host.

He drove me through brand new developments and streets burnt out from the previous year's rioting. We watched the Apollo 11 blast-off on TV – in colour, I noted. I went with him to a lecture at George Washington University (he was doing an MBA at the time) and to Bolling Air Force Base (he was a reservist). He took me to a shopping centre: 'All inside, very good shops, air conditioning, aviary, trees etc – and especially [parking] space for a number of cars.' It was the first I had seen.

His circle of friends included the receptionist for Vice-President Spiro Agnew, and she gave me a book of vice-presidential matches as a souvenir. She also arranged for me to go on the Saturday morning White House tour. 'Not very impressive and the crowd very big, although it's a VIP tour,' I wrote – rather churlishly, in retrospect.

When Bill was at work I visited three Smithsonian museums, two courts, a probation office, the FBI Building, the Lincoln Memorial, the offices of Congressman Jonathan B Bingham (Democrat) and a Senate debate (well, more of a monologue, and I fell asleep). In what looks to my 72-year-old self like an aberration, I'd decided to walk up the Washington Monument rather than wait for the lift: 'Oh Boy! About 900 stairs and 500 feet.' At the top I realised I had run out of film, which does seem more in character.

I had a couple of encounters that shook my mid-20th-century British complacency. The first took place when I found myself chatting with a staff lawyer in a canteen in the basement of a Congress building. I wrote:

> He turns out to be very southern/conservative (though professes to
> be a Democrat). 'Commies are the lowest of the low'; 'We must smash

communism wherever it rears its ugly head'; 'In Cuba all men are slaves.'

The second came at the end of the FBI Building tour:

Finally [we go to] the shooting range, where an agent demonstrates efficient killing. All the little kids clamour for the cartridge cases and the man-shaped target. Horrifying! My shock is compounded by hearing that one in two people in Washington carry a gun. There is much concern, but what can be done now?

On the upside I received an unsolicited act of kindness. I was chatting to a Texan standing with his family alongside me in the queue for the Senate. I told him my plans, and he handed me $2 to visit the living history museum in colonial Williamsburg.

On this trip, however, I am not expecting to be offered any handouts. (Spoiler alert: I am to be proved wrong.)

This time I only have two days in Washington, so to get restarted I have reserved two places on a 'free' tour of the National Mall.

The tour starts at 9 am to avoid the worst of the midday heat. The temperature is already in the 80s (26–32°C) when we arrive, and we hug the shade wherever possible. Our guide is Chelsea – young, articulate and a history teacher in her day job – and she introduces us to the magnificent landscape around us. George Washington was keen that the country should buy this land, she tells us, and some of it was his to be bought. Politics and property development, it seems, have long been intertwined in America.

She tells us about the Washington Monument. A drive for public subscriptions ran into trouble when a group called the Know Nothings objected to a contribution from a group of Catholics (ah, these religious wars!). The Know Nothings took over the construction but made a mess of it, and it remained a stump for many years. When finished in 1884 it was the tallest structure in the world – but only for five years, until Gustave Eiffel completed his tower in Paris.

I am relieved to hear that this summer the monument is closed to repair damage caused by a 2011 earthquake and restore the lifts (the ones I could not be bothered to wait for in 1969). So I am spared the decision of climbing the 900 steps or admitting that I can't.

We continue through the Mall, dodging sweaty joggers and not-so-sweaty electric-scooter riders. Off to one side we get a good view of the White House. Ahead and around us are the remains of the two Independence Day events just 36 hours ago – a symphony concert at this end of the Mall and Trump's military event at the other. Curiously shaped patches of grass show signs of wear, barriers are stacked up, and empty toilets stand in line, their civic duties over.

To mark Independence Day the National Park Service has put up comment boards. One asks: 'What rights should be inalienable?' Answers, in a variety of hands, include: love; freedom of expression; life, liberty and the pursuit of happiness; abortion; birth; education; health care; and air conditioning. I am impressed to see no expletives and no crudely drawn genitalia.

We go to the Vietnam War Memorial, built to a design by Maya Lin, then a 21-year-old undergraduate at Yale University, chosen in a public competition from nearly 1,500 entries. Her concept was to create a wound in the earth that would heal: it is a low black stone wall in a V formation. There's no triumphalism; it's just a calm place of remembrance.

Until I reread my diary I had forgotten how much Vietnam overshadowed our lives in 1969. On one bus at that time I spoke with a USAF sergeant, a teacher by trade, who bitterly attacked the war, and I wrote that so far everyone seemed to oppose it. I also met a veteran of Khe Sanh who, I was shocked to find, was the same age as me:

> [He] swore he would rather go awol than return. Didn't like being shot at. America seems to be in a bad way over this war. Few like it, many bitterly oppose it for personal and idealistic reasons. But I suppose if you have a culture that deifies materialism it is difficult getting people to fight and die.

Our guide Chelsea takes no sides: 'What everyone can agree upon is that the veterans were the ones most affected. If we as a country dealt with it and honoured those who died, it would be a healing moment for the nation.'

We pass a wreath and a poem to SP4F Floyd Watts, born in 1943, killed on 4 July 1969. On that day I was partying on a yacht off Connecticut.

I speak to a family on our tour. The two youngsters say they know nothing about the war. The father says his uncle went, but never talked about it. I look around and realise that we are the only ones in our group who lived through that period. What was raw then has become a peaceful walk in a park.

What **rights** should be inalienable?

Thomas Jefferson wrote that people are "endowed by their Creator with certain inalienable Rights." Inalienable means something that cannot be taken away.

Celebrating liberty: one of several comment boards marking Independence Day put up in the Mall by the National Park Service.

At the end of the tour we call an Uber. When it arrives, the driver says that the temperature has risen to 91 degrees (33°C). He is an African American who was born in Washington, but now lives in Maryland. He says more and more people in Washington are being pushed into less and less space. He reels off three problems: congestion, humidity (the city is built on a swamp), and rodents (who grow fatter as humans get fatter).

We are on our way to a museum. The Smithsonian has 17 of them (plus a zoo) in Washington, all of them free – but it is not any of those ones. Instead we have chosen the Newseum, independent and with an entrance fee, opened in 2008 – at a cost of $450 million – by a group led by the founder of the newspaper *USA Today*. The intention was to promote the principles of free speech in general and good journalism in particular. In this era of fake news a supportive visit seems the least we can do.

The Newseum's intent spills out onto the pavement, with today's front pages from a selection of newspapers throughout the world. As we enter we see the tools of modern communication: a TV van and a news helicopter. There are six floors of exhibits, and we start at the bottom with an introductory film: the take-home point is that only 13 per cent of the world's population have a free press.

Just outside the little theatre is an FBI exhibit, 'Fighting Crime in the Age of Terror'. I am pleased to see it because although the FBI Building still has tours it is open only to US citizens and those with green cards. This should be a good alternative.

The exhibit deals with cybercrime, electronic surveillance and face recognition – and how the media cover them. Artefacts on show include the handcuffs used to detain the 1993 World Trade Center bomber and the car used in the attempted bombing of Times Square in 2013. A sophisticated video is rolling on 'how the FBI is working to stop terrorist attacks at home and abroad'. One of the talking heads is James Comey, looking a lot more relaxed than he does now, after his firing as FBI Director.

The tone of the displays seems softer and more nuanced than in 1969, when the idiom was goodies vs baddies, end of story. Captions here are sensitive to the tension between the forces of law and order and the free press. And thankfully the display does not end, as the show did in 1969, with a glorification of the shootout.

A few floors up is a special display commemorating the golden jubilee of the Stonewall Riots, and the changes in the media that followed. The eponymous inn was an illegal, mafia-owned gay bar in Greenwich Village, New York. Police raided it often, but on the night of 28 June 1969, lesbians, male prostitutes, drag queens, transgender people and others started to fight back. The six-day uprising set in motion a wave of activism, leading in the short term to the first Gay Pride March the following year – and in the long term the acceptance of LGBTQ groups, though sadly not by everybody.

In the month I flew back home (October 1969) the *Time* magazine cover was 'The Homosexual in America'. Now it would be considered offensive; then it was a giant leap. The tone changes: the June 1998 cover is 'The War Over Gays'. More coverage follows on the Aids epidemic, same-sex marriage and more. A video is running of landmark films and TV programmes showing how once-taboo topics are now routinely portrayed.

My 1969 arrival in New York overlapped with the Stonewall Riots, but I made no mention of them in my diary. It's been a big shift.

We pass to another key event of the last half-century: 9/11. The exhibit's centrepiece is the battered radio mast that stood on top of one of the

Twin Towers, but the most powerful image is a wall of front pages from the USA and around the world. A common theme is 'USA under attack'. But the tabloids are less restrained: 'BASTARDS'; 'TERROR'; 'HORROR'; 'DEVASTATION'. At the memorial site in New York a few days ago we saw dignity and pain; here is the initial reaction: anger in thick black capitals.

Not far away is a history of newspapers, shown in cabinets filled with newspaper front pages and with news stories year-by-year on the tops of them. The two exhibits for 2016 read 'Rise of Fake News' and 'President Attacks Press'. Above them is a quotation from the newly elected President Trump: 'The Fake News Press hates it when I use what has turned out to be my very powerful social media of over 100 million people! I can go around them.'

The gallery is sponsored by News Corp, part of the Rupert Murdoch empire along with Fox News. I wasn't expecting that.

As we leave, the Newseum is filling up with people, and I'm not surprised: I find it a credible display of democratic values at their best – freedom of religion, free speech, free press, and of course integrity. But there is a twist: at the end of the year the museum will close and the building will be turned into a prestigious postgraduate centre for Johns Hopkins University. The reasons for the closure are not clear. Mismanagement? Indifference? A surfeit of museums? The entrance fee? A climate of hostility to journalists and journalism? The public affairs department tells me they are giving no interviews, which sadly undermines their position.

I hope that the Newseum will be missed, but I am not sure it will be by enough of the people who count.

We are staying in the suburbs with Barbara's friend Debbie, in the house where she has brought up her two children. She is a former editor of government agricultural handbooks and she is a constant source of good advice on my writing. That evening she holds a small gathering for us to meet her friends: most are of our age and are Washington types: retired civil servants, engineers, health professionals.

I ask them what they think has changed since 1969. Their answers include: greater income inequality; technology; a change in the role of women; and guns (someone mentions that America has more guns than people). They doubt whether I will see much of these trends on my bus journey. (Another spoiler alert: they're wrong.)

Sunday 7 July

A day of preparation. Before I hit the road tomorrow I have 16 tasks to do, half of which are concerned with sorting out my two companions, Geoffrey the Go tablet and Morris the Motorola. Morris is particularly annoying, beeping at me every five minutes to tell me I have a message that I am not interested in. I want to turn off his beep, so I ring the helpline number I was given in England. But it doesn't seem to work so I google another number, probably the same call centre in the Philippines. As I start to explain, an automated voice intervenes: 'You have exceeded your data.' And cuts me off.

I finally sort it with a visit to a T-Mobile store, but I can't help thinking I am not cut out for new technology.

The 1969 BUNAC guide was uncompromising when it came to warning us about Washington. 'Unescorted girls should not go out after dark.' Also: 'Drive up 14th Street and absorb the atmosphere of gutted buildings, boarded windows, soul brothers, frustration, and lack of opportunity.'

This was the street where a year previously, triggered by the assassination of Dr Martin Luther King, riots had resulted in 7,600 arrests, 1,097 injured and 13 killed. The government deployed 13,600 troops, and nearly 2,000 buildings were damaged, some completely destroyed.

When my host Bill drove me through there, I was shaken. I wrote:

> Down 14th Street, where the riots were. The only white faces are ours. We have to lock our doors – in case. Rather an eerie situation, and the oppressive aggression of the place is exacerbated by our fears and the burnt-out carcases of buildings.

This year Debbie drives me to the corner of U and 14, which was the centre of the rioting. We find a parking space easily and start walking around. The area has been transformed. Many of the older buildings still exist but are now overshadowed by large modern apartment blocks. Street art in the alleyways depict African American heroes: the Obamas, Muhammed Ali – but not Bill Cosby, in prison for sex offences and whose likeness has recently been removed. We see a sign for a heritage trail, but agree it is too hot for us to walk it.

We stop for tea on the main street at Busboys and Poets, a flourishing Washington institution that combines healthy eating options with live performances and books for sale about the struggles of the dispossessed and marginalised. It is a 'community where racial and cultural connections

Washington DC: 'Street art in the alleyways depicts African American heroes'.

are consciously uplifted' says its website. The founder is an Iraqi American and the name comes from African American writer and activist Langston Hughes who worked as a busboy before being recognised as a poet. The place is doing good multicultural business.

When we drive back Debbie does not have to advise me to lock the car door; the car does it automatically. Another sign of changing times.

That evening two more of Debbie's friends come over. One of them is an 80-year-old lawyer, still practising and formerly in politics, when he had a political job in Reagan's administration. He does not like Trump (to put it mildly), but says, despairingly, that he can't bring himself to vote Democratic. He says that the Republican party has turned into the party of angry white men. The Democrats are upscale, transformational, multicultural and diverse, and the Republicans are afraid of them.

SOUTH

1. Knoxville: a lightning tour

Monday 8 July

The sun shines bright this morning but not for long. As I eat my porridge, Morris the mobile starts to whimper: 'Alerts – flash floods in your area.' Up to four inches of rain is threatened in some places, and Washington is already the scene of 'active water rescues'.

It does not augur well for the day that I am going solo. Barbara will fly back to England this afternoon and the safety net will be dismantled. Over the next five days my schedule has me travelling some 1,200 miles.

I have some hard riding in front of me, though not as hard as in 1969. Then I left Washington at 3 o'clock on a Saturday afternoon and travelled pretty well straight through to St Petersburg in Florida, arriving at 11 o'clock on the Monday morning. On the way I stared out of the window at mountains and swamps, read large chunks of *War and Peace*, and chatted.

> Some interesting people, including three black teachers (two female, one male and blind), an aggressive, garrulous boy who let me read some of his comics, a hillbilly who kept saying 'Very interestin' … and knew all about England and 'Queen Margaret and Queen Elizabeth'.

My route then took me first via Williamsburg to Knoxville, Tennessee, and through the Great Smoky Mountains to Asheville, North Carolina. 'I really enjoy the ride', I wrote. 'The road is comparatively small and twists and turns through tall wooded mountains. We climb up, down and around, and the hazy silhouettes are continually changing.' After that we travelled east to Jacksonville, Florida: 'No character at all', I wrote.

Fifty years later I am going again from Washington to St Petersburg but this time stopping at some of the places I rushed through last time.

We set off for the bus station in Debbie's car as soon as we can. After a short distance the thunder grumbles, then roars – and the rain starts. It's not an effete British drizzle but tropical bucketloads, hammering on the car roof and overwhelming the windscreen wipers. Debbie struggles bravely with rush-hour traffic and unfamiliar one-way streets, and though we get near our destination we can't find the entrance. In the end she drops me at the front of the train station. In the eight seconds it takes me to run into the entrance I am soaked, as is Barbara, who has come in for a goodbye hug.

I watch her get soaked again as she runs back to the car, and then I find a dry route through to the bus station. A friendly lady books me in and labels my case, and I settle down in the lee of a sign: 'Waiting Area for Bus Patrons Only with valid same day tickets' (their capitalisation). Underneath is a list of transgressions – loitering, soliciting, panhandling, alcohol, smoking – with a promise that transgressors will be escorted immediately off the property. I now know the rules. Rain still hammers down on the station roof.

As soon as it seems decent I join the line to board, well placed at third from the front. The minutes tick away and the line grows longer. We pass the 9.45 departure time. More passengers join the queue, which starts to snake back on itself. I assume these people have come off coaches that have been delayed in the flash floods; I wonder if they have been involved in an active water rescue.

At about 10 o'clock a Greyhound official in a high viz vest comes to tell us that anyone with connections past Charlottesville (as I have) should go back to the ticket office. I do so, and the same cheery lady who waved me off just over an hour ago issues me with a new ticket that will take me to Roanoke via Richmond, leaving at 1.20 and arriving just in time for a late supper at 8 pm. Could be worse, I reckon. Exceptional circumstances.

With three hours to kill, I go back next door to Washington Union Station, and I have time to look at it properly. It is unexpectedly splendid, with a marble floor and high vaulted ceiling. I look up the history: it was built in the first decade of the 20th century to enable trackwork and terminals to be removed from what is now the Mall (the open space, not the shopping centre), and at the same time make it fit for a capital city. Accordingly it included a presidential suite to allow visiting dignitaries to be greeted appropriately – and away from a would-be assassin's gun.

I didn't see the station when I was here in 1969, but it was in decline. Since then it has been renovated, and between the arches of Potbelly's Sandwich Bar ('Ya Gotta Get it Hot') I see a plaque to Keith Kelly (1923–94), the project director. The citation ends in pathos: 'In 1994, on the day

Waiting Area for Bus Patrons Only with valid same day tickets.

- No Trespassing
- No Loitering
- No Soliciting or Panhandling
- No Sleeping
- No Alcohol or Smoking

(intoxication or being under the influence of a ontrolled substance will result in your removal)

Violators will be escorted off property immediately at Security's discretion.

I have to wait three days and five hours before getting on my first Greyhound bus — and there are rules to follow.

he was to die, Keith Kelly made his last visit to Union Station as the man who led the building's return to glory.'

I pass time by buying a poncho and looking for a model of a Greyhound bus. Fortified by a Pret A Manger sandwich, I go back to the bus station and join another line. As before, the start time comes and goes, and the line gets longer and longer. I suffer the first pangs of what I will later label Pre-Embarkation Anxiety Syndrome.

A bus turns up and we leave at 1.45, a mere half-hour late. I ask the driver if I will miss my connection, and he shrugs. 'They'll put you on the next one – and you won't have to pay.'

This bus looks as if it has been pulled out of the reserve stock. Seats are of a tired cloth and my armrest looks as if it has been nibbled off. The electric plugs do not work. Almost every seat gets filled. A man across the aisle shakes his body spasmodically and mutters loudly to himself. About this time Barbara is boarding her plane home.

We make it to Richmond with 15 minutes to spare, and I make the connection. The new bus fulfils the website promises: spacious, leather upholstery, WiFi that works, and even little holders for our coffee. Our driver is a tall white man with white hair and a clipped moustache who might have been a figure of minor authority in a Disney movie. The bus is half-full and we can spread out. This is better.

We head towards Roanoke, passing through lush landscapes and cider apple farms, and are soon circled by hills. I play with Morris the mobile and come across a news story from the previous day. What appeared to have been gun shots in Washington Union Station sent people scattering for cover. Later the deputy mayor for public safety tweeted that the sounds were probably fireworks: there was no shooting and no casualties. I'm glad I didn't spot the story while I was in the station.

Shortly before 7 o'clock we arrive at Lynchburg, in the foothills of the Blue Ridge Mountains. The approach is charming, over a bridge with a view of the town ahead and on one side. We go through side streets, past clapboard houses with verandas.

It looks a pleasant place and probably is. But when I passed this way before (and unknown to me) the large building known as the Virginia State Colony for Epileptics and Feebleminded was still taking in women from all over the state and sterilising them. In the late 1970s the American Civil Liberties Union brought a class action, and the victims received formal apologies and an offer of counselling. The colony was renamed the Central Virginia Training Center.

At the bus station a new passenger is waiting. I see him through the window and start taking notes. He is a big man with a long greying beard, wearing a forage cap and army fatigue trousers and carrying a bulging army issue rucksack with a bedding roll on top. He boards the bus and sits just across the aisle from me. I wonder whether I should speak to him but he goes straight to his mobile phone with no eye contact.

When I was going through this area in 1969 I talked to all kinds of people. One I described as a 'ponced-up young (rich) male' from Florida who was rather 'tuned in and insipid'; the other was a girl of about 16 from Lake Michigan who 'said how boring everything was, how the world was in a mess and how we could do little to change it'. But this time so far I have spoken to nobody.

At 8 o'clock we arrive at Roanoke. It is a mere 15-minute walk to the Holiday Inn Express, and I think the fresh air will do me good. I set out gamely, with my rucksack on my back, wheeling my case behind me. I have been assured at the bus station that the streets are safe.

I pass a couple of men sitting on the steps with a miscellany of belongings around them and a bottle each. A little way down the street a couple more are drifting around a lamp post. I pass a shop and a woman offers to give me directions – and asks me for money. The streets are otherwise deserted and it starts to rain. The scare stories about travelling by Greyhound bus have penetrated my head – and I go into a restaurant to call an Uber, which speeds me in comfort and safety to my hotel.

There is no food on offer when I get there and no food outlets nearby, so the celebratory dinner for my first solo trip is some instant porridge that Debbie has thoughtfully stuffed into my rucksack. 'I won't need that,' I thought at the time; now I eat it gratefully and focus on tomorrow's breakfast that I have already paid for.

Tuesday 9 July

On my copious hotel breakfast buffet is something that looks like mushroom soup with lumps of oxtail swimming in it. The server tells me it is 'sausage gravy', a white sauce to be eaten with a slice of sausage meat and biscuits (not to be confused with what we call biscuits; more like scones, though without the elegance).

One taste of the gravy is quite enough for me and instead I learn to make my own waffles. Breakfast over, I talk outside to a man with a large beard and no front teeth, who smokes three cigarettes in quick succession. He is a truck driver from Ohio and says that the sausage and gravy down here is the best he can find. I also talk to one of the receptionists; his other job is as a part-time member of the Roanoke City Ballet. I neglect to ask him if he likes sausage and gravy.

And so to the Greyhound bus station in Roanoke. In daylight I can see that it has a practical wooden floor, a waiting area with healthy pot plants at each end, and toilets that are clean. There is no shop so I can't continue the search for a toy Greyhound bus that I have set as one of my secondary objectives from this trip. Just before I left, my personal trainer Nicole, who has had a tough job getting me in shape for this trip, presented me with a card ('Keep calm and jolly good luck') and a book about Greyhound buses (*Hounds of the Road; a history of the Greyhound bus company*, Carlton Jackson, Bowling Green State University Popular Press, 2001). The least I can do is bring her back a souvenir to show I made it to the bus station.

In this one there is one member of staff on duty: Thomas, a calm man with a jolly laugh. He needs both attributes: his first task is to break the news that my bus to Knoxville has broken down. It was the morning bus from Richmond: had I stayed there last night (which looked probable at one stage) I would now be on it – or more probably on a verge beside that bus, waiting to be rescued. Repairing the bus or bringing up a new one will take several hours.

Thomas assures me I have plenty of time to look over Roanoke. I am surprised to hear that there are no lockers; half a century ago I used them regularly so I could roam the street unencumbered with my oversize suitcase. Today I will have to drag my luggage with me.

The streets feel safer in daylight, with more people and cars around, and I make it back to a little market and chat with a lady selling peaches. She tells me that the first bottles of Dr Pepper were bottled in Roanoke, and that just outside the city on Mill Mountain is the Roanoke Star, which shines over Roanoke and surroundings.

The star was originally a Christmas decoration, first lit in 1949. It is made of 2,000 feet of neon tubing, stands just over 1,000 feet over the town and is lit every night, sometimes in different colours. According to the official Blue Ridge Mountains website it is 'the largest free-standing, man-made illuminated star in the world'. I am sorry I missed it last night: it might have cheered me up.

My friend the peach-seller suggests I go to the Texas Tavern, another local landmark. I tug my luggage along the baking streets and find a tiny white-bricked diner, nestling up against a much larger building. It is emblazoned with signs: OPEN ALL NITE, HAMBURGERS $1.50, CHILE $1.90. EAT.

The inside is retro, with a counter and red-topped stools, and mildly curmudgeonly chefs in mustard yellow T-shirts and small white paper caps. A sign hangs on the wall: 'We feed millions ... ten at a time,' and I later see this has been turned into a postcard. I ask the chefs what the place looked like in 1969 and they say probably the same as it looks now.

The tavern was founded in 1930 by an advance man for Ringling Bros Circus who was looking for somewhere to settle down. His great-grandson now runs it. As for the chefs, they are relative newcomers, having worked there only for 30 years or so.

I go back to the bus station. Thomas says there is no sign of a bus, so I face down my Pre-Embarkation Anxiety Syndrome and go out again to buy a sandwich. I find a local delicatessen run by a former New Yorker and I tell him I have been reading about the opioid epidemic: has it affected the town? (*American Overdose*, Chris McGreal, Faber & Faber, 2018)

'Hell, yes,' he says. 'People from West Virginia would come here and have their prescriptions made out. Then they'd go back home and have another one made out. A lot of times you would see dumb crimes – it would be one of the grand-kids. They knew where to find the money and the medicine.'

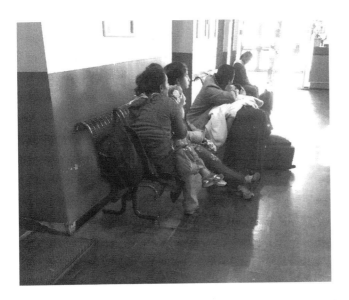

Roanoke Bus Station: a family from Guatemala waits for their 'amigos'.

I drag my belongings back to the bus station. Some of the people I saw on the streets last night have reassembled outside. One asks me for money but ruins his chances by calling me 'Pop'. Back inside the bus station I remark to Thomas that I don't remember seeing so many homeless people last time around. 'You were younger then,' he says. 'And there are more of them now.'

As the day wears on – and my Pre-Embarkation Anxiety Syndrome kicks in with a vengeance – I sit down in the bus station and start typing up my journal. A man with a mane of curly hair and more luggage than he can keep track of starts to curse Thomas, who escorts him off the property. The warning notice I saw yesterday isn't a joke.

A few benches down, an American lady is speaking fractured Spanish with a family of four who until now have been sitting quietly among their suitcases. I join her. We find some common ground with the elder daughter, using my distant memories from Spanish O-level, a bit of mime and the dictionary in a mobile phone app. The family has travelled from Guatemala: a husband and wife, daughters aged thirteen and two. He has been a corn cutter. They are tired after their long journey. And no, they have not had any trouble with the police. They are going to stay in

Roanoke, where they have 'amigos'. The parents look worried, the younger child looks defiant, and the older girl's smile is full of confidence.

One of their 'amigos' turns up to collect them. She is a well-dressed woman. I notice there are no hugs or other signs of joyful recognition. She leads them, not offering to help with the luggage, away across the car park across the road. I watch them go and hope they will be safe. I am not confident that they will be.

At 4.30 a bus turns up with a splendidly cantankerous driver. It is one of the good buses, and again not full. We are on the road by 5 o'clock, seven hours late.

We are soon well into our journey. Hills surround us and on one, puzzlingly, I see what look like three crucifixes. The hills get bigger. Our first stop is Wytheville, a pleasant-looking place that markets itself on an idyllic rural situation, a unique name and a water tower made up to look like a hot air balloon. I dig a little further and find that in 1926 it was the site of the last known lynching in Virginia: an African American who had a child with a white woman.

We reach Knoxville at about 10.30, too late to see the Sunsphere (built for the 1982 World's Fair), or the Women's Basketball Hall of Fame. Rain still lashes down. A small group is smoking and milling about outside the bus station, and the friendly security guard advises me to stay inside until I see my car arrive.

I have booked a room at the Crowne Plaza and it is plush: I wonder what persuaded me to book it, and I am sorry I won't be able to stay long enough to enjoy it. This is because my next bus is due to leave at 6.10 am, and I work out that my truncated stay is costing me about $30 an hour.

Over the last two days I have spent 12 hours waiting for buses and 14 hours travelling in them, to cover 700 miles. Barbara has flown 3,000 miles back over the Atlantic in 7 hours.

Wednesday 10 July
Five hours later my alarm call rings out. I shower quickly, repack the few things I have dared to take out of my case, and drink a glass of water for my breakfast. As I wait by the lift I see a picture of a huge plate of food: 'Our delicious breakfast buffet stretches almost as far as your imagination.' But breakfast here doesn't start for another hour, and I don't find that sign helpful.

My route today will take me to Atlanta, where I am scheduled for a six-hour stopover, and I should arrive in Unadilla at 6.55 this evening for a two night stay The Knoxville bus station is heaving when I get there, full of people who have been travelling through the night. I find a seat next to a young man in jeans and a bright checked shirt, probably from the Indian sub-continent, who, turned to the window, does not respond when I speak to him in English. I fall asleep.

When I wake I turn to Barbara. Except she isn't there. The silent man next to me is still turned to the window, at one with his mobile phone. Others around are in the same foetal position: I have no choice but to leave them to their own devices. Literally.

I join the club and play around with Morris the mobile, collecting a message from Barbara. I note that my friend Richard Smith has tweeted about my journey; he recommends that the 'old-timer' will be worth following. I wonder if he expects a disaster blog.

2. Atlanta: Morris goes missing

I want to spend my short time in Atlanta wisely, so I have pared its many attractions down to a shortlist of two: the World of Coca-Cola and the National Center for Civil and Human Rights. I opt for the latter, partly because I am sure it will provide more insights into the last half-century than a fizzy drink, but mainly because I realise how little I know about this part of American history.

The Uber drops me at the foot of some 50 steps. It's 10 am and already baking hot. I could not find anywhere in the bus station to stow my luggage, so I have my rucksack and my case-on-wheels still with me. I drive myself upwards with the thought that each step I climb is taking me closer to the cloakroom (where I can deposit my bags) and the coffee shop (where I can at last have breakfast).

At the top there is no cloakroom and no coffee shop. I drag my belongings across a small square for breakfast. On the way I take my second selfie of the trip and tweet it.

'Is the strain showing?' I ask.

'OMG. Are you OK?' tweets back my friend Nurse Catherine. That answers the question.

After a coffee and croissant I go back to the Center. Security is tight and I am asked to open my luggage. I kneel on the floor, open my case and expose my knickers to the world. My 1969 diary makes no mention of searches of this kind.

Such inconveniences are quickly put in perspective as the Center establishes its narrative: 'The South was caught in a current of change.' The first room starts with the statements of post-war segregationists, including this sentence from Lester Maddox, Governor of Georgia at the time I was visiting the USA: 'Inequality, I think, breeds freedom and gives a man [sic] opportunity.' I find it chilling.

Next an exhibit lists the southern states and the segregation laws they lived under. In one state non-whites were forbidden to go to the beach where white people swam, to use the same entrance at hospitals, to ride in the same part of the bus, to marry someone of a different race, and even to publish and circulate printed information. I knew about such laws, but not in such detail. And it had never occurred to me that publishing might be on the banned list.

A docent explains Jim Crow laws to me. The phrase originated from a jimmy and a crowbar, signifying breaking into white society. A popular minstrel of the time called himself Jim Crow and it became a shorthand for the struggle for change.

I go into another room, where contemporary film is showing pictures of a burnt-out Greyhound bus. This is the story of the multi-racial Freedom Riders who rode together into the South in 1954. Their bus was stopped by a mob and torched. Those inside escaped when the gas tank exploded, only to be beaten up with clubs for ten minutes, until the police arrived. 'OK folks, you've had your fun,' one officer said to the mob. 'Time to go home.'

Next I am invited to sit at a replica Woolworths counter to experience what happened in Greensboro, North Carolina, in 1960, when a group of black people sat, against the rules, in a whites-only area. I slide up on a shiny, red stool and a friendly guide slaps some large earphones on me and tells me to place my hands on the counter. The sounds in my ears start gently, as my colleagues speak reassuringly and tell me to be calm. Then the mob comes in. The mayhem starts. I find it difficult to describe what I hear, though for a moment I think I can feel the hot breath of an attacker as he leans into my ear and curses me. I read on the web later that I am not the only one who 'felt the breath' and was terrified.

I have lasted the full 1 minute, 30 seconds. It was terrifying and felt longer. As the docent takes away my earphones he tells me that quite a few people give up before the end, particularly Europeans. He has no idea why; later it occurs to me that it was our ignorance of these events.

I speak to an elegant African American woman I estimate to be in her 60s who is visiting from Alabama. I ask her whether she thinks things have changed. 'Sometimes I wonder whether we're back to where we were – the drop-out rates in college, the poverty, the violence. We were given the opportunity but it didn't take hold … It hurts.'

In room after room I see atrocities confronted with extraordinary courage and finally legislation. I feel ashamed that I know so little about these horrendous events, even though most took place only a handful of years before my first trip to this area.

The scope broadens. As we go up and through bright and airy rooms I see a huge quote from Martin Luther King: 'Injustice anywhere is a threat to justice everywhere.' The content moves to include white farmers in Zimbabwe, Christians in Burma, disabled people in many places, LBGTQ, slavery, labour practices. And then a wall of heroes and heroines, such as Mahatma Gandhi. Nelson Mandela and Eleanor Roosevelt – and another quote from Martin Luther King: 'The fight is not over.'

I am drained and want some lunch. I drag my luggage across the park to the CNN Center, where I am told there is a food court. A security guard stops me: suitcases aren't allowed in. I just want a sandwich, I say, and she relents. After I eat my sandwich I want to go to the restroom. She sighs, but relents again, though not before I produce the 'Can't Wait' card I carry for my ulcerative colitis.

'There's a camera over there,' she says, pointing. 'This could cost me my job.'

When I return she has been replaced by another security guard. I trust this is because her shift has ended, not her career.

I call for an Uber. I miss the first driver because I can't work out how to answer the phone when he calls. I manage to connect with another driver, who takes me back to the bus station. I have developed a ritual for checking when I get out that my pockets still contain wallet, notebook and Morris the mobile. As the driver pulls away I perform the ritual: Morris is gone, presumably still in the back of the car I now see turning the corner at the end of the road.

I check my pockets, ransack my rucksack, scour the gutters. I seek help from the Greyhound staff, who phone my phone, but no-one answers. I seek help from the security guards who phone Morris again. No answer.

I am now standing outside the bus station, which is crowded with smokers and more. One young lady, who has been talking to the security guard in friendly terms, offers to phone Uber, but we fail. She then offers to sell me her phone, at which point I make my excuses and go back inside. My immediate reaction was 'What else is for sale?', which in hindsight I realise was terribly unfair.

Time ticks on, towards the time that my bus is scheduled to leave; unlike most of my buses so far, this one will of course leave bang on schedule. I have to decide whether to take the bus and leave the phone behind, which is what the Greyhound staff suggest – or wait and carry on tracking down the driver. Someone suggests that I might find help in a T-Mobile store.

That clinches it: I decide to stay on, and I watch as my bus pulls out and leaves.

A taxi rank is just across the street. The drivers have already seen my plight and, as I am about to discover, their predatory instincts have been roused. I am ushered into a battered and rusting white car with a large driver who speaks with a French accent. He says the nearest T-Mobile store is in Midtown and quotes me $15.

When we arrive he asks for $20. I refuse. At the time we are standing outside the cab in the searing heat, and he takes a step forward. He is, as I said, a large man, and I am a small one. I settle for $17, or it may be $18. I am not in a mood to remember. I am shaken by my ineptitude and his aggression.

The T-Mobile store is an oasis of cool. I am assigned to Amoshia, a young African American who is calm, knowledgeable and sympathetic. I have Geoffrey, my tablet, in my rucksack, and she handles him deftly, seizing on the fact that I have a copy of the receipt from my trip. She finds the driver's contact number and rings it. He rings back. He has Morris in his car and will bring it to me within the hour. Job done.

Amoshia now helps me to find somewhere to stay, which is not easy since a big design conference is in town and the delegates have taken all the best rooms. She works the internet and finds a room at the Emory Conference Center Hotel – built to a visionary Frank Lloyd Wright design with 'luxury guestrooms in a resort-like setting', according to its website. But it's eight miles from the bus station and even more expensive than my hotel last night (unless you cost it by the hour, since I will be in my room for ten hours this time, not six).

I need to eat and Amoshia is about to take a break, so I ask if I can buy her supper. She clears it with her manager and we go to a bar and restaurant across the street.

She is 24 and comes from Columbia, South Carolina. Her father was a soldier. She has just enrolled for a master's degree in writing at a local college. And she makes sure I know early on in our conversation that she is a committed Christian, a member of the Young Christian Apostolic Church. When our food arrives, she says an extemporised grace.

'Less than a year ago I found Jesus,' she says, hinting that things had not been going well; I am not inclined to probe. I mention my Catholic upbringing and my concern that what some US churches seem to be preaching – that wealth is godliness – does not conform to the Christian values I learnt, and still value.

'You can get wolves in sheep's clothing,' she says. 'Some folk label themselves as being Christian and they act against the Word.' She adds: 'You can speak truth without bible bashing.'

Turning to politics, she believes Trump was sent by God for a purpose. She also believes that 'there will be mass destruction'. She talks a little about her writing, and when I press her she says that she wants her journalism to reflect her faith.

Her short break time is over and she goes back to work while I finish my meal. I write in my notebook: 'A most impressive young lady.' I don't agree with some of the things she has been saying, but she has a serenity and purpose – and I am grateful for what she has done for me.

She returns when I am on the point of paying the bill. The driver has arrived and wants to see a photo ID so I go out with her and show him my passport. He explains that the next passenger found my phone, but wanted to go to the airport which is why he didn't bring it back to the bus station. He looks a little shamefaced.

I take another Uber back to the bus station; the fare is $15, $5 less than the taxi driver asked me for earlier. I exchange my ticket for a seat on the bus that leaves at 7.30 tomorrow morning: I have to fork out a $20 fee even though I have paid extra for a flexible fare.

I get another Uber to my hotel. The second driver, Sandra, turns out to be a political science graduate and flight attendant who drives to pay for her holidays. I tell her about Amoshia, and my concerns about the type of Christianity that preaches wealth is godliness. She calls that 'Prosperity Preaching'. She consoles me by saying I wouldn't believe how many people leave their phones – and their keys – in the back of her car. She also points out the strip joint just across the road from the bus station. We later follow each other on Twitter.

I console myself with the fact that in the first eight days of my 1969 trip my diary records my anguish at losing important items on four separate occasions: my wallet, my address book and my camera (twice). It's nice to know that I'm not forgetting things because I am an old-timer; I'm forgetting them because that's what I do.

And tomorrow is another day. I have lost one of my two nights in Unadilla, but I still have almost a full day in the town to look forward to.

3. Unadilla, Georgia: the centre cannot hold

Thursday 11 July

I came across Unadilla, Georgia, a few months into my planning for the trip. I had been determined to get to some small communities away from the big cities, and found it listed as a Greyhound bus stop between Atlanta and Orlando. I started to trawl the web – and the more I read about the place the more I liked the sound of it.

According to the town's website the name comes from an Iroquois word which means meeting place. It is a second-class city (presumably a category not a judgement) with a population of about 3,600. It is in Dooly County, which has been close-run in recent presidential elections, with the Republicans taking it back in 2016 with a 51:49 split. The city has a Yard of the Month competition, and the mayor is a man called Myron Mixon.

I turned to Mayor Myron Mixon's personal website, which featured a jolly-looking cove with plenty of facial hair, and the strapline: 'Winningest Man in BBQ.' Looking further, I found he is a well-known TV chef, the chef/partner in a restaurant near Augusta, and a *New York Times*-listed best-selling author. I had visions of holding mayorally curated ribs in one hand, and in the other the July certificate for Yard of the Month that I was about to present to the winner – along with the tasteful gift I had brought over from an English garden centre.

I emailed the mayor's personal assistant. 'What a wonderful road trip ahead of you!' she wrote back. 'Unadilla is a very small town that was established because it was a frequent stop for the railroad. Everyone knows everyone here and we are the epitome of southern hospitality. I cannot confirm if the Mayor will be available on July 11. Summer is obviously his busy season with barbecue. I will see if I can schedule a sit down with the two of you.'

That was most encouraging, but as the weeks passed I heard no more. By then I was getting used to emails not being answered and was only moderately worried. I phoned from the bus station in Washington and got through to an answering machine, which made me a little more anxious, but not hopelessly so.

Now, leaving Atlanta in the early morning, the bus ride goes well, despite a chronic sniffer seated directly behind me. The bus arrives on time and I step down at the bus stop a mere 16 hours behind my original schedule. The bus stop is at the All State Truck Shop, which is also a gas station, a repair shop, a 24-hour restaurant and a general store with a wide range of products (though sadly no model buses).

I chat to the manager about whether Greyhound buses have changed. 'Society has changed,' he says; '90 per cent of passengers are on welfare. At night times they can be dangerous: they hit on young girls, drink alcohol (which they're not meant to) and if you fall into a deep sleep they'll take your money.'

I tell him about my Golden Jubilee Bus Tour and he is intrigued.

'This was a neat little county town until Walmart came along and everyone started to shop out of town,' he says. 'Downtown is nothing more than a couple of shells and a few hardware stores ... But you must see the mayor.'

I tell him I hope I will.

I then call up my Uber app to find a car to take me the mile to town. For the first time on this trip Morris can show me no baby Ubers cavorting in the vicinity. I ask the manager where I can find a taxi, and he chortles. 'Taxis? None here.'

I reckon I can walk a mile easily, even with luggage, so I stride out towards the town. I quickly find out that a mile at home in Surrey is not the same as a mile in Georgia, USA. First is the heat, now in the 80s and rising. Second is my realisation that a small, hot Englishman struggling along with rucksack and suitcase might look like an attractive proposition to a predator. I retrace my steps to the All State Truck Stop, put on my bewildered Britisher look, and ask if there is any way I can get a ride.

One of the cooks takes me to a battered man with a battered car. He drives me into town, past a fine-looking building that he says used to be a bank. We pass other empty buildings in various states of disrepair, and some farm machinery rusting by a broken-down shed. I see no people. He deposits me between a derelict building on one side of the road and a newer office block on the other, which turns out to be City Hall. I offer to pay but he declines my offer. I tell him how grateful I am.

Unadilla, Georgia: the view from City Hall.

City Hall is blissfully cool, with comfortable seats and a jolly poster advertising the summer reading club. I tell my story to the young woman at the desk and ask if the mayor's PA is there. After a short while she comes back looking embarrassed. The mayor is not in town, she says. Can I see the PA? She is not available either.

This is bad news. I don't know whether I have offended the mayor, or his PA, or both. Maybe he really was out of town and busy? Or maybe he disliked something in my CV? Whatever the reason, I am now stuck in a near-empty, apparently run-down town with no transport. My hotel is over a mile away and the temperature is now in the 90s.

I defer a decision by strolling along what appears to be Main Street. Of the nearly dozen store fronts, only three have signs of occupation: a dog grooming parlour, the Lions Club and a diner (currently closed for a vacation). I go to an antique shop filled with stuff and lined outside with rusty implements, but it looks very closed: when I read the flyer in the window it is for a Grand Night of Singing at a nearby Methodist church 16 months ago. The only sign of life is a man with a truck who is using an unusual red bark to mulch some trees along the pavement. His radio is blaring. I begin to feel like the cowboy hero striding into a town so deserted that the only other moving thing is the tumbleweed.

I walk up to a parallel street, which as far as I can tell from Google Maps will take me nearer to my hotel. I see more empty buildings. I also see a garage with a Mercedes pulled up, taking petrol at an unmanned station, and I walk towards the driver to check if I am on the right road for my hotel. Although he's twice my size the driver recoils angrily: 'I have money out. Keep back.' And he quickly closes the car window,

I ring the hotel, but they have no-one free to pick me up. I have no alternative but to keep on walking. And here the picture changes: I am no longer among run-down, empty buildings, but in a leafy street with neat houses, tidy gardens and a variety of cars – some large. Among the houses is what was obviously a school, now boarded up.

I pass a sign saying suspicious people will be reported to the sheriff and wonder what non-suspicious-looking people look like and whether I fit the bill. It then dawns on me that reporting suspicious people to the sheriff may not be the first choice of action here. How many of these respectable homes have a firearm of military strength propped up by the front door? I walk faster.

I check with Google Maps, and a prison has appeared within range. I walk faster still.

At last I pass a garage, cross the I-75 over a bridge and find my motel, a Travelodge, one exit away from the one my bus took for the All State Truck Stop. I'm greeted by one of the staff, who (like several others I see in Unadilla) is of Indian sub-continent origin. 'I like this town,' he tells me. 'I like this country. I like the President.' Unadilla is very safe, he adds, though I remain unconvinced that this extends to mad Englishmen wheeling suitcases along residential roads in the midday sun.

For most of the afternoon I recover in the air-conditioned cool of my room, writing up my journal. I take a break, and talk in the car park to a woman struggling to get into her car with a bag and a crutch. She and her son are staying at the motel because her air conditioning has broken and she is waiting for it to be repaired. She is not insured.

She has lived in Unadilla all her life. 'You should meet the mayor,' she advises.

When it gets cooler I walk back to the garage on the other side of the freeway. On either side of the road, under huge and billowing American flags, are substantial retail outlets. One is a Ford/Chevrolet dealer, with several hundred large vehicles – mainly white – parked outside. The other is a huge discount clothing store called Clothing Carnival.

I go into the latter and chat with three staff members standing by the tills. They tell me that Unadilla does have a community life, such as a senior citizens' centre and a community centre about to be set up in the former bank. But, like many other small rural towns in the US, many of the young are heading out to colleges and cities, and have been for some time. It is an interesting conversation and later one of them emails to wish me well with my book.

So Unadilla is not dying – but you do need a car. Back in my hotel I phone the nearest taxi/Uber driver, who lives a couple of towns away. He agrees to pick me up tomorrow for $20: for me it will be a 1.5-mile journey, though for him it will be a lot longer. I have no option.

Friday 12 July

Next morning I find several messages from friends warning me that Hurricane Barry is heading towards New Orleans, as am I. As I eat my breakfast the Governor of Louisiana talks on CNN about the impending danger. He has called out the National Guard and has put 300 buses on alert. I try to convince myself that I have plenty of time to change my route.

My taxi driver picks me up: the trip takes less than five minutes, hardly enough for a proper conversation. 'I'll only charge you $10,' he says when we arrive, and I thank him.

The bus comes and I climb aboard. I collect my thoughts on Unadilla. The town centre was desolate and many services lacking, but most of the people I met were friendly and generous. I would have liked to have talked to the mayor about this – but never mind, I have another Unadilla coming up later. Let's hope I can speak with the mayor there.

4. Orlando: street life and bedroom conversations

I am on my way to see how Orlando, Florida, has grown. The only mention of the city in my 1969 diary is a brief stop at the bus station to have breakfast: 'Sat next to a soldier who was going home on leave to his wife after six weeks intensive training – some of his excitement rubbed off on me.'

My 1969 BUNAC guide, my travel bible, didn't mention the place at all. This is not surprising because it was then a small town of under 300,000 people, known mainly for an airbase that had been transferred over to the navy the previous year. Today it has a population of nearly 2 million people, attracts about 75 million visitors a year, and is considered the theme park capital of the world.

It has clearly been a half-century of huge change, so I have booked two nights at an Airbnb to investigate further. This will be my first solo Airbnb experience: the only other time was for a week in England, and I went with Barbara, who had made the arrangements.

My chosen destination describes itself as a 'charming studio apartment' and I receive a friendly e-note from my host, Melissa, explaining how to let myself in. She tells me to look for an illuminated sign of welcome and asks what time I plan to arrive. I try to reply on my Airbnb app, but for some reason it won't let me. I assume she'll be able to help me sort it out when I meet her.

My driver drops me in an area of upmarket suburban houses. A tropical storm is raging and the rain is belting down. The sign of welcome is a beacon of friendliness. However, I have to squint at and fiddle with the key box, and by the time I get in I am soaking wet.

What was once a garage has been lovingly converted into a living room/bedroom, bathroom and kitchen, all well equipped. Cold drinks are in the fridge and welcome snacks on the work surface. A stack of electronic equipment is on the dresser, and images on the television are moving silently around the screen. I try to tune in to a terrestrial station, but a notice comes up on the screen to tell me there is no service.

Next to the television I see an unfamiliar semi-spherical object. A note tells me this is a Google Assistant (hereafter to be known as GA, not necessarily affectionately), and explains how I can introduce myself.

I speak to GA, a little tentatively at first; after all, this is our first date. She handles my early questions competently, telling me the outside temperature and Boris Johnson's current occupation, but is less successful at providing me with music. When I ask for something classical it is so quiet I can hardly hear it. I look for a way of stopping it. As with so many modern gadgets there is nothing so simple as an on/off button, so I tell GA to shut up. It works most satisfactorily.

That evening I leave GA to her own devices and brave the rain to walk the mile into central Orlando. The houses are upmarket and bursting with shrubbery. A lake gleams as I pass. There is no-one walking the streets but me. I sit at the bar at an elegant sushi restaurant and chat to the couple next to me. They talk about a film they have seen recently about a flood in Orlando which brings all the alligators out from the lakes, who then start gobbling up the population.

My glass of wine goes to my head. Foolishly I decide to walk back. It is still pouring with rain. As I walk I scan the shrubs carefully in case two large alligator eyes are looking at me hungrily. (I hadn't worked out what I was going to do if I saw them.) I pore over my Google map in the dark trying to find the house, until I realise I am outside it and that the Welcome sign has been turned off. GA neither welcomes me back nor asks what took so long.

I feel I have been transported onto a different planet, stuffed with gadgets just beyond my competence. I can't even open the little packets of treats that have been left out for me. I go to sleep thinking I am in a film – and one that is unlikely to end well.

Saturday 13 July

In the sunshine, the streets seem friendlier, and I see joggers but no alligators. As I walk through a pleasant park, I notice a small group in red T-shirts handing out little care packages and cards to a handful of homeless people. They hand me one of the cards. On one side is written: THIS CARD COULD CHANGE YOUR LIFE FOREVER; on the other I am invited to one of their church services. They are a group called EpicLife: my bus schedule won't give me time to attend the service, but later I look up their website.

Their core beliefs include giving generously to the church: their website quotes scripture (Malachi 3: 10–12) and says 'we honor God with the first fruits of our increase; the 10% of our income that is the tithe.' I watch a couple of videos from their services, each ending with an impassioned plea for donations. The message seems to be if you're worried about money you should give them some because God will provide: 'Our worship with God is with giving … When we tithe we lay up treasures.' I can't help wondering about this all-loving God who's happy for the poor to divert scarce funds away from themselves and their families …

I am on my way to the Orlando Public Library. Early in my researches I had made contact with Matthew David, one of the managers. It was not easy: my emails bounced, so we had to use the phone, then Skype, then Twitter. But he managed to give me good advice on what to do in Orlando and invited me for a tour of the library.

As I approach I see a banner proclaiming that it has been awarded a 2018 National Medal for Museum and Library Service. Matthew is on holiday, so I am met by Kim, who has worked there since 2001. She shows me the Melrose Center, opened in 2014 with a $1 million grant from an Orlando businessman in memory of his late mother, a great supporter of the library. I find myself in a huge central space around which are audio, video and photography studios, meeting rooms, a lab with 3D printers, an interactive media wall and more. They are there to give residents the skills they need in order to use modern communication tools, and then the facilities to put their new skills into practice.

I tour four other floors. There are shelves and shelves of books, of course, ranging from Atlanta yearbooks over the ages to two copies of *How to Hire a Nanny*. But there are also lines of computers, meeting rooms for local groups, a used book store run by the Friends of the Library, special areas for children and young adults, a sewing room, workshops for citizenship classes, and the Disneyworld archive (including not only the full range of copies of *Eyes and Ears*, the lavishly produced magazine for staff – but also the plumbing code used in the construction of Epcot). A Right Service at the Right Time computer allows anyone, not just those with a library card, to see information on (for example) how to find affordable homes and how to apply for food stamps.

There are plenty of people about, even for a Saturday morning, and clearly the library is providing plenty of useful personal and community support. I tell Kim that where I come from they are shutting libraries, not expanding them with innovative ideas. How can they afford it? She tells me that library services are a 'line item' on the property tax bill. They are free to residents, and non-residents can access most of the benefits for a fee.

'We show we are relevant and offer services of value,' she says. 'We try to be proactive, to find services which help people get involved in the community. That's why our residents are such staunch supporters.'

(As I write this up a few months later, I see a report that the UK's Chartered Institute of Public Finance and Accountancy's annual survey of UK libraries shows that 773 have closed since 2010.)

I go next door to what used to be the courthouse. In 1998 the court moved to a new 24-storey building, which seems like a lot of space for litigation – but then this is America. The old courthouse is now the home of the Orange County Regional History Centre.

I am looking for the story behind Orlando's transformation and find it under a sign: 'Welcome to the Magic Kingdom'. A few years before I passed this way in 1969, rumours went around that someone was secretly buying up large tracts of what was thought to be worthless marsh land. Some thought it might be Walt Disney, already doing well with his Disneyland theme park out west in California, but no-one was sure. And he wasn't saying. According to the museum, when someone once spotted the man himself they were told: 'I get mistaken for him all the time. If ever I run into that SoB I'll tell him what I think of him.'

In 1966 Disney went public with his plans. The museum shows the first rough sketch he made, with a park, hotels, a lake, a golf course and a tourist trailer camp; it looks a bit like a multi-petalled flower. The resort was opened five years later on 27 October 1971 – 'the day we changed', according to the museum. Within two years it had attracted 20 million visitors. By 1989 the urban area had expanded 200 per cent and the population by 140 per cent.

Orlando has also played a major part in space exploration and was the site of a major aeronautics firm that merged with Lockheed. The rockets sending astronauts to the moon were launched only 50 miles away, at Cape Canaveral. They included a local boy, John Young, who was Commander of Apollo 16 and walked on the moon. The highway I was driven along, coming in from the bus station, is named after him.

A more recent, though unwanted, claim to fame was the 2016 shooting at the gay nightclub Pulse which killed 49 and injured 53. A couple of floors down in the museum is a temporary exhibit inspired by the tragedy. In the aftermath a local art retailer offered free materials to those wishing to commemorate victims, and the results are shown here. They include photos of two male hands clasping and of a sea of rainbow flags; a series of pictures by a single artist, one for each of those killed; a recipe book and a book for children. Bright colours and the word 'Love' abound. You can't help but be moved.

For lunch I find a branch of the global sandwich chain Subway, not one of my favourite haunts but at least the menu won't hold any surprises. As I am about to leave after my meal I notice a young woman with (unusually for America) a cracked front tooth. She is standing at the till with an emaciated, ill-dressed man. She pays for what's on his tray and hands him $5. When I go up to her she looks alarmed, but softens when I tell her about my trip.

'There are times we have to do something,' she says. She is a Christian – a Baptist, but not a regular churchgoer and not preachy, she says. Her job is cleaning the offices above where we are eating, and she is on her way to start work. She earns $8.50 an hour.

'They think being poor is somehow bad. I don't think they should criticise,' she says. 'I went through 15 years of bad stuff. I didn't have a job until a year ago. I was living with someone who abused me. I got out and now I live with my two children.'

She indicates the homeless man. 'I was almost there for some years. The government have turned their backs on them.'

I feel humbled and guilty. I would like to give to the homeless I see around me but don't have the nerve (or the local knowledge). I offer her $10 and she looks startled again, until I explain my motives.

'I'd like you to give this to someone who needs it,' I say. She seems pleased.

As we chat I tell her I am on Twitter and a few hours later I see that she has tweeted about the 'kind English gentleman' who gave her money to give to the poor. I look her up and find that she set up the account after we met. This is the good side of America.

I return to my lonely high-tech garage. My phone still won't let me connect to my hosts via my Airbnb app, which warns me not to contact them directly. I disobey and ring the phone number on the message they have sent me. I get connected to Falcon Bar and Gallery. I hang up before finding out whether my hosts own it, sing in it, cook in it, or are just having a drink.

They clearly live in the house in front of the garage, so I walk the few paces to their front door. On one side a sign says, 'Knock if you like Satan' and on the other, 'Guarded by ADT'. An extra line of defence appears: a gruff pug makes eye contact from the bottom of the other side of the door. It bares its teeth, then barks. I retreat to the safety of the garage. I do not tell GA what I have just done.

That evening I go out to eat. I take my rucksack on the grounds that in a country of guns having an Epipen (for my wasp allergy) in each trouser pocket might be misinterpreted as carrying arms and lead to trouble. Back in the garage later I have another go at turning on the TV: I want to find out more about Hurricane Barry, which is still threatening New Orleans. I still can't make the TV work.

'How do I get a signal?' I ask GA.

'The Orlando Signal Company is ten minutes by car,' she replies.

'Are you any use?' I ask.

'I've got to admit I'm not quite sure.'

Is she showing a human trait? Come to think of it, is uncertainty a human trait anyway these days? I go to sleep. In my dreams no alligators come to eat me.

Sunday 14 July

My most urgent job today is to restore links with Airbnb. They want me to give them some personal information I have already given them. I try again but my password won't work, though I'm sure it's the right one. I ask for it to be reset, only to find that part of the procedure will involve their contacting me by phone – which would have been fine had we not put the relevant SIM card on Barbara's phone, now languishing back home in London.

I start once more. I put in my new US number. Then I am told that to verify this they are sending a message to the number that I thought I had just changed. I give up.

And all this to speak to someone whose doorstep I can walk to in under ten seconds.

I ask GA the temperature. 'A high of 95,' she threatens. I ask what time the bus goes to Tampa: 'I'm sorry. I don't understand.'

As I go, I say goodbye. She answers in Hindi; at least that's what she tells me. Smart-arse.

I go downtown for brunch. I look forward to broadening my conversational skills beyond robots, and approach a couple of elderly ladies (my age perhaps?) and ask if they know where I can get something to eat. One of them reaches into her purse to give me some money. I explain my situation and decline. America's kind streak again.

Kindness does not extend to my Twitter followers. When I tell them I have in effect been mistaken for a homeless person, one tweets back: 'Next time look in the mirror before you leave.'

Today's Uber driver does not sound kind either, and his sympathies are not with the homeless: 'It's their own fault,' he says. 'There's plenty of work.

Soon I am comfortably installed in my bus and speeding past what looks like a tacky Roman Coliseum. A notice says: 'The Holy Land Experience'. Holy Shit!

My attention taken, I keep looking out of the bus as the hoardings flash by: Fun Spot – Stop, Drop and Roll; Hagrid's Motorbike Adventure; Toy Story Land; Infinity Falls, World's Tallest Drop. A rocky mountain glides by, complete with waterfall and a tangle of waterslides. Then comes a tethered balloon. The playgrounds proliferate – and we are still miles from Disneyworld.

When I came this way in 1969 I dismissed my surroundings curtly as 'palm trees, farm land, swamp etc'. Today I see wide roads, grassy patches, little pools at the intersections, squadrons of well-groomed palm trees, carefully sited in their rows. High-end hotels and higher-rise blocks of holiday apartments hide behind huge gates. Nature has largely been banished, and replaced by an ersatz world of order and entertainment.

We pass what looks like a hawk, up in the sky. By now I have no idea whether it is real or a plastic model.

I change buses at Tampa, and as I am climbing on board my new driver says: 'You do know that this bus no longer goes to St Petersburg? It will stop at Largo instead.'

Actually I didn't. Call me old-fashioned, but I usually believe what is printed on the ticket.

We get dumped in a car park 15 miles away from where I want to be. Quite a few of us get off here, but most of the passengers knew the score and have lifts waiting for them. I try to contact an Uber. It's baking hot with no shade and sun so bright that I have trouble reading Morris. The driver, when he appears, offends me by asking if this is my first Uber trip.

He is from Cuba and has been in the United States for 24 years. I mention immigration.

'We can't take everyone,' he says. 'They're taking our jobs. Trump could be the best president; he could be the worst. But the Democrats are always reacting – you can't win that way, you got to be creating. He's not suited to be a president, but that's what you get when you get things wrong.'

I ask the all-important question: 'Will you be voting for him?'

'Yes. There's nobody else.'

5. St Petersburg: ageing gracefully

My whippersnapper self was scathing about St Petersburg in 1969, cruelly writing it off as the place where Americans go to die. I can't wait to see what I make of it now that I'm approaching the age of those I pilloried.

At least back then the bus station was in the middle of town. I arrived early in the morning: 'Walked down to the beach – the streets nearly deserted with only a few octogenarians around. I change in the public restroom, rather frightened by the lifeguard who had just been bitten by a jellyfish. Go in for a swim – the water very warm.'

I then sat on the beach chatting first to lifeguards, next with a group of small boys who stole my cigarettes. Later I took a walk past a long pier, around a reconstruction of the Bounty and into the history museum. When I got back to the beach a lifeguard who had promised to show me the town had gone off with a girl instead. 'Who can blame him?' I wrote in my diary. I think I'd be less tolerant now.

I also chatted with an 'old lady' who told me that the world had only seven years to go, and that that the Kennedys, the Popes and the Arabs were all evil. 'Such people do apparently exist!' I confided to my diary.

I wrote home: 'Aged Americans, preserved unnaturally by the best (and most expensive) of American medicine, pass their days keeping in the shadows. The chief industries seem to be medicine, investment advice and undertaking.'

For this trip I have booked into a 30-room independent hotel not far from the waterfront. The Inn on Third has been a hotel since 1937 and has wooden furniture, brass handles and a slew of daily newspapers in the lobby. I am greeted by Stephanie, who has run the hotel with her husband Brian for nearly 15 years. She advises me where to eat (writing on a paper map to show me how to get there) and where to get my laundry done (in the hotel). She adds that, as an extra touch of hospitality, each night guests are offered a beer or a glass of wine with nibbles in the lobby. These are proper snacks in a bowl, not confined to packets that I can't open.

I take the suggested route down to the waterfront. The dreary streets

Rui Faris, director of the St Petersburg Museum of History:
'It's a good thing we are no longer God's waiting room'.

of 1969 have transformed and are packed with busy restaurants and fashionable art galleries. Tables are out on the pavement. A pair of heavily tattooed young women pass, holding hands. An elderly man wheels a toddler up and down in a little cart. A young woman with a small dog unzips her ukulele and puts up a music stand, ready to busk. A saxophonist lets rip. It is lively and cosmopolitan. Now that I am back with real people I am starting to enjoy myself again.

Today I am going back to the St Petersburg Museum of History where I have arranged to meet Rui Faris, a former sports journalist who is now its director. The museum is small compared to Orlando's, but its attractions include a replica of a 1913 Benoist Airboat hanging in one room and what it claims is the largest collection of signed baseballs in the world. It also has one of the green benches that used to line the waterfront; I must have sat on one in 1969, so I sat on one to take a selfie (my third on this trip) against a background of 1930s holidaymakers.

Rui is shocked when I tell him I was offloaded in Largo. The bus station I had come into in 1969 moved to a new site soon afterwards, and this is the one that has now been sold for redevelopment. And there have been other changes: the pier I mentioned was remodelled in 1972 but taken down four years ago, after sea water had fatally eroded the foundations. A new pier is being built and the entire area, including the beach, is closed while the work is being done.

The traditional economic drivers have also gone. 'The last citrus grove in Seminole was sold two years ago for housing,' says Rui. 'Now the oranges come from Brazil. Tourism drives the economy now.

'It's a good thing we're no longer God's Waiting Room, but people need to be wary what they wish for. Old Florida is fast disappearing. The prettiness of it is being lost. The towers are going up – apartments in the latest block were selling for $900,000, and they were sold out before they were finished.

'And,' he adds, 'it's now almost impossible to find a parking space downtown.'

He first came to the city in 1967 when he was four. His parents were from Portugal, and they bought and ran a 30-bedroom hotel dating from the 1930s. Its clientele was mainly retired people, and it was half-full in summer and full in winter, with a handful of people living there all year round. The hotel is long gone, and the site is part of the Johns Hopkins Children's Hospital. 'Had my father hung on another ten years and sold to them, I would be retired right now,' says Rui.

St Petersburg has festivals, concerts, world class museums, the largest gay pride festival in the south – and a slew of small businesses. 'A city of swamps, orange groves and cow pastures is now a city of hipsters. There are murals in the streets. People are eating outside. There used to be ordnances preventing that!'

On Rui's advice I walk along the waterfront to the Vinoy Park Hotel, an opulent resort listed on the National Register of Historic Places. Like the city, it has had its ups and downs – and has had the good sense to record them in a little museum, which Rui helped them install.

Built in 1926 the hotel could claim for a while that it was the 'finest luxury hotel on the west coast of Florida'. It was open only from December to March, but was so successful that it needed a three-storey dormitory for staff, and had two sittings for dinner for the guests.

By the time I was here in 1969 it was out of fashion and in decline; by then, visitors preferred to buy their own apartments in the city. In 1974 the hotel closed, the contents were auctioned, and the building was left vacant. It was resurrected in the early 1990s and last year sold to the Glazers, the family who own the Tampa Bay Buccaneers and Manchester United, for a reported $188.5 million.

I walk further on towards a beach which Rui thinks may have been the one where I chatted to lifeguards and my cigarettes were stolen. It doesn't look familiar, but it has been 50 years. The heat is intense. I call an Uber and for once am too tired to talk.

Tuesday 16 July

A group of teachers are staying in my hotel, and I hear them talking as they have breakfast. I go to join them and manage to inveigle my way into their conversation. They are here on a conference run by the International Forum on Language Teaching and are talking about the value of taking students away on exchanges to countries such as France. What they say has a familiar ring.

'Language teaching is not a priority,' says one. 'There's a big trend towards testing, and teachers' hands are tied more and more. Funding is going down.'

'I don't think people see any value in it,' adds another.

I tell them about my American wife who half a century ago majored in French at an American university and how – unable to afford an exchange – spent a year in a 'French House' on campus speaking French.

'I don't know anyone majoring in French these days,' comments one.

I mention the British perception that so few Americans own passports. Brian, the proprietor, immediately produces figures from the internet showing that the proportion has gone up from 20 to 40 per cent in the last 25 years. We discuss it: has the introduction of cruising made a difference?

I am gently rebuked for talking about 'foreign languages'. 'We use the term "languages other than English",' says one.

'We say "modern languages",' adds another.

Back to my room and the business of the day. My first task is to sort out the flight I have booked from Tampa to New Orleans on the low-cost Spirit Airlines, and I spend 15 minutes grappling with Geoffrey and the airline's robots. First, in order for me to take luggage into the cabin, the airline whacks me $59 on top of the $91 I have already paid, and then another $10 to reserve a window seat. (I feel it is my duty as a reporter to look out over an area that Hurricane Barry might well have devastated.)

I opt for uploading my boarding card and am notified that it has been sent to my phone. Morris hasn't got it, so I try Geoffrey, who has. It means that when I board the plane I will have to flash a tablet, not a mobile. That is, if it works.

I check out how much a Greyhound bus would have cost. A ticket to New Orleans tomorrow would have cost me $90 – that's $1 less than the cost of the flight plus the bag in the hold. The flight time is just over an hour, compared with a 17-hour 45-minute journey on the bus, which I would have spread out over two days.

I am feeling guilty that I spend so much time indoors fiddling with Morris and Geoffrey but this seems to be modern life. It's great when it works but can eat up time when it doesn't, and it's almost impossible to find timely support. In the shower I have a flash of insight. I am travelling not in one country but two, each with their different and unfamiliar languages and customs: USA and Technonia.

But I am also voyaging into my own hinterland, so maybe that should be three countries?

Organised and clean, I talk to Brian about the hotel.

'From day one it took off,' he says. 'This country has grown hugely. We've worked hard, the city has worked hard, and everyone has benefited … I want our children to have a nice life. It's always been a great thing to be American. I would like that to continue.'

What about the President and what appears to be his racism?

'He is brash and difficult. But one may think that he is making great corrections to the American machine.'

I tell him about the incident in the Subway in Orlando, and he tells me that around here people at a drive-in food counter often pay for the people behind. Sometimes the chain can extend to six people or more.

'This is a country without a safety net. It's extreme in terms of opportunity. But that's why people come here … I do believe that deep in their hearts most people are good. That explains the lady in Orlando with the sandwich.'

For lunch I walk up – slowly, in the heat – to a neighbourhood that Rui said would give me a taste of St Petersburg as it used to be. I pass quirky little stores, charming arcades and some challenging pavement signs. This one was outside a hairdresser's: 'I gotta get my life together … This damn heat makes me realize I can't go to hell.' I see a restaurant that promises 'Tiki Tapas Billiards/ Cold dead fish'. This is the place for me and my lunch.

My devices continue to give trouble. I am waiting to be served and reading a newspaper online when I press something I shouldn't and Geoffrey blurts out: 'Once upon a time disease was believed to be a punishment sent by God.'

I somehow manage to stifle the voice. I look round. Nobody seems to have noticed.

Later I take a shuttle bus so that I can stay in a motel near the airport at Tampa. The driver turns out to be a former Boeing engineer; the other passenger is from Dallas. They have been talking about Trump, they say, and ask what I think. I say I worry about what he is doing to the notion of truth. This goes down badly: they are scornful of the 'liberal dictatorship' and loathe the idea of the Green New Deal that some parts of the Democratic Party are now promoting.

They talk about how the county we have just driven through can't afford to recycle waste, so they send it to landfill or a mega-large incinerator (presumably to belch fumes into the atmosphere). Next they talk about how taxes are too high and ask if our health service is good for sick people; I say yes. Their faces tell me that's the wrong answer.

They start to talk approvingly about how one local authority has raised a lot of money through taxes to build a local sports stadium. I refrain from saying it's good to see socialism at work.

6. New Orleans: Katrina and Barry

Wednesday 17 July

My plan to fly to New Orleans has got me into Twitter trouble. Some of my followers have tweeted that not taking the bus is cheating: 'Surely that's not allowed?' asks Richard Smith. I reply that in the interests of objective reporting I will be able to compare two different types of low-cost travel.

I soon come up against one of the downsides of flying: the need to arrive two hours before take-off. My flight leaves at 7.10 am, which means arriving at the airport at 5.10, so I set a trio of alarms to ensure I get up at 4.10. My Pre-Embarkation Anxiety Syndrome is not confined to buses.

Then the upsides come in. At 5.10 in the morning Tampa International Airport is bright, bustling, full of passengers and staff. There are plenty of model planes on sale, though not surprisingly no model buses. As for food, instead of a row of vending machines (most of which are out of order) I have a choice of options: Chick Fil-A, PF Chang's, Starbucks, Hard Rock Café and more. This terminal is a far cry from the small, ageing, sparsely staffed bus stations I have been passing through.

I manage to print out my boarding pass and luggage tag, then go to the desk to query the $59 I paid yesterday for my cabin baggage. I was wrong to do so, I was told: my rucksack is not 'cabin baggage' but a 'personal item'. Who'd have known?

The nice lady tells me that she cannot reimburse me but tells me to ring the airline who, she assures me, will pay out. (She does not lie: a few days later I find the amount back in my account.)

On the plane I sit next to a couple who have moved to Florida from Jersey City, and they are happy to put their devices down and talk. This will be their first time in New Orleans, and they are going for a Michael Bublé concert. It seems to be the concert season; the Stones were here at the weekend, despite the threat of Hurricane Barry.

She used to work at Standard Chartered Bank in the World Trade Center, New York, and one of her roles was to help operate the recovery site across the Hudson River held ready if a disaster happened. By chance she was already at the site on the morning of 9/11, preparing for an audit. When the planes crashed into the Twin Towers she helped to switch the computers over from the main office to the recovery site. She had a 'prime view'.

'I could see things that were horrible. People were jumping. When the first building fell everything shook. It gives me goose bumps still just thinking about it ... I didn't get home until 5 am, and then I had a quick shower and went back.'

She tells me about their landlord, Jan Demczer, who had worked as a janitor at the World Trade Center. He used his squeegee to prise open a lift and free some workers, and then led them and others out of the building shortly before it collapsed. The squeegee is now in the World Trade Center museum with a gold commemorative plaque. She describes going to visit him a few days after the incident: 'He was still shaking.'

'The attack brought a lot of people together,' she says. 'The unity was amazing. We never thought we would see so many people work together.'

'What do you think has changed after 9/11?' I ask.

'The morals of people. What has been a democracy has been ruined. Hate and racism have come back. It's the way this president picks on people, degrades women. He does not understand what the United States of America represents.'

As she talks, I keep looking over my shoulder to check whether other passengers are reacting to our conversation. I worry that her views might provoke a reaction. I don't remember such a concern in 1969.

Soon our plane is losing height, passing over from the calm waters of the Gulf of Mexico towards well-ordered, prosperous suburbs. There is no sign of flooding. I take a shuttle bus into the city and the driver tells me that the recent scare stories about Hurricane Barry were 'a bust'.

Hurricane Katrina was a different matter, though, he says. 'I had five foot of water in my home. It scared everybody. I had to move away for a while. But things are now back to normal. They rebuilt. Some areas still need some work but that's because some people didn't come back.'

In the afternoon I go to see for myself. I have booked a tour, and our guide – a former pilot who drives, talks and plays us jazz CDs – takes us to some of the areas flooded in 2005. He points out one of the levees that infamously failed to keep out the floodwater. We pass a couple of houses still showing the marks made by inspectors to alert rescuers to the state of the house and to indicate if any occupants were still there, dead or alive.

One or two streets are still being repaired, and here and there is a new house, built prudently on stilts. On to the more fashionable areas: large ornate houses with painted wooden shutters, intricate ironwork on the balconies and an aura of private wealth. They have recovered well. Our guide points out which ones have been used for films and TV programmes (most of which I haven't heard of) and which celebrities live there (including Sandra Bullock and Nicolas Cage, who I have heard of).

I remember watching on television harrowing pictures of the aftermath of Katrina and wondering how the city could ever recover. From what I can tell so far, it has managed well.

I have booked a hotel in the French quarter, which I was much taken with in 1969, not least because it was the first time on that trip that I was able to have a cup of coffee *outside*. Now, in America as elsewhere, tobacco regulations have encouraged customers to spill out into what without irony is called fresh air.

I walk across the road to the Mississippi River, as I did in 1969. Now, as then, a paddle steamer is moored on the bank and in the middle distance is what last time I described as 'a splendid new bridge across the river'. It still looks splendid and from this distance has worn a lot better than I think I have. Around me the grass looks spectacularly green, a sign of summer rain.

I speak to a walker about Hurricane Barry. 'It was all hyped up by the newspapers. By the Wednesday evening everyone here knew we were going to be OK.'

Back in my hotel Morris still won't allow access to Airbnb, though Geoffrey has received a bland email saying how much they appreciate my problem, blah-blah. Through Geoffrey I write my first Airbnb review. Since I'm new to this and feeling vulnerable, I put down something bland, and award my hosts more stars than I think they deserve. This unlocks their review of me: 'He left the place clean.' It reminds me of my school reports which ended with faint praise: 'He is always polite.'

I am beginning to resent the constant requests for me to review where I stay, what I eat, what I see and how I travel. I care little about adding to the constant stream of five-star ratings seasoned with one or two spitefully low ones from those with axes to grind or blood ties to the competition. Nor do I want to spend time choosing my words so that they can be later used as free advertising copy. And anyway I fear that the results will be used less to improve the service than to bully the staff.

New Orleans: a house still bears the marks put there by inspectors after Hurricane Katrina.

That evening I stroll along Bourbon Street. There is plenty of neon and noise, though I hear fewer trumpets and saxophones than I'd expected, and more guitars. Tourists speaking many languages clog the street. A panhandler (I learnt this word at the Washington bus station) holds up a creative sign: 'For weed and socks'. A pair of young street dancers skitter past; a few moments later I see why: two policemen are walking down the street.

As I walk through this tourist trap I suddenly realise that none of those trying to entice passers-by into their establishment are bothering to entice me. They did last time. Here's another difference that half a century has made to me, and I am not sure I like it.

Thursday 18 July

'Went for a stroll around the old quarter,' I wrote in 1969. 'Much to look at in the quaint streets and arches, especially paintings. Went into museum (25¢) but little of great interest: exhibits on Mardi Gras, old costumes and old toys, including a splendid clockwork train set.'

Today I am going back to the same museum, the Presbytère (admission $7 for seniors). It still has a Mardi Gras exhibit, but I have come to learn more about the horrendous events of 2005.

The exhibit is *Living with Hurricanes: Katrina and Beyond,* and the first room gives the back story. The previous 'big one' had been Hurricane Betsy in 1965, which claimed 58 deaths, flooded 22,000 homes and prompted Congress to authorise the Corps of Engineers to build a prevention system. They never finished it.

The second room shows how Katrina started. As the storm built, the warnings were grave and a state of emergency was declared. Some residents left, others started to take refuge in the Superdome, walking along the car-deserted freeways to get there. The storm hit on the weekend of 26–27 August 2005, working up to a Category 5 hurricane with winds of 160 mph.

The next room is in darkness, punctuated by lightning-like flashes, and gives us some sense of the full force of a major hurricane. One wall is taken up by a screen on which runs film recorded by some extraordinarily brave people: heaving expanses of water, palm trees bent right over, a fleeting image of a pet dog cowering in the wreckage and another of what looks like a dead hand hanging off a balcony as the rain beats down. There is no need for a commentary: nature speaks for herself.

Next we see the start of the floods. In some areas the water rises fast, forcing people to climb up to their attic, smash a hole in the roof and climb out. People start to die – of dehydration, stroke, heart attack, lack of medicine. At that time the over-75s made up only 6 per cent of the population – but almost half of the deaths.

A relay of screens presents first-hand testimony of those caught up in the unfolding disaster. Conference delegates wheel their cases to a bridge, attracting more and more followers as they go, only to be told that there are no buses; they are then fired on by sheriffs. A pair of doctors see Marine One approach and they discuss who will be chosen to meet the President when he lands, only to watch the helicopter fly over and recede into the distance. Snipers fire on medical staff as they work in their hospital. The horrors multiply.

The Superdome becomes a disaster in its own right as thousands of people are packed into the arena amid stifling heat, bursting lavatories, inadequate supplies – with no mobile phone coverage and no coordination. The National Guard is responsible for conditions in the Superdome, and the army for evacuation; an officer is quoted saying that they do not speak to each other.

Whoever wrote the narrative pulls no punches: 'Shock turned to frustration and anger as millions watched desperate citizens trapped on rooftops or stranded at triage points, with woefully inadequate food, water and medical supplies … Government at all levels seemed stymied by the catastrophe.'

The event was 'a natural force with an outcome compounded by human error'. Systems and structures were 'incorrectly planned and engineered.' Preparation 'fell far short of acceptable levels'. And all this on a community made particularly vulnerable by a combination of poverty and environmental changes – crucially, the loss of its wetland buffers.

The first breach of the defences was on 29 August. An exhibit shows in 26 steps how the waters occupied the city, area by area. It was not until 11 October that the streets were fully 'unwatered'.

Among the first-hand accounts are items taken from the wrecked city. An axe used to break out from an attic to a roof. An abandoned teddy bear. A pair of jeans on which someone had written their phone number, just in case. Fats Domino's Steinway grand piano upended, just as Katrina left it. Also conserved is a wall fragment taken from a demolished house on which a stranded resident wrote a diary. One entry reads: 'Sunday. Nice weather. But it will never be normal.'

The final death toll was about 1,800. Looking back, national institutions failed to an extent that we would have found hard to anticipate in 1969.

And the danger is not over – as one sign in the museum warns: 'Louisiana can expect the Gulf waters to rise by 2–7 feet over the next century.'

A highlight of my 1969 trip was my visit to Dixieland Hall to hear Louis Cottrell and his band: 'a dingy hall, no air conditioning, no liquor but a great atmosphere. Dancers most amusing.'

The hall and Louis have long gone, but Preservation Hall, which was also open at the time of my visit, is still going strong. That evening I leave the air-conditioned cool of my hotel to stand in line, just past a beggar and her dog with the sign: 'She eats before I do', and between a couple of Irish pubs. Opposite is the Voodoo House, where a knot of black-clad heavily tattooed people are preparing to take the popular 'haunted New Orleans' tours. The line is exceptionally orderly, thanks to a well-mannered and apparently unarmed security officer who several times intervenes to stop people jumping the queue.

When the doors open we pay our $20 cash and file in. We sit on benches. It's simple but not dingy and definitely has air conditioning. The band enters – six African Americans of mature years followed by someone who comes in looking like a tourist, a little lost and clutching a bottle of water. She turns out to be a Japanese jazz pianist, Mari Watanabe.

The music comes from Guy Stafford and the Presentation Jazz Band, and I love it. The young woman next to me sways enthusiastically. Guy sings 'Careless Love', in which he hitches up his trousers and does a passable falsetto. He moves on to 'I'll be glad when you're dead', and tutors us to join in the chorus: 'You rascal you!/ You rascal you!'

The performance is less than an hour, which is not enough time to get bored. I speak to the woman at the door, who tells me that nothing has changed in 50 years. I speak to one of the band members, who tells me he is 87 – and a former lorry driver. The audience leave plenty of dollar bills in the hat.

Later I learn that Preservation Hall reopened only eight months after Hurricane Katrina hit the city.

The story in the news last night is President Trump's speech in Greenville, North Carolina, in which he attacks 'the squad' of four ethnic minority Congresswomen. He gets the crowd to chant: 'Send them home; send them home.' This is dangerous stuff: somebody tweets, 'What's next? Armbands?'

At the same time the Democrats seem weak: too many candidates, internal squabbles and lack of a real programme other than, 'We need to get this man out of the White House.' A headline in the *New York Times* says: 'Democrats say they won't repeat the mistakes of 2016. They don't agree what they were.'

The Cuban driver in St Petersburg who predicted that Trump will storm into a second term is not the only one telling me that. But many say the opposite, though I doubt things will go as far as the prediction of a woman I talked to in a bus queue: 'He thinks he's getting away with it but they'll take his money and give it to the poor.'

Later that day I go to a coffee shop and start chatting to the server about my golden jubilee bus trip. Two ladies start listening. One gets up and comes over: 'It's great what you're doing. Let me pay for your tea.'

So this is America: one group baying to evict all immigrants, another buying welcome treats for visitors. Where will it lead?

Friday 19 July

This was the first time for a couple of nights that my coughing hadn't kept me awake, possibly because I bought some cough mixture yesterday. It has a child-proof cap which I managed to get off last night, but this morning, with my fingers stiff from sleep, I can't do it. I go downstairs and take it to the efficient lady on the front desk who slaps down the palm of one hand on the cap and twists it off with the other.

'I'm not cut out for the modern world,' I say.

'Most of us aren't,' she says. 'We're just faking it.'

7. Covington: a nice place for tea

In 1969 I had arrived in New Orleans early in the morning and by lunchtime was tired from the walking and the heat. It was the custom among us Greyhound riders to use our pass to take a siesta. We would ride a bus for an hour or so out of town, spend an hour so exploring, and then take a cool and relaxing trip back, ready for the evening's activities.

I chose to take a trip to a town called Covington, a place I hadn't heard of. The route would take me over Lake Pontchartrain, which I hadn't heard of either, along the longest bridge over water in the world, at just under 24 miles (38 km). It sounded interesting, and it was, though the monotony of the drive soon sent me to sleep.

In Covington I came across a state park. I wrote:

> Not only is there a beautiful river but also a beach, a number of small boys from a summer camp, various families etc. These swim, fish etc. Bit of rain. River mucky, trees dark green (with moss), soil sandy. I see an old negro and a young boy fishing together.

I took a couple of photographs, which I have still, and they remain among my favourites. The old man was wearing a dark brown felt hat and a brown coat, and the young boy, aged about 10 or 11, had spectacles and a yellow T-shirt. What makes the photograph special is that it was taken in Louisiana, in the Deep South.

I took it as a welcome sign that the world was changing for the better.

It goes without saying that I want to go back. I don't expect to see them still fishing, or even a comparable scene, but I hope to find the river and learn more about the town.

I contacted the office of the mayor in good time. Bridget, his executive assistant, promised to help: 'Mayor Mark will not be in due to outside work meetings, but I would love to meet with you and share information about Covington. Also, I have a couple who would love to share Covington's English connections with you.'

My favourite photographs from 1969, taken in Covington, Louisiana.

I take an Uber: one major change since last time is that there are no longer any scheduled bus routes from New Orleans to Covington. The bridge is still there, but with extra carriageways added.

However it is no longer in the *Guinness Book of Records* as the undisputed longest bridge in the world. That went to Jiaozhou Bay Bridge in China in 2011. The decision was challenged, and Jiaozhou Bay Bridge took the title of 'longest bridge over water (aggregate)', and the Pontchartrain Bridge the' longest bridge over water (continuous)'.

Bridget greets me in her office with a smile and a bag of goodies – a map, a magazine, a bicentennial scrapbook, branded lip salve, pen, sunglasses with green frames, and a superior key chain with torch. She is enthusiastic and welcoming, and tells me that she has lived in Covington since she was eight.

'When you were last here it was a small country town; now it is an affluent suburb,' she says.

She drives me to the museum at the Covington Trailhead, scene of concerts, a twice-weekly farmers' market and the start of a 31-mile paved trail. I am introduced to Debbie, who puts me in front of a video about the history of Covington: 'A little old town where the rivers meet.' It was a transport hub, then an oil town (there is oil offshore) and a resort. Now it is bigger than it ever has been, with 10,000 people in the city and 250,000 in the parish, many of whom moved out of the city after Hurricane Katrina and now commute back across the bridge.

'We have had growing pains,' says Bridget 'but it's an interesting place. People come from everywhere. And there are more and more young people.'

One of the problems has been opioid addiction and resulting suicides, which seem incongruous in such a comfortable community.

'It starts with an operation, and the doctor over-prescribes,' says Debbie, a graduate in social work and former teacher. 'These are normal people and they get addicted. It takes people who otherwise would go down life's trail with a productive outlet – and it just cripples them.'

'I get a lot of calls from people in trouble,' adds Bridget. The former police chief had started a 'great program' which meant that anyone walking in off the street and asking for help could get referred to various programs. It sounds encouraging.

Bridget drops me and my luggage off at the Southern Hotel, where, at her suggestion, I have booked in. The city is clearly proud of the hotel, which opened in 1907 when Covington was a major transport hub. It had 43 rooms – and hot and cold running water. Since 1983, over three decades, it has had a mixed career as courtroom annexe, government offices and bar. In 2011 it was bought and expensively restored, and is now doing well. My room is charming, with soft pillows beckoning. It's not cheap, but I'd reckoned it would be worth paying for a bit of pampering at this stage in my travels.

Bridget has an appointment but drops me off at the English Tearoom where I can have lunch. It is in a small side street but easy to spot because outside it a dummy in a peaked cap sits at the wheel of a London taxi. A few yards away a cut-out of the Queen seems to be emerging incongruously from a red phone box.

Inside, the walls are lined with shelves over-populated with china teapots (I sneak a look and they are made in China) – plus an eclectic range of British memorabilia. I sit facing an advert for an early Beatles concert, with on one side an oil painting of half a phone box, and on the other a framed picture of the 2013 Codebreakers reunion at Bletchley Park. In the washroom, the toilet has what looks like a gold seat and a chair upholstered with a Union Jack.

The catering is as eclectic as the decor. I look at the menu and make a

The English Tearoom 'where the catering is as eclectic as the décor'.

rough count with one of the young serving staff: we reckon nearly 200 different types of tea. Food is ostentatiously British: Marmite sandwiches, bangers and mash, crumpets, Scotch eggs, cheese and Branston pickle. I notice a few infiltrators, presumably for the local market, such as bagels and lox (marinated salmon) – and I can't see a toad in the hole. I choose cheese on toast.

Back in my hotel I check my timings for tomorrow's ride from Baton Rouge to Houston. Problem. I find I have made a mistake: the 12.00 trip I am booked on is for midnight tonight not midday tomorrow. If I take it I will have to forget about the luxurious pillows and start packing immediately.

I decide to change my journey time. Now that I know Greyhound demand $20 for a 'flexible' ticket, I decide to buy a new ticket online rather than change the one I have. All goes well, until at the point of delivery the app flashes up a number I must phone, and shuts down. I call the number and not for the first time on this trip find myself talking to someone in the Philippines speaking a brand of English I struggle to recognise.

We muddle through and I am issued with a ticket. But Morris isn't showing it. I ring Greyhound back and they email me one that I can print – except I haven't got a printer. The hotel receptionist kindly agrees that if I forward it to her she will print it for me.

I need some air and walk through the town. Unlike Unadilla, there are several signs of prosperity. I find a couple of clothes shops, an ice cream shop, several restaurants (one threatening Open Mic Night tonight), a bank and an ironmonger's that looks as if it has changed little from the last time I was here. I see two lawyers' offices – another sign that there is money around.

Now it is getting cooler I go to look for the park where I took my photograph in 1969. Down by the river I find a band setting up for tonight's community picnic. I show them the picture and they are intrigued, suggesting that the place I took it might be a little further down. I follow the path they suggest and come to a park, deserted but for a brace of kayakers. There is no-one fishing but the river bends and the bank is sandy. I take some photos of the river: it is still a peaceful spot.

I had hoped to meet Tim and Jan, the owners of the English Tearoom, at lunchtime, but they were not on the premises. As I dine in the restaurant attached to (but not part of) the hotel I receive charming emails from them both, inviting me to their monthly special event which is getting under way. It is curry night.

I go over. The event is in full swing, complete with trivia, costume competition, a belly dancer and tea pairings for each course. The place is packed out: about 60 people at $40 a head. While Jan busies herself as the evening's compere, I chat with Tim. He has a trim white moustache and wire-rimmed glasses, and wears a grey peaked cap (even indoors). He is an anglophile who used to be in real estate. When he burnt out he set up a small tea room, and it took off.

'The state is very French-oriented. But my ancestors came from England; we are English-oriented. We have travelled a lot in England and we get treated there better than anywhere else,' he says.

I ask about the signed Bletchley Park reunion photograph. It was donated by a customer, now aged 93, who was a codebreaker before being whisked off to the USA as a GI bride.

And why no toad in the hole?

'We used to have it on the menu. We still have Marmite sandwiches, but nobody orders them. We had to Americanise things a little. I wanted to have English china, but it got so expensive.

'You know, there's one English politician I really admire,' he adds.

I wait and wonder. He has a portrait of Thatcher and an entire room devoted to Churchill.

'Nigel Farage,' he says.

I think this is the spot: half a century later the river at Covington is as peaceful as it was.

As I leave I pass a notice for the next gala evening: Doctor Who night. It is already sold out.

The town is buzzing as I walk back to my hotel. The oyster bar across the road looks packed out. The corner café advertising open mic has a flautist playing and he finishes to polite applause as I pass. A wedding party, bristling with bonhomie, is gathering in my hotel's public rooms.

What do I make of Covington? It looks like a nice place to live. But I am aware I may only have got one side of the story.

Saturday 20 July

My elegant hotel does not do breakfasts, though they can sell me a little box of breakfast food at the bar. There is no way of getting to Baton Rouge by public transport, and since Ubers are rare in Covington the hotel has booked me a taxi. It will cost $110; another reminder that this really is a country for private cars.

As I wait, I talk to one of the staff about Covington. She has moved here earlier this year and likes it, though it is 'full of old white couples'.

I say I am finding people are kind face to face, but not when they get to their mobile phones.

'I don't have any social media,' she replies. 'They never bring the good stuff out. They don't tweet about someone going out to Africa and feeding 10,000 people. It's very negative. But people need to be open to others … It'll get better, I hope.'

The taxi driver is late and I start pacing. The hotel has to ring him. He arrives looking dishevelled and smelling of a quick cigarette. He says he overslept. I fear he has had a late, wild night.

As we drive I try to draw him out about Covington. He says he has lived in the city (that's what they call it – cities don't need cathedrals here) long enough to have seen the highway rebuilt three times. 'There are a couple of areas you don't want to go into,' he says, and leaves it at that.

At Baton Rouge, while waiting for the bus, I decide to try something new and buy a packet of Buster Rind's chicken skin snacks. It's probably a sign that I am missing Sunday roasts at home. Too late I read the label:

'INGREDIENTS: chicken skins (soybean oil and/or canola oil) (with TBHQ added to help protect flavour and dimethylpolysiloxane added to help inhibit foaming,) Flour (bleached wheat flour, malted barley flour, niacin, iron, thiamine mononitrate [vitamin B1], riboflavin [vitamin B2] and folic acid), seasoned salt (salt, sugar, spices including paprika and turmeric, onion, corn starch, garlic, tricalcium phosphate, paprika oleoresin and natural flavour) (spices, garlic powder, onion powder.) (Salt, sugar, spices, dehydrated garlic, monosodium glutamate, citric acid, smoke flavour, extractive of paprika.) (2% silicon dioxide) soy oil.)'

I find no discernible taste.

Three hours later we are passing a town called Lake Charles, Louisiana. It seems very industrial. I look it up on Morris and (without asking) am shown the top three local news headlines:

Lake Charles man accused of raping 9-year-old girl

Lake Charles Police say incident on Lucille Street investigated as murder suicide

Lake Charles Diocese knew of abuses years before listed dates.

We seem a long way from Covington already.

8. Houston: the moon and a fallen star

'The Eagle has wings.' I see this tweet on Morris shortly after 1 o'clock as my bus speeds through the Texas countryside. Today is the 50th anniversary of the first moon landing, and I have just discovered @ReliveApollo11, a Smithsonian project that is tweeting us through the momentous events in real time. This message tells us that 50 years ago *to the minute* the lunar module freed itself and started its descent to the moon.

Some eight hours later the Eagle has landed, and I, along with the other 12.4k followers, receive this sequence:

Neil Armstrong is completely outside of the lunar module, standing on the porch of the LM …

Armstrong: 'I am going to step off the Lunar Module now …'

People watching TV around the world cheering. Over 10,000 gathered in Central Park …

Armstrong: 'That's one small step for man, one giant leap for mankind.'

As I write this I have goose bumps. At the time landing on the moon was the future; now it's history – as far removed from us now as World War I was removed from us then. And I am looking forward to visiting tomorrow the place from where it was masterminded: Mission Control Houston.

Meanwhile my lodgings reflect another Houston shrine. My Airbnb for the next two nights takes up the ground floor of a modern condominium in an up-and-coming area a little out of the city centre. My new temporary home is called the Astrodome Suite: on walls are pictures of the iconic sports arena and a couple of shirts worn by the baseball team that played there. On the shelves are what would now be called merchandise, and in the hall outside my bedroom are two orange seats, numbered 5 and 114. I have happy memories of a visit to the stadium in 1969, which is why I have chosen to stay here.

Sunday 21 July

I am not surprised to find that the Space Center Houston – a non-profit Smithsonian Affiliate Museum – is heaving with visitors today. By the time I leave in mid-afternoon, the counters on the turnstiles have clocked in more than 5,000 people, nearly twice the daily average.

I start by waiting half an hour in line for a little tram to take me (and a couple of hundred more) to the NASA Johnson Space Center next door. This is government property, still active, and surrounded by a fierce-looking security fence. First impressions are of an upmarket university campus with bicycles, some of which we are told have been in constant use 'since before man stepped on the moon'.

We have a 15-minute wait – this time outdoors in the heat – before being taken to the Christopher C Kraft Jr. Mission Control Center. This is named after the cigar-chomping flight controller for Apollo who later became the Center's director. We file into a flight control room; this is the one they keep in reserve, though in the future it is expected to be activated for the push to Mars.

Over the last half-century I have seen many shots of the control room on films and TV but today I am seeing it from the back, through a glass panel. It is still impressive. Our guide points out where the flight director would have sat, with a place on his right for CapCom, the capsule communicator.

'Fifty years ago yesterday we took a humungous leap. Not only could we get a man into space, but they could live on the spacecraft, land on the moon and come back safely to earth,' says our guide. 'There's only eight generations of grandma between the moon landing and the time Galileo identified the planets. This room is the past, the present and the future of the space craft industry.'

Impressed though I am, I don't have the energy to swelter in another long queue to see the next landmark, the Training Center. I start walking to the tram that will take me back through the fence and to the Visitor Center. On the way, in a long shed, is a Saturn rocket; it is massive. I pace it out: it takes 130 of my long strides, the equivalent of six cricket wickets.

Back in the Visitor Center I am plunged into a world more Disneyworld than Smithsonian, with several ways of persuading me and my fellow visitors to part with our money. We can choose between three different simulator flights. We can experience the disorienting effect of zero gravity. We can have our picture taken and doctored to look as if we are standing

Mission Control Center, Houston: 'Fifty years ago yesterday we took a humungous leap'.

on Mars. And when we are done, the gift shop offers furry little space monkeys, freeze-dried vanilla ice cream sandwiches and astronaut bibs.

Away from the crowd are some historic pieces of kit: the Skylab trainer, the Apollo Center Command Module, Mercury 9, Gemini 5, a Boeing 747-12 with the space shuttle on its back. How dated much of it looks! Did those chunky computer monitors really get us into space? And what's with all those switches and dials? So much of the equipment – campus bicycles excepted – looks horribly outdated.

On my way out I pass a column of Chinese students waiting patiently for their visit. They all wear T-shirts proclaiming *USA History Tour*. I wonder how many US students are standing, with *China History Tour* T-shirts, at the Great Wall.

For the price of my NASA visit I also get a bus tour around the city. We gather in a waiting room which features a lamp fashioned out of a Colt .45 and a cowboy hat. Our guide tells us: 'We carry guns and are very friendly – that's *why* we're very friendly!' I don't see people carrying guns, apart from those in uniform, though I don't look too closely.

As we tour the city the superlatives come quickly. An I M Pei-designed building is the 'tallest five-sided building in the world'. According to *Forbes* magazine Houston is the number one city in terms of job creation, starting a business and starting a family. It is also energy capital of the world, with more than 5,000 energy-related firms, and has more than 11,000 restaurants. The zoo 'has one of the largest elephant exhibits in the entire world'.

The Roman Catholic Co-Cathedral is said to be 'the only one in the world'. That's not what they'll tell you in Valletta, the capital of Malta, which I visited earlier this year. I say nothing.

We pass the Rice Hotel, where President Kennedy spent the last night of his life before going to Dallas. We also pass a 160-year-old building that now houses a bar which still uses candlelight at night, has the old cash register, and (like many other places in America, it seems) is said to be haunted.

One dull office block has hundreds of small windows with the handles on the *outside*. "This was a mistake," says our guide, but I find it hard to believe him.

The guide does not mention the Astrodome, which in 1969 I had thought was the ultimate in American indulgence. I wrote in my letter home:

> This is the enormous indoor stadium (which costs millions of dollars and still leaks) controlled by computer, with the 'longest bars' (Texans are obsessed with size), a scoreboard which has a 45-second coloured light sequence wherever there is a home run, a flat for the boss etc. However, due to the absence of sunlight, the grass needs to be plastic, and this is cleaned with beer and kept together by THE LONGEST ZIPPERS IN THE WORLD. Hooray for American achievement.

How time destructs. I couldn't believe, when researching for my golden jubilee trip, that the Astrodome was now closed and derelict. It even has the true mark of obsolescence, a preservation society. For the past 15 years it seems that its main use has been emergency refuge for victims of natural disasters: Katrina in 2005 and Harvey in 2017. Now bits have been dismantled and the rest stands empty.

At least I have found an Astrodome-themed place to stay in. My hosts are Jonathan and Kelli, and tonight they invite me to go upstairs and meet them.

Their living room takes up all the first floor, is filled with striking modern furniture and has great views. Jonathan says they wanted their Airbnb to represent Houston. He and Kelli used to work for an NBA basketball team (Houston Rockets), which is where they met. He now works for a real estate development company and she for City of Houston Tourism.

As for the seats in the hall of my suite: 'People became very nostalgic. They

A Texas lamp: 'We carry guns and are very friendly – that's why we are friendly.'

wanted to buy seats, beer holders, bits of Astroturf. We had a three-hour wait to buy them and it cost us $100 for the pair.'

He gives me the background. 'The Astrodome was an all-concrete, multi-purpose indoor stadium, built for multiple events. Other cities copied it. It was a killer revenue-making machine, but that fad went away. Most have now been torn down – Seattle, Atlanta – but not New Orleans. There was no charm in the Astrodome – apart from "This is new, this is neat." That didn't last.'

He tells me about Minute Maid Park, which is where the Astros now play baseball, and where he is a tour guide in his spare time. 'Now we have smaller, single-purpose arenas, with more character, more charm. It's all about how close you can be to the action. And Minute Maid Park also includes the old railway station, and when we have a home run a train moves and shoots fireworks.'

It also, I read later, has gone back to real grass.

We change the subject and talk about travel. A few years ago Jonathan and Kelli took nine months away from their career paths and drove all over the USA in a converted van. They show me a beautifully illustrated book of their journey. I ask them if they will repeat their trip in 50 years; they say they have been talking about that – and yes.

They ask me what I have found on this trip, and I tell them I have found it fascinating but not easy. They are sympathetic and interested, not least in the fact that I am taking notes in a notebook with a pen – in shorthand. At one stage Jonathan turns to Kelli: 'He's a bit of a time capsule.'

My next driver is an African American woman. We chat about the area I am staying in; until not long ago it was predominantly African American. Some of the small wooden houses still stand among the condos, but the inhabitants are dying and their children selling their homes to developers. She is not clear where the African Americans now live.

Then I take the plunge. One or two people (all white) I have spoken to have implied that the race issue has been exaggerated. So I ask my driver: 'What's it like for African Americans these days?' From the back seat I see her broad shoulders sag.

'Because of this president, people are more open with their opinions and their racism. Some folks get into the car and want to know who I am. I have to reassure them – that I am a teacher and have a master's degree.

'People are more open to voice their opinion. We see the racism. "If you don't have my money you have to stay over there," they say. "If you are not of my colour you have to stay over there."

'The President is a disgrace, and so many of his race are covering up for his foolishness.'

Monday 22 July

I have a few hours this morning before my bus leaves, and I suddenly decide to make a pilgrimage to the Astrodome. The Uber driver, a long-standing resident, tells me that 'they' were going to pull it down, but now the decision has been taken to turn it into a conference centre. 'It was billed as the eighth wonder of the world. Elvis performed there – and Evil Knievel.'

As we approach I see it is dwarfed by another building: the NRG stadium, home of the Houston Texans, the Houston Rodeo and other events – the Rolling Stones are about to perform here. The mantle has passed.

The Astrodome stands next to it, surrounded by car parks, and the only splashes of colour come from a bed of marigolds and pink begonias sponsored by a local landscaping firm ('Beautification is our trademark – we are the best in our field'). The stadium is a bleak concrete shell, stripped of the razzmatazz of a major public venue. In 2008 it was declared a fire hazard (officially – 'not compliant with the code') and five years later part of it was demolished. Various rescue plans have been mooted,

Houston Astrodome: once dubbed the 'eighth wonder of the world'; now stripped and redundant.

including one to make it into a car park with an exhibition centre on top, and another to strip it back and keep the basic structure as the focal point of a public park.

The current position is a stalemate. Earlier this year the Harris County leadership went from Republican to Democratic, and developing the Astrodome is not seen as a priority now. On the other hand, it is a State Antiquities Landmark, and any change will have to be approved by the Texas Historical Commission.

I take a train back to the centre of Houston and reflect. Fifty years ago I was captivated by what was going on in Houston. All that enterprise and invention was going to make the world a better place, wasn't it?

At the Greyhound station the systems are down. The lady at the desk sees me struggling with my suitcase, and says I am as decrepit as she is. She has been working for the company for some time: 'Things are not the same. It seems as if everyone is angry about something. When I started it was a fun job and it was nice to come to work. Now it's not.'

Another long-serving employee chimes in: 'It's more than just technology. Half the people who come up to me here don't know how to use their phone. The hardest thing about travel is getting adult people to listen. Common sense is not common any more.'

9. Austin: drumming for God

Austin is the last stop on my first leg. The three-hour journey there is uneventful, and for once I arrive a little early. Barbara's cousin Laurie picks me up and tells me that the temperature today has reached 106 degrees (41°C). Thank goodness for air-conditioned buses.

I am hoping that Laurie's student daughter Sarafina, being young, will be able to help me with a technical problem that has dogged me throughout my journey: how to answer Morris when he starts ringing. She punches in the number – and her face crumples. The phone is ringing – but she can't find a way of answering, either. She tries a couple more times, and we conclude that it's not the old-timer being incompetent – there really is something amiss. When I get home, I will have to take Morris to an expert.

I have booked into an Airbnb in a spacious hut at the bottom of someone's back yard. It has a pleasant terrace with sunshade, though I assume that for most of the day it will be too hot to sit under it. I put my breakfast banana into what I think is a fridge but is really a freezer. Some hours later rigor mortis has set in; by the morning it is brown mush.

Laurie tells me that a cold snap is on the way: tomorrow's temperature is expected to be a mere 92 degrees (33°C).

Tuesday 23 July

The America I visited in 1969 was still largely the America of Lyndon Johnson, whose term as president had ended six months before. Today I am going to visit the Lyndon Baines Johnson Library and Museum to find out more about his legacy.

A sign at the entrance warns that I am entering a smoke-free and weapon-free zone. I then step past the custom-built limousine that LBJ used in his post-president years. Once inside, the library is packed with information: TV news clippings, original documents, photographs, even selected clips from the 643 hours of recorded presidential conversations. There are extracts from LBJ's speeches:

'I want to be the President who helped to end hatred for one's fellow man.'

'Will you join in the battle to build the Great Society?'

'It's all of us who must overcome the crippling legacy of bigotry and injustice.'

As with Russian President Gorbachev two decades later, I am puzzled how conventional roots can produce a radical reformer. LBJ's early life provides the clue: after growing up on a ranch he trained as a teacher, and his first job was in a small school for Mexicans and Americans in a small town in Texas. He saw poverty at first hand.

His achievements are clearly listed: the Civil Rights Act, the War on Poverty, the National Trail Systems Act, the Economic Opportunities Act, public broadcasting, seat belt legislation, nuclear non-proliferation treaty, Medicare/ Medicaid. An African American is quoted as saying: 'New doors opened. They swung open for you. They swung open for me. We really couldn't believe a man with a Texan accent could be on our side.'

On the downside was the tragedy of the slaughter in Vietnam which was, the exhibits suggest, the reason why he did not stand for a second term. Johnson was succinct about it: 'The biggest damn mess.'

I speak to some ladies of my generation who are also touring the library 'He wasn't a perfect gentleman,' said one. 'But at least he was honest in terms of public policy. He had legislative knowledge to push things through.'

'What about the present president?' I ask, with my usual timidity.

'I think he's an arsehole, and I still can't figure out how he got elected.'

Her friend dissents, politely. 'He (Trump) can't do *everything* for Mexicans. I feel sorry for them, but at the same time their own president is not doing anything for them. They have to support themselves. They have the absolute right to come in; we have the absolute right to keep them out. It is time for a businessman to reorganise things in America – though I'm not sure he's the right man.'

There's also a temporary exhibition about Motown which neatly spans the half-century I am writing about. It is a remarkable story, not just of the one man – Berry Gordy – who drove the music and the performers, but of the huge range of talented musicians he nurtured from a small area in Detroit: the Supremes, the Temptations, the Four Tops, Stevie Wonder, the Jackson Five, Marvin Gaye.

The exhibit has glass cases full of extravagant costumes. There's plenty of music, and we are invited to do a bit of karaoke and a bit of dancing; I try a couple of steps when I think no-one is looking, but for the sake of the other visitors refrain from picking up a mic.

We are also shown the less glamorous side of being a black musician in a white America. In a filmed interview one of the Supremes recalls that their bus was shot at – and when they got off they were shocked to see the bullet holes that proved it.

On the TV that night I see that the head of the FBI has told the Senate Judiciary Committee that the Bureau has made about 100 arrests in domestic terrorism cases in the past nine months. 'The majority' of these cases involved a form of white supremacy.

I am reminded of the LBJ quote I saw on the wall in the little cafeteria at the library: 'Our mission is at once the oldest and most basic of this country: to right wrong; to do justice, to serve man.'

Is this still current presidential policy?

I also find a poignant postscript to my Houston visit in the *New York Times*:

> Christopher C Kraft Jr, the legendary founder of NASA's mission control, who directed America's first piloted orbital flights, oversaw the Apollo 11 lunar landing and was director of the Johnson Space Center in Houston, has died today in Houston, two days after the 50th anniversary of that historic moment on the moon. He was 95.

That night I am taken out to a Tex-Mex restaurant. I fear that my opinion has not wavered since 1969 when I wrote in my diary: 'Ugh!'

Wednesday 24 July

Today's visit is to the University of Texas. Laurie's husband Jim drops me in the middle of the campus – full of portentous buildings, well-manicured lawns, elegant trees and building sites. One hoarding put up by the College of Natural Sciences promises: 'We are catalyzing innovation.' It makes no mention of what it is doing to the English language.

Dominating the campus is the 27-floor Main Building, or Tower. Jim tells me it is notorious for a mass shooting in 1966, when a former marine stabbed his wife and mother to death and then took guns to the observation deck. From there he killed 14 people before he was shot dead,

90 minutes after he had started to open fire. It was found afterwards that he had a brain tumour, which may have been responsible for his violence.

'When this happened a lot of people went home and got their rifles. This plays right into the hands of the NRA (National Rifle Association) lobby,' says Jim. 'Now the rhetoric is: the only way to stop a bad guy with a gun is a good guy with a gun.'

He tells me that some years ago when he was researching a short story he enrolled on a day's gun class.

What were the people like?

'Just ordinary moms and people like that ...' He seems as baffled as I am about this need to carry arms.

I go into the tower because I am trying to find the offices of the student newspaper *The Daily Texan*. I wander around the first few floors; there seems to be no security. I see a notice about a visitors' centre just off campus and walk there. The centre is lavish and generous, giving out maps and advice and free bottles of water, a thoughtful gesture in this heat.

Back on the pavement, electric scooters whizz by. As I stand waiting to cross the road, I ask a woman next to me how long they have been around. Since last summer, she says, adding that their speed is restricted to 8 mph on campus; normally it is 15 mph. She says she finds them 'pretty scary' and I agree.

I enter a building which I realise is the wrong one, but not before I see this notice: 'License holders for a concealed handgun may not enter the premises with a concealed handgun.' I cross to the William Randolph Hearst building which houses the offices of *The Daily Texan,* but no-one is there. I have lunch at the Students Union food hall, where there is a long queue for Chinese food but only one person at the salad bar.

As I walk back, I hear a bagpipe striking up 'Scotland the Brave', accompanied by two drummers. I go to investigate and am immediately approached by two young men. They are well turned out, wearing chinos, jacket, shirt and tie, and hat (not caps). One thrusts a leaflet into my hand. I scan it: *10 REASONS to protect the unborn.*

I talk to the shorter one as the bagpiper segues into "Auld Lang Syne". They are from an organisation called The American Society for the Defense of Tradition, Family and Property – 'For the present, for the unborn and against abortion'. He says they are Catholics.

What about poverty, I ask? It nonplusses him for a moment. Then he goes into a story of how he took someone off the streets, put him up in a hotel and offered him a job.

'When we went back he had been taking drugs ... There are some who are poor who want to be poor.'

'Does he like the President?' I ask.

'Yes. He's against abortion.'

I don't pursue that line.

Instead I tell him that I had eight years of Benedictine education, which seems to soften his tone. His group numbers about a dozen, standing on the pavement on all four corners of a crossroads. The bagpiper stops but the drums remain, and they have a sign: 'Sound your horn if you are against abortion'. Quite a few drivers respond.

'Are there any women in the group?' I ask.

'Not today,' says one of them. 'But we had a couple the other day.'

One of his colleagues approaches a slight young woman as she starts to cross the road. She declines a leaflet and avoids eye contact. She looks distinctly uncomfortable. I try to make a light comment to soften the tone, and she ignores me too.

I feel uncomfortable. Underneath the smart clothes (uniforms?) these young men remind me of the school bullies I used to know. I worry about their presence on the streets: they are unlikely to change minds and perhaps they don't mean to. It is a show of worldly strength.

Later I look up the group on their website and on Wikipedia, and discover I have witnessed one of their 'caravans' that tour campuses and other places (where presumably they are likely to run into opposition). The group has been going since 1973 and claim about 120,000 members. Their views are anti-abortion, anti-LGBTQ, anti-socialism, and anti-the current Pope. They claim to occupy the 'front lines of the Culture War, peacefully defending the values of tradition, family and private ownership'.

I drag up from the past my memories of a Catholic education and can't recall any of the monks encouraging us to go on the streets to defend private ownership. I do remember, though, 'Love Thy Neighbour'.

I return to *The Daily Texan* offices. It is a large space, with some glass cubicles for the editors, and a table tennis table in the middle, which I learn later is used for editorial meetings as well as for ping-pong. There are two people around: one is Spencer Buckner, the editor, who is happy to speak to me.

The University of Texas is one of a declining number of universities still with a proper student-run newspaper, and during the school year a print version is published every weekday. The editorial team numbers about 300 and it is all extra-curricular. Spencer, who is 20, will be editor for a year.

I ask about the future of journalism.

'Wow! That's a can of worms.' He pauses.

'I'm in journalism school,' he continues, 'and within the journalism community there is definitely a sense that things are changing. I was at a conference of college newspapers last week. There are funding cuts. Papers are publishing less often, or they are digital only.

'The people I am studying with are proud of what they do but there's also an anxiety about it – what's it going to look like five years from now? It's kind of a weird place to be.'

'What about the traditional notion that truth is something journalists should aspire to?' I ask.

'One of the big questions is how do we get people to trust journalists again? You can have publications that do everything right – getting facts, being persistent. But people just don't care. There's a whole aversion to facts. I don't know how we will work with that.'

The issues he anticipates for the coming year are sexual assault and misconduct, the cost of college, the cost of living in Austin, how to make a more inclusive campus, and climate change: 'This is an existential threat. We are moving towards disaster.'

He is in his third year but doesn't think he will be a journalist when he graduates. Instead he is thinking of law school, or policy, or academia. 'I love journalism. I don't know if it's something I want to do after college.'

This is not good news. Is the current onslaught on journalists causing the brightest and the most principled to go elsewhere, just when we might most need them?

I walk a mile – slowly – to the Briscoe Center for American History building, which now houses the statue of Jefferson Davis, President of the Confederacy and a hero of the Right. It used to be in a prominent position on campus. Now, after protests (and some paint daubing), it has been moved indoors. A notice says: 'No longer an object of commemoration, the statue now forms part of an exhibit exploring its history and significance as both a work of art and evidence of the past.'

It seems a reasonable compromise – of the type that some might say makes America great.

Student editor Spencer Buckner: 'How do we get people to trust journalists again?'

Thursday 25 July

I am offered a free coffee this morning at the little shop I have been frequenting. They may have spotted my buoyant mood: this evening I fly home. I could do with the break, and am particularly looking forward to being in the same place for more than two days, eating food that I have put on my plate myself, and waking up next to my wife in my own bed with the alarm turned off. Oh – and not frying in the sun or shivering and sniffing in the air conditioning.

I call an Uber to take me to Laurie's. The driver is a tall, fair Texan with a pony-tail; his car is a huge, white Honda Pilot. He has a master's degree in education and he taught for 12 years. 'I was trying to change the system from inside. Now I am free and not implicit in the dumbing of America.'

He combines driving with writing, and has four screenplays on the go. As we arrive at my destination he starts telling me about one of them, involving a flamenco rock band and hallucinogenic drugs. Before I can get out of the car he starts telling me about another, involving a robot teacher. 'I would like to get Arnold Schwarzenegger for that one,' he says.

I flee, noting that he had asked me no questions. And he a writer …

Then, as the big white car starts to accelerate down the road, I realise that Morris the mobile is still in there, alone on the back seat. Again. I panic of course, but am accumulating a little experience on how to deal with Morris's disappearances. I borrow a phone to ring my own number, and start to go through the automated Uber systems to see if I can contact the driver directly.

I am beginning to despair that the robots will not let me through when there is a knock on the door. My driver has brought Morris back. I tip him generously, and feel guilty for any unkind thoughts I may have had about him. He says that he heard the phone ring, but couldn't work out how to answer it. I really will have to get Morris sorted out.

In 1969 I wrote admiringly about the wonderful new shopping centres that were springing up. In Britain we were still some way behind: our first out-of-town centre was London Brent Cross in 1976. Now I have been told of what appears to be a new form of the genre – an open-air shopping mall, with housing built over and next to the shops. It sounds suspiciously like what we used to call a town.

The development at Austin is called the Domain, and I start in the Northside, still under construction. Last year it aroused a storm by publishing a brochure that looked as if it had been lifted from a PowerPoint pitch. The 'quintessential' customer was described as a 'classy, well-heeled woman between 30 and 60 years old' who most likely identifies as 'Anglo, Jewish, or Asian'. She (yes, *she*) 'cares about how she looks and feels, and spends generously on the upkeep of herself and her family'. There follows a litany of luxury goods, few of which mean anything to me, and further details about the putative customer: 'This woman is married, but highly successful in her own career.'

Social media has been incandescent. 'It couldn't be a better parody of itself,' says one person. 'So much to hate here,' adds another.

I go into a 'residential' office to find out how much it would cost to live in one of their dwellings. The young man views me suspiciously, and tells me that the price of accommodation can be found on their website, goodbye. I should have carried a branded handbag.

I walk towards the older part of the development. It is midday and a tolerable 86 degrees (30°C), and I chat with a friendly man walking with his pug. He spent a year in London in the 1980s, living in a squat in Camden Town and helping to build Chelsea Harbour. Now he lives in the Domain where, he says, you can get a studio for $1,500 a month. I ask him if there are any homeless people.

A new shopping centre in Austin, Texas; 'I see row after row of discounted clothing'.

'They run them the hell out of here.'

I find a main street, lined with shops: J Crew, Victoria's Secret, Ted Baker, Louis Vuitton. I go into one and talk to the two members of staff.

'Business is good – we wouldn't be here otherwise,' they say.

It's all very swish, with fine trees, shaded sidewalks, a fountain and more restaurants. I lunch in one and have some edamame dumplings in broth with dashi, white truffle oil and Asian herbs plus a glass of watermelon-flavoured lemon juice. It costs me $20.

I go into Macy's, one of the 'anchor' stores. Up on the second floor, in the middle of the men's clothing department, I see row after row of discounted clothing, including 50 per cent off USA T-shirts. I see no customers, and not even someone to take my money. On the floor below I find a few people, and I chat to two ladies. 'This is too hot to have an open air mall,' one says. 'And people are beginning to buy everything online. I don't think they're doing very well.'

What will happen if people stop going there to shop? Will we see writ large the desertion and decay I saw in Unadilla? In a world which increasingly shops online, it seems a brave experiment.

That night, in the back of a near-empty plane, I have a row of three seats to myself. With the first leg safely navigated, I sleep the sleep of the righteous traveller.

WEST

1. Los Angeles airport: the adventure resumes

Monday 19 August

I feel a bit teary as I wave goodbye to Barbara and get sucked up again into the tedium of Heathrow security. The Golden Jubilee Greyhound Bus Tour Part Two is now under way. I have spent just over three weeks at home, where I visited the gym and the osteopath, weeded my garden, restocked my pill boxes, took Morris for a service, enjoyed the temperate climate, had another bout in the dental hygienist's chair (thankfully no more grand ideas), tidied up the 40,000 words I had written on the first leg, bought some more notebooks and tried to sort out my next set of adventures.

I am determined to go through with the trip. But I can't stop thinking about the tough stuff that lies ahead: the early starts, the crowded bus stations, the lonely and oversized meals, the technological hiccups – and that sinking feeling when Morris the mobile disappears over the horizon in the back of yet another car.

My first five nights should be a gentle enough reintroduction. I will be in one place: Pasadena, California. I want to find out what has happened to my old newspaper, and see if I can repeat some of the activities I wrote about 50 years ago: taking lunch with the senior citizens, having my hair cut, riding in a police car. I also want to catch up with my friend Martha after 32 years.

My brief stay at home had been busy. I had postponed making full plans for the second leg, because I thought once I had ridden the buses I would make better plans more easily. That didn't happen. I had the usual trouble with recorded phone messages that promised and didn't deliver, and unanswered emails that might not even have been delivered. But my worst experiences were booking the Greyhound bus tickets.

When planning a visit to the small town of Grinnell in Iowa, I managed to find Greyhound buses that would get me there, but none that would take me out. I discovered www.Rome2rio.com, an excellent site that will tell you all the different ways of going from one town to another, and quickly found a Trailways bus that would take me out. Then I realised that the departure time was exactly the same time of day as the arrival time a few days earlier. It had to be the same bus (and indeed it turned out to be), with Greyhound compelled by some legal stitch-up not to admit its existence. Madness.

Another morning I was issued with five tickets for the same journey and a few days later two tickets for three journeys instead of one for each. The first were reimbursed after a lot of haggling but my appeals about the second went unanswered. I resigned myself to the reality that I could kiss goodbye to the money I had spent. It had cost me £90.30 – and my residual respect for the Greyhound website.

Meanwhile Eva, a young and feisty relative of Barbara's from America, who was staying with us while I was trying to book my trip, suggested that I had become a willing victim in an abusive relationship. As she said it she laughed, but a tad unconvincingly.

My administrative difficulties were overshadowed by news of more violence in America. During my first weekend back home (3–4 August) gunmen killed a total of 31 people in El Paso, Texas and Dayton, Ohio. One had an anti-Mexican manifesto; the other's motive was not immediately clear. Only a few weeks after stirring up a crowd to shout: 'Send them home!' President Trump made a formal speech attacking racism.

Eva commented: 'When the Columbine school shootings happened in 1999 I was in middle school. I was in the first group for whom this became a regular thing. Since then it keeps happening. Nothing much changes in a meaningful way. This kind of terror is fundamental to American society. We love performing our shock and our sadness. But this is becoming the norm, and we are feeling sad about things we could fix.'

Meanwhile, on the plane to Los Angeles, my flight is as uneventful as the one to New York was back in July. After 11 hours the landing is smooth and my trip through immigration effortless, taking less than an hour from touchdown to exit past customs. The immigration robot works well, except that the picture it takes makes me look like a sick old lag on the run. I mention this to the live official doing the final screening, but he doesn't seem unduly sympathetic, nor does he arrest me for looking suspicious. He asks what I am doing in America, and when I tell him about my project he wishes me luck. At least – and unlike his counterpart in New York – he doesn't laugh at me.

And so to my first Airbnb of the second leg. I have not booked a self-contained shed or a promoted garage, but a single bedroom in a condominium. I am looking forward to meeting my host. We have already had email contact, and since my phone is not yet reconnected to a US network I am encouraged by her message saying she should be around when I arrive.

She is not, and I find the outside gate securely locked. I knock on the door of a neighbour – a charming young mother of Polish origin with two small boys – who gives me water and sympathy and helps me to connect Geoffrey the Go to her WiFi.

We find a message from my host apologising for not being there and giving me two combination numbers to get through the outside gate, then the front door. I enter: the heavy curtains are closed and while the sun shines brightly outside, inside the house is dark. I find a light switch, which reveals a flight of stairs with a line of shoes at the bottom. I take the hint, take off my shoes and go up.

On the small landing are four doors. Two are closed but two are open – a bathroom and what I assume is my bedroom. I also assume one of the other bedrooms is for my host. My room is basic. There is no chair and no table. There are no pictures on the wall, though I can see hooks still there. The bedside lamp has a switch that is hard to locate (and later in my stay I knock over my glass of water trying to find it in the dark). There is no television. I don't know the code for the WiFi and I can't find anything that tells me.

I am back on the trail.

My first priority is to re-establish Morris's links with an American network, so I walk a half-mile or so to T-Mobile to reactivate my US account. The shop staff are as friendly as ever – and so they should be, considering what I am paying. Then I stroll a little more. In the main street I see a building which has an awning with *Pasadena Star-News* written on it. I go to investigate: it looks as if it has been empty for some time.

I have particularly fond memories of Pasadena and the *Pasadena Star-News*. In the middle of my 1969 bus tour I stayed here for four weeks in the YMCA while having what would now be called an internship on the paper. I was thinking of trying to become a journalist and had managed to get the job through the good auspices of my friend Martha's father, who was the paper's insurance broker – and a friend of the editor.

In what was a turning point of my life I ended up writing articles every day. My farewell piece talked about the 'dreaming spires and drooping palm trees and pseudo-Spanish palazzos and smoggy sunshine and half-hidden mountains and bustling buses and blood-chilling beer'. I ended: 'I really will miss it all. So don't cry down there in the front office. I may well be back.'

And now, half a century on, I am.

Pasadena still looks like a good place to be. The spires are still dreaming and the palm trees drooping, the pseudo-Spanish palazzos have been replaced with functional condominiums, the mountains are no longer covered by smog, and the buses have been replaced by a light railway. I haven't tried the beer yet, but in half a century I have got used to drinking it at other than room temperature.

The streets seem safe (especially compared with other places I have been in on this trip). I am staying just off Colorado Boulevard, which used to be Route 66, about one and a half miles out of the centre. I come across some interesting shops, including two second-hand bookshops, in one of which I am presented with a free bottle of water.

I settle on a little sushi restaurant for my dinner. The food is delicious – up with the best sushi I can remember eating – indisputably fresh and cheerfully served. I take a glass of Californian chardonnay. This is the first restaurant I have been in on this trip that has a fixed service charge (15 per cent). This is 'to be fair and to give everyone a living wage', according to the manager.

When I get back to my digs the house is still dark, though slits of light shine under the doors to the two other bedrooms, one presumably belonging to my host and the other to another guest. At 8 pm local time (but 4 am my body time) I go to bed, trying to block out sounds of revelry from around next door's barbecue.

When I wake up it's quiet again – but only midnight. I am dying for a pee, but the bathroom door is closed, with the sounds of someone showering within. I have no idea if there is a downstairs toilet, and don't dare explore in the darkness to find out, so have to exercise some self-control.

When I finally get into the bathroom I find that my torso and upper legs are covered with hives. I take an anti-histamine pill, and wonder whether I have developed an allergy to sushi. Or America?

As restarts go, it's not great.

2. Pasadena: back after half a century

Tuesday 20 August

The morning fails to brighten my situation. I have slept badly since midnight and a rash still covers my body from navel to knees. While shaving I get the plug stuck in the plughole, leaving the communal sink full of my dirty shaving water. I find my host downstairs and greet her with the news of the damage. She goes straight to the cupboard under the sink, takes out a bent knife, and starts prising. She has done this before, which makes me feel a little less guilty.

I leave to find breakfast. The recommended café just across the road is closed on Tuesdays so I ask a passing couple if they know of any alternative to the McDonalds down the street. They say they don't but are determined to find one. As they stride on towards the centre of town, I go into McDonalds and order a huge breakfast, most of which I leave. Later I stand in the sunshine and speak on the phone to Barbara, who is starting to prepare her supper back home. For the next couple of weeks our lives are going to be out of kilter.

On the way back to my room I pass a hotel which looks as if it might have chairs and tables, and go in to see if they might have a room I can transfer to. They quote me $149 dollars for Tuesday and Wednesday, then $370 for Thursday. $370? The reason is that the Rolling Stones will be giving a concert in the Rose Bowl on Thursday and the cost of finding a roof has, well, gone through the roof. I decide to stay where I am, and anyway I have something to look forward to: Martha has hired a car and we are off to visit a Queen.

In 1967 the city of Long Beach, 32 miles from Pasadena, took the risk of spending some of its oil revenue on buying a redundant transatlantic liner – the RMS Queen Mary, war hero, holder of the Blue Riband (for fastest transatlantic crossing) and star of the Cunard Line. When I was in California two years later, the ship was still being refitted for a second career as a holiday resort. My editors at the paper came up with the bright idea of sending me there by public transport, mainly as an excuse to have

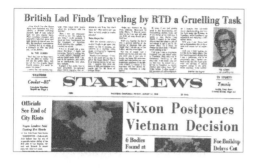

'My editors came up with the bright idea of sending me to see the Queen Mary by public transport'.

me experience a long and tedious journey with the Southern California Rapid Transit District (RTD).

The article I wrote was published on the front page of the Sunday edition precisely 49 years and 361 days ago under the headline 'British Lad Finds Traveling by RTD a Gruelling Task'. In fact, I had travelled 7,000 miles to get to California, so was relatively unphased by a 32-mile journey. It involved two buses, plus plenty of confusion and hanging about – and took just over three hours to get there and three and a half hours to get back. I was at the dockside for less than 20 minutes. I described the brief moment:

> I am gazing through the barbed wire fence at the Queen Mary, 81,327 tons of rust-brown painted steel. I feel no regret at not having bothered to see it when it was ours. The guard prevents me from getting closer, so I buy a souvenir guide to pretend I did.

Our journey by car today takes about an hour, despite Martha's fears that we might get stuck in one of the area's notorious traffic jams. As she drives, I look out the pictures of my previous visit: they show the ship empty, shorn of all but one funnel, stripped to the bare minimum, with its lifeboats stranded in what looks like a car park.

Today the ship is surrounded by huge car parks and colourful flower beds, and we park not far from where the lifeboats used to lie. The Queen has shed its rust, and now stands in the dramatic colours of black for the hull, white for the superstructure and black and red for the funnels. All three funnels are now back in place and beneath them the lifeboats are back on their davits.

The Queen Mary is soon to celebrate half a century as a resilient tourist attraction and hotel, offering 347 cabins or staterooms plus events and attractions playing on nostalgia and the current obsession with the paranormal. It is regarded as the world's most haunted ship, according to

The Queen Mary 1969: 'empty, shorn of all but one funnel, stripped to the bare minimum'.
The Queen Mary 2019: with original colours and all three funnels back in place.

its website, and offers tours that 'may connect with those who still call the ship home'.

We are more interested in the Art Deco interiors, which have been beautifully restored. On our tour, led by a guide kitted up as an officer with two gold rings on his blue blazer, we see fine woods and original works of art from the 1930s. The first-class rooms are magnificent, including a rehearsal room with a white piano that looks as if it was played by Liberace (and of course was), a playroom strewn with expensive toys, and a dining room that looks like it comes from a swish hotel (not surprising since one of the original designers also designed the Ritz in London). The second-class public rooms look fine to me but are definitely more Lyons Corner House than Ritz. We see little of the third-class accommodation.

What is striking – as indeed was the original intention – are the ostentatious class distinctions – and we hear of the lengths taken, not always successfully, to ensure there was no mingling. Not surprisingly: the cost of a first-class ticket was $1,070 in the 1930s which we are told is the equivalent of $18,000 today. It's a reminder that extremes of wealth and its ostentatious flaunting are not new.

We take lunch in the Promenade Café then leave. Martha's fears about the traffic are again not realised and the journey back to Pasadena takes about an hour. Later I look up on Rome2Rio the different ways of taking the trip. The journey by car should have taken 36 minutes had the roads been clear. The two-bus route that I took in 1969 still exists and should today have taken 2 hours 45 minutes, not a great difference from before.

But there is now a faster way: the Gold Line, a 31-mile light railway running through Pasadena to Los Angeles, with 27 stations. Passengers from Pasadena to Long Beach can save more than an hour by taking one of these trains into the centre of Los Angeles and then a bus out to Long Beach. The service is part of the Los Angeles Metro network, which is still expanding. It seems that public transport in the city area has been taken seriously.

One of the selling points of the Gold Line is that it runs through Old Pasadena, and that evening Martha and I wander around the area. It is small scale, with quaint alleys, eclectic restaurants, plenty of bare brick facades – and many customers. Back in 1969 this was the red light district (though there is no mention of that in my diary). In 1980, using federal tax incentives, it became part of a controlled redevelopment scheme. Now, according to its official website, it has 200 retail outlets in 22 'historic blocks' and 100 'world class restaurants, sidewalks cafes and bistros'. It has a slogan: 'Old world charm; modern conveniences'; I wonder whether the phrase has been carried over from its previous red light existence.

Martha and I eat in an Italian restaurant. When we first met she was spending a year in London with her mother, who lived down our street in a London suburb. Martha now lives in Oregon and has flown down to see family, friends and me. Much has happened since we last met, and she spends her time keeping fit, travelling and worrying about what is happening to America. She has not forgotten how to wind me up, not least by recalling aspects of my behaviour half a century ago that I thought I had suppressed. I do my best to reciprocate.

We talk about the summer of 1969. My diary records a busy social life: going to parties, visiting pubs, going to the beach, sitting in traffic jams, dipping in and out of swimming pools. We were given tickets to the Pasadena Playhouse to see the world premiere (in rehearsal) of *1491*, a short-lived musical about Christopher Columbus by the man who wrote the song 'It's beginning to look a lot like Christmas'. 'Good fun and relaxing, though I doubt it will be a hit on Broadway,' I wrote. Good judgement: it never made it there.

On my first weekend in 1969 I went with Martha to the wedding of her best friend's sister in a Roman Catholic church. I wrote in my diary, 'It is rather sad because the couple have already eloped to Las Vegas. It is very hot in the church and the chief bridesmaid faints. Thunderbolt??' Martha tells me that the couple are still married to each other – but the bride's mother later divorced her (second) husband and married the groom's father.

I also wrote in my diary that the young people I met seemed obsessed with marriage.

'Yes, yes, yes,' says Martha. 'Some years after I graduated from college, I realised that several people I knew had been searching for husbands. This did not cross my mind. It was a time in our culture when things were changing.'

3. Pasadena: the newspaper that changed my life

Wednesday, 21 August

My career in newspapers started where the cliché says it should: in the post room (or in this case the Dispatch Department). My first job at the *Pasadena Star-News* had me filling in forms and taking copy up to Typesetting on the fourth floor, which didn't take up much of my time. After three days I was offloaded onto various salesmen, which didn't take up much of my time either. They forgot to take me out with them, and when they remembered I was shocked how little work they seemed to do. One cooked his dinner and collected his laundry between calls; another took me for a leisurely lunchtime swim.

I must have lobbied effectively because after six days I got my chance to move up three floors to the newsroom. I didn't do much there either at first, until on the second day I remarked how much I was hating the smog.

'Write us a piece about it,' one of the editors said.

So I did, and it was published the next day with a photo byline. Under the headline 'Blimey! Oh for some English Fog', I wrote: 'Smog is frustrating: from the mountains you can't see Pasadena; from Pasadena you can't see the mountains. It took me a week before I knew they existed.'

It was on the day it was published that my editors came up with the idea to send me to the Queen Mary. After that I wrote articles nearly every day, some on the weather and some on touristy things like finding British beer and identifying interesting things to do in Pasadena.

My new colleagues welcomed me warmly, and none so much as Russ Leadabrand. He was the travel editor (he still has ten guidebooks to California listed on Amazon) and resident humourist. He was bearded, twinkling and clever, and the first person I had met who was paid to write bits of whimsy. He was also generous, helping me with my copy and nursing me through a joint project which ended up as one of the featured stories in the Sunday edition.

Under the headline 'Slippery Hands Across the Sea', it took the form of a spoof questionnaire devised by the entirely fictitious Meskatonic

University to probe the differences between Americans and Brits. The questions (which he also devised) ranged from: 'How do you greet the new day?' to 'Did you fight much in your early schooldays?' We each had to supply witty answers, and even in retrospect I think we did. We also gurned together for the photograph accompanying the piece.

I learnt so much just by being around him and absorbing how he worked – and what he wrote. He published occasional Open Letters to Tim Albert, which he personally sent to me long after I had gone home, and they are exemplars of satire, still relevant today. Take this description of America:

> We have indigestible takeout food stalls in rows where you can get indigestion at a different spot every night and we all love the shops. We have beaches that are among the most beautiful in the world that are polluted with garbage, sewage, oil and tin cans. On some of them, at night, you will be mugged. The US is a pretty comical place – considering we sent a man to the moon (a serious endeavour).

(Russ Leadabrand, A Tribute to a Fellow Scribe, 2 September 1969).

I was lucky to ride on his coat tails, and ended up being recognised in restaurants (much to Martha's disdain). I also received a couple of fan letters, including one referring to 'those adorable articles … such a darling point of view' and another from a 16-year-old who described herself as a black Aquarian from Cleveland who should have been born in Liverpool. I was invited to the California Institute of Technology, where I was given an official tour followed by lunch at the swish Athenaeum. On my last night, in a double-breasted tuxedo loaned from an advertiser, I went with Beverly, the society page reporter, to California's 200th Anniversary Ball.

It was an extraordinary experience and it changed my mind – and my life. Until then I'd been lining myself up to become a social worker.

Very early in my preparations for the repeat trip I googled the *Pasadena Star-News*. The title still exists, but the website now calls it a 'local news source'. It is part of the Southern California News Group, which owns every daily paper in Southern California except the *Los Angeles Times*, and is the title for a website and a much slimmed down daily edition.

One of the named journalists on the website is Larry Wilson, who joined the *Star-News* in 1987 and was its editor for 12 years until it stopped being a free-standing paper. He is now public editor for two papers in the group, and a writer of regular columns and editorials, based in a small satellite office in Pasadena along with two district reporters.

I have been in touch with him, and he has invited me for lunch today. He picks me up in his red Mini, and by coincidence he is taking me to none other than the Caltech Athenaeum, the swish restaurant where I was taken 50 years before. Then (my diary tells me) I chose soup, shrimp and beer – and didn't rate the cold beer. This time I choose soup, club sandwich and beer – and enjoy the cold beer.

Larry is a fourth-generation Pasadenan. 'It's unusual because most people came yesterday,' he says. His great-grandfather was a farrier, his grandfather a theatre manager/impresario, and his stepfather a rocket scientist at Pasadena's Caltech and the Jet Propulsion Laboratory. His father, also a rocket scientist, now 92, grew up across the street from Caltech.

Larry grew up with Russ Leadabrand's columns: his father was an avid reader of the *Star-News*, and the two of them used to start the day reading the papers together. Larry went on to Berkeley, where he was an English major and rock music critic for the *Daily Californian*, the well-regarded student newspaper. He went to *Rolling Stone* in New York as a fact checker for the book-publishing arm, then came back to work first for the then newly-founded *Pasadena Weekly* and later for the *Star-News*.

The paper occupied a prime site on Colorado Boulevard, had five storeys and two basements, the first for the printing press and the one below for storing paper. The newspaper left the building in the late 1990s, moving to the office further along Colorado Boulevard that I saw on Monday night. 'I remember the day we gave the presses away to anyone who could take them out of the basements,' says Larry. 'It went to a Filipino newspaper, who used a crane to take them away.'

'Twenty years ago most people would know who the editor of the *Star-News* was,' he continues. 'Now no young person would know because the paper doesn't come into their heads. When I was a kid the little league scores were in the paper the next day. Now they are online somewhere immediately.

'In my neighbourhood I go running every morning. We get three newspapers delivered. But only one out of ten other households have a paper delivered, and in this case it's only one, usually the *Wall Street Journal* or the *Los Angeles Times*.

'The implications for newspapers are terrible. They used to tie communities together: for instance I had a full-time education reporter covering the schools. That was invaluable. We chose a profession – or practised a trade – that was about communicating, and a community paper had to be community-friendly. We used to give talks to Rotary, schools. Nobody does that any more.'

He talks of the internet company Next Door whose product came into his neighbourhood ten years ago. 'It doesn't bring a community together. There are appeals for lost dogs and cats, but one of the most common stories is: "There's a young Latino in his car outside my house. Should I call the police? FYI." It's a portal where a bunch of facts get fed in, a Petri dish of paranoia. It's not the newspaper way.'

I repeat the question I'd asked the editor of the student newspaper in Austin: 'Are you optimistic about the future of journalism?'

'We shouldn't be chauvinistic about newspapers. There are a lot of non-profit web-oriented organisations like Politico or LAist. There's a lot of good news reporting being done. But I am afraid that so many people are still watching Fox News. Everything on it is being tainted by the reactionary views of its owners ... We can't believe them ... I don't watch them.'

With that he goes off to get his pass for tomorrow's Rolling Stones concert at the Rose Bowl.

That afternoon I perch on a stool downstairs in the Airbnb to write. I can't find the light over the table and the perching is not fun. A fellow guest comes in, a young scientist from the British Geological Survey who is visiting the Jet Propulsion Laboratory in Pasadena. He is interested and interesting, and we agree to have dinner tomorrow night. I find out that he has the room that I'd thought was our host's. He thinks she may be sleeping in the basement.

Martha collects me and we go on a quest. I have two photographs I took in 1969: identical shots of a street view, one with mountains as the backdrop and one with no mountains. I had forgotten where they were, but as soon as I got back to Pasadena I realised that this was where I had taken them, to show what the smog could do.

There is a street sign in the photos so we should be able to identify the exact spot. Martha has been scouting the area today, and she takes me to an intersection at the end of the road where she and her father were living.

The view has gone completely; instead there is a boring multi-storey car park, built across the street as part of a shopping centre complex – a slice of street cut out and repurposed. We walk around to the other side of the car park and are relieved to find that the mountains are still there. They are not hidden by smog.

Thursday 22 August

As I go out of the house this morning, I notice that someone has been sleeping on the living room sofa: could that be our host? I head out to Andy's Coffee Shop, the diner over the road which looks as if it has changed little since the 1950s. The red coverings on the banquettes are worn and splitting, and the tiles pitted with use. Lining the walls are pictures of Marilyn Monroe, Audrey Hepburn and the annual Rose Bowl Parade passing the café. I am not surprised to hear that the diner is in demand as a period location: some of *Madmen*, for instance, was filmed here.

I am meeting Rick Politte, area director of the YMCA, in order to find out what happened to the YMCA hostel where I'd stayed last time. He tells me it lost out to the competition from cut-price hotels and is now owned and operated by a group called Abode Communities, a non-profit formed by idealistic architects in the 1960s to provide 'service enhanced social housing'. It provides 144 single room occupancy homes for formerly homeless people.

Rick, who has been with the Y for 37 years, is now responsible for carrying on the YMCA traditions in the area with child care, summer day camps, sports and a recreation centre. 'Bringing people together is an important part of our work,' he says. 'Although we are connected electronically, we don't have warm personal relationships. We need to teach people to care for others. Next week we are having a Pot Luck party, with about 100 people. It's the 96th birthday of a member. He lives alone. He never married. We are his family …

'In my workplace I am regularly coaching my young directors that part of the job is standing in the hallway talking to people. Everything I understand about being a Christian is that we are accepting and loving of people despite their sins. But you see this other side that is just the opposite.

'I don't know how things will evolve,' he continues. 'Are we just going through a generational phase? I just don't know.'

I seem to remember that we were asking that same question 50 years ago.

Pasadena's disappearing mountains: two photos from 1969 showing how smog can block out a good view, plus a photo from the same place in 2019 showing that urban development can do the same thing.

4. Pasadena: lunch for old-timers

The editors of the *Pasadena Star-News* had fun working out my assignments, and one day they sent me off on a visit to the local senior citizens centre. I took with me the hubris of a 22-year-old, gently ribbing the old folk I met. I condescended to play games with them – shuffleboard. pinochle, bridge, canasta and chess – and lost every time.

My article appeared with the following strapline: 'Not yet senescent enough for lavender and old lace, our visiting British exchange student paid a visit to a senior citizen center. (He spells it *centre*.) Here he tells how his precocity was not quite enough for shuffleboard or pinochle.'

Of course I had to go back. Perhaps I would be less condescending this time? I emailed the center/centre and they invited me to lunch.

I am clearly expected and am greeted warmly. One of the staff comes out to show me round. What strikes me is the centre's size and vitality. People in the library read newspapers or work on computers, others in the centre are packing up a 'boutique' (bric-à-brac) sale, playing dominoes, doing their tai chi exercises or playing solitary chess. I pass adverts for other activities, such as driving courses and tutorials on how to use mobile phones, and for a series of talks by a retired professor of journalism on fake news.

My guide sits down with me to help me go through the four-page registration form. Fifty years on I have moved from youthful observer to potential liability.

The questions are many. Sample: Are you urban or rural? Do you have help at home? Are you straight or same-gender-loving? (This was not a binary question; there were other alternatives.) Do you have problems with your mouth that make it difficult to eat? (On this one I successfully resisted the temptation to write: 'Yes. I find it hard to stop talking.')

I finish the paperwork. 'You are now an official member of the Pasadena Senior Center Lunch Bunch,' says my new carer.

I still have to pass the scrutiny of a brace of formidable ladies officiating at a table just inside the door. They give me a number to put on the table where I want to sit, and they hand me my knife, fork, spoon, napkin and straw. I have to sign another form and then I am free to go through.

The room is filling up and I find a place on one of the few tables still with vacancies. Soon after I have sat down, a woman hands me my lunch from a trolley: a compartmentalised plastic tray, plus a carton of apple juice and a carton of low fat milk. It's not my lucky day. Ever since 1953, when the nuns at my convent school forced me to finish food even if it was making me retch, I have had trouble with mincemeat and onions. Today the main course is spaghetti and meatballs, and true to form I start retching (discreetly I hope) at the first taste of the spaghetti, without even getting onto the meatballs. I drink my juice and play with my food.

I try to chat up my table companions. They direct me to a nearby table to see George. He is from England, an engineer and businessman who came over from the East End of London 45 years ago. He is what I have been having trouble finding: a Trump supporter who is not afraid of saying so.

'I love hearing the President speak,' he says. 'Sometimes he goes too far, but I'm not wanting to marry the guy – he's running the country.'

He takes me through familiar Republican views: FBI corruption … the myth that Trump is a racist … left wingers wanting to turn the country into socialism … a single pay health care system run by big government … killing history by pulling down statues … the New Green Deal … no real consensus that fossil fuel is bad for the environment.

'I despair about it all – for my grandkids,' he continues. 'If it doesn't go the way of Trump again it will be a disaster. It will kill the economy.'

'Where do you get your news?' I ask.

'Fox. They are not biased. In my opinion they look at the truth and they look at the lies. NBC, CNN – all they are doing is bad-mouthing Trump every day. Why? No-one likes him. He's embarrassing them.'

Seeking to understand, I ask if he used to watch *The Apprentice*; he tells me he did.

'I don't necessarily agree with everything Trump says. But one thing you can't deny is that he loves his country. I have been self-employed since I was 25. One thing I have learnt over the years is how to read people, and there's one thing I can tell you about Trump – he is consistent. He does not lie.'

I was sure my eyes betrayed my surprise but I managed by a small margin to keep control over my lower jaw.

I walk down a corridor and into a parallel universe. The executive director of the centre has invited me to see her and I am shown into her office, which is large and bursting with books and papers and goodwill.

Akila Gibbs is a cheerful African American woman, a former TV journalist who was in corporate PR, then worked for the Alzheimer's Society and has run the centre for ten years. She gives me the statistics: 10,000 people coming each year and 80,000 units of service (counselling and other support). They do a lot about 'food insecurity' (seniors not eating properly) and partner an LA food bank. The city provides the building, but they have to raise operating funds themselves.

'The biggest change is that older adults have gotten younger. People used to come to the centre all dressed up in hats and gloves and would never have thought of sweating in a gym. Now we have dance classes, we have people trying to keep in shape, we have people trying to write the great American novel.'

I ask her about race.

'My great-grandfather was a slave,' she says. 'I have a position that he would have thought was unthinkable. When I got this job my father, a former navy man, asked unbelievingly: "You get to tell white people what to do?" '

She tells me her husband is a psychologist and he got a similar reaction from his father: "You really have white clients, and they listen to what you say?"

'Then,' she continues, 'I look at my daughter who has had so many opportunities – she won a silver medal in bob-sledding at the 2018 Winter Olympics. That would have been unimaginable.'

She shows me a picture of her daughter with the medal and talks of her pride for her country. Ivanka Trump was at the Olympics, and her daughter talked with her because she felt it was the polite thing to do; she received a lot of nasty emails from people who disagreed.

'Are you an exception?' I ask.

'Maybe I am if you compare me with the black population, but not if you compare me with the general population. I remain hopeful, although I think Trump is just a hateful individual. I don't understand his meanness. Every ethnic minority that has come to the United States had had a hard time – there's a lot of ugliness out there. But I have had so many people of all races be kind to me. There are so many good things going on – but they are not news.' She laughs, with a hint of resignation.

The Pasadena Star-News building: now a cookery school.

On my way back I realise I am famished. I pass a familiar building, standing stolidly on a crossroads, with a decorated door and clock, over which is written *Star-News* in a script that would not have looked out of place on the Queen Mary. It's my old place of work – now a culinary school with restaurant attached. I can't resist.

The lunch rush hour is over and it's almost empty. I sit in what used to be the front office, just inside the main door where a group of young women used to sit taking small ads over the phone. One of them kept changing her hair style (and colour), and I started to mention her in my articles. We went out in a group for a drink one evening and I wrote in my diary that she left early because she had a blind date with a mortician. I never found out how it went.

I order a soup and a sandwich, and they are pretty high-end. My waiter today is a young man who hovers. He asks me where I come from, and when I say London he says he was just there – on his way back from performing at the Edinburgh Festival. He was part of a college group, and it was clear that this was his trip of a lifetime. I say I hope he has written a diary; he has.

I go and have a look round the ground floor, and see the lifts I would use to take the copy upstairs. I do not descend to the basements; they now contain a gym and swimming pool. A fine building once devoted to feeding the mind has been converted to one feeding and exercising the body. Is that telling us something about modern life?

That evening I go with my new scientist friend Ekbal to Urban Plates 'where real food is made from scratch'. This is an upmarket cafeteria, with stations for sandwiches, meats, salads and more. I take some chicken, which comes with two sides and a slice of bread. My request to have a half-portion of sprouts is denied as contravening company policy.

My friend is Cambridge-educated, a blogging polymath and a public speaker. We discuss big issues. Is the trajectory of history leaving people behind? Why do we have to politicise things that are universal? We speculate about whether the human race is going to destroy itself and he talks about the things that could do it: nuclear war, climate change, disease, a meteorite, and 'something we don't yet know about'!

It's been a good conversation, and lifts my mood, but only as long as it takes for him to show me his room. It is clearly superior and has its very own en suite bathroom. I am jealous: shouldn't old-timers get priority?

I go to bed wondering whether the human race is going in the right direction. And whether the book is too.

5. Pasadena: be careful out there!

Friday 23 August

When we were growing up in England our view of America was formed first by cowboys and Indians (*The Lone Ranger*) and next by cops and robbers (*Highway Patrol* and *Perry Mason*). So not surprisingly when I was in Pasadena in 1969 I was drawn to the police station, just a short walk from my YMCA lodgings.

I started off under the protection of the paper's police beat reporter.

> Reporter socially inclined and keen on black–white community relations. Pasadena seems to be doing well on this front: has a group of community workers who operate 'at street level' rather than 'governmental level' … Interrupted by a police officer in charge of community relations (heavily moustached) who wants to discuss plans for a police forum. Very impressive ideas etc but it must be difficult for a man to talk about communication, love etc with a gun in his pocket.

One evening I wandered back to the station to see if there was anyone still in the press room, and a woman police officer recognised me from my articles. We started to chat and were quickly on first name terms: she was Mary Ann. Soon after she fixed a ride for me in one of the police cars.

> First we spot a drunk and warn him. He says thank you, pitifully. Then a woman with a twitch and a long story about turning her cousin out of her home and him or a strange man in a van coming to the house. Then a call to 'malicious damage' – a shot up windscreen, one of a series. Take details and then back to the station.

They gave me a copy of the Radio Code Book (which I still have): Code Four: Emergency. Use Red light and siren; Code Seven: Out of service to eat.

My new friend Mary Ann took me under her wing. One Sunday she drove me to the Los Angeles Arboretum, among other things the location for the first Tarzan films. I have a great picture of her feeding a peacock.

I didn't hold much hope of finding her 50 years later, but I still wanted to go back to the police station – and perhaps ride in a police car again. From England I sent emails and left phone messages but heard nothing.

When I met Larry from the *Star-News* for lunch he advised me to go down to the police station and mention his name, which I did. Soon after, I got a phone call (which was now answerable – some progress since the first leg) from the Chief's personal assistant and was given an appointment to see the Chief himself.

The police headquarters has moved to a purpose-built building across the road from where it was. The front desk is now protected by a glass screen, and the only way to talk to a police officer is via microphone and speaker. I would never have got past these defences 50 years ago.

The Chief's very friendly PA takes me up to a well-equipped suite of offices, and I am ushered into the Chief's office to wait. Tucked at the side of the sofa is his bulletproof vest. I look at his bookshelf: *New York City Riots*; *De-policing America*, Sun Tzu's *The Art of War*; *Terrorism and Counterterrorism*. I suspect he has read them all, since he later tells me that he has a PhD in public administration and keeps a copy of *Elements of Style* (Strunk and White's legendary book on clear writing, and one of my great influences) on his bedside table.

The Chief comes in. John Perez is an engaging man who talks fast, and who has been with the Pasadena police for 34 years, working his way up from police cadet to what he calls 'office manager'. About 18 months ago the then Chief retired, following some controversial incidents and plenty of negative publicity. John, who was recovering from a double heart bypass, was asked to fill the gap.

'Pasadena is now a world hub of activity socially, culturally and in terms of business. The little old lady from Pasadena is more alive, more youthful, more socially involved – and drives a faster car.' There are 150,000 people and 240 police officers; Santa Monica has roughly the same number of police for only 80,000 people.

'The 1980s was a terrible period,' he says. 'We had shootings, the highest level of incarcerations, gangs and drugs epidemics. Police work was difficult. It produced a need for teams – tactical teams, community policing teams, school teams, bicycle teams. But after the 2001 recession there was an anomaly – crime dropped. One reason is that we are using social media in many positive ways, getting messages out, putting notices on Twitter.

'On the other side we have had the highest level of active shooter events, more this year than ever before, fuelled by social media outrage and YouTube. It's really about mental health – these people have psychological problems and social media drives them on.'

'What the hell is going on with guns?' I ask.

'I should say the same,' he replies. 'We have too many guns, and getting numbers down will take decades. The problem is that most of those who own guns are very responsible gun owners – they truly believe they are the best. So new laws impact them. But what they don't understand is that there are people out there who aren't responsible.

'And there are no national gun laws. California has tough gun laws with as much on safety as on the guns themselves. I am not a gun nut, but I have two – and I keep them in a large safe bolted to the floor. We need national laws on safety, licensing and training.'

The Chief's current concerns are use of force by the police, community relations and police–community oversight. The use of force by Pasadena police officers has dropped by 35 per cent. He has brought in active officers to talk to communities about policing. And he has called in seven people 'who didn't like me' to be an advisory committee; it meets every two months.

He says the media needs to know what is happening, and he has set up a scheme called Policing 101 (ie, basics of policing). They take journalists out to the police range and take them through various scenarios. He tells the story of one journalist who was firing at the target and said 'I don't know why I'm firing', but continued to do so as he said it.

'We need more education. We google something and the first response we get we assume is the truth. We need more discussion and discourse. We want to make sure we are not living through the last days of the Roman Republic. I look at where we're at – the best time of our lives with science, medicine and space exploration – but the unanswered question is how are we going to meet *that* challenge?'

I ask him if there is a chance of having a ride in a police car, as I did in 1969.

'Sure,' he says. Before I can get over my shock he has introduced me to a commander who takes me down to meet Field Sergeant Rudy Lemos, who has been on the force for 27 years. Sgt Lemos takes me into the garage and opens up a huge black and white car. I ask him if a field sergeant is like the man in Hill Street Blues who used to say, 'Be careful out there.' He says yes.

We drive first through the old town, which he says is so lively at weekends they have to bring in extra police officers on overtime. We cross a bridge over a freeway and he points out the tall fences put up to stop people jumping. Soon we are cruising along the streets of the rich – lined with oak trees and rambling houses with spotless lawns, neatly trimmed hedges, and rubbish bins twice the size of those used by normal folk.

We skirt the Rose Bowl, the huge stadium best known for the New Year college football game, where they are cleaning up after last night's Rolling Stones concert. As our progress is held up by a tractor pulling a line of toilets – 'porta potties' according to Rudy – I ask him what's changed in policing.

'My father was a police officer, and when I started I had the same weapons as he had carried – a revolver and a night stick. Now we have a collapsible baton, a rifle and a shotgun in the car. We never had to do this, but because of the bad guys we have to arm ourselves to the teeth.'

He explains that the North Hollywood Shootout in 1997 'changed the mindset of policing'. This was a prolonged battle between police and two heavily armed and armoured bank robbers. The police were outgunned and had to commandeer an armoured car and semi-automatic weapons. In the ensuing battle nearly 2,000 rounds of ammunition were fired, twelve police officers and eight civilians wounded, and the two gunmen killed.

I realise that the space between us is filled with two large firearms – a shotgun and a rifle – stacked side by side. 'That's the world we live in,' he says. 'But I'm trained to use them. My job is to make people safe and put them in jail.'

'Have you been fired on?' I ask.

'Yes. In a pursuit. I fired my gun. I was not the only one to shoot, so don't know whether I hit the target. But I didn't sleep for two days.'

We move back across the city centre into another area of town, where live the less affluent, mainly African American and Hispanic. The houses, gardens and bins are all a lot smaller. As we pass housing and welfare officers we see little knots of people hanging around, but they don't react to us.

A poorly dressed woman shuffles along the pavement, Rudy lowers the window.

'How're ya doing?'

'Bad.'

'How bad?'

'Bad.' She shrugs and shuffles off again. An addict, he says.

He sees some young people across the street. 'Those are gangs,' he says.

Posing with Field Sergeant Rudy Lemos before my repeat tour of Pasadena in a police car.

'Do you see they're wearing red?' By the time he has finished saying it, they have slipped over walls and behind corners.

We turn a corner where a man tinkers with his car outside his home. He smiles broadly when he sees Rudy and they chat happily. As we drive off Rudy turns to me: 'He was a dealer. Now he sells cars.'

He goes on to say that the man was shot at, but not hit, during another named firearms incident – the 2014 Summit Street Shooting. 'A neighbour took out an AK-47 and started shooting. Killed three people. He'd had a fight with his girlfriend. Killed her, her father and one other.'

Then he tells me of the Halloween Murders in 1993. Some boys who had put on costumes for the festival were mistaken for rivals by some gang members, who started to shoot. Three boys were killed and three more injured. This was personal for the Pasadena police: one of their crime scene investigators was a parent of one of the boys who were killed. I am horrified.

Later I looked up the records. Three gang members were sentenced to death for what was called at the time 'a crime that to many symbolised the intrusion of urban-life horror into the haven of the suburbs' (Abigail Goldman, *Los Angeles Times*, December 23, 1995). They are still on Death

Row along with more than another 700 inmates in California, where executions have been stalled in political and legal fights over the legality of capital punishment. Only 13 convicted murderers have been executed in that state since 1972, the last in 2006. In March 2019 the new governor issued a moratorium. One estimate by a US appeals court judge is that the death penalty has cost California $4 billion.

Then something tugged at my memory and I dug some more. In August 2018 Pope Francis declared the death sentence 'inadmissible because it is an attack on the inviolability and dignity of the person'. I wish I had known this when confronted by the pro-Lifers in Austin.

Back in the sergeants' room Rudy introduces me to a colleague responsible for the homeless unit, currently made up of three police officers who are each partnered by a health professional when they go out on patrol. 'Our job is outreach, to focus on the ones that have mental health problems – that's like 90 per cent of them,' she says. 'A lot of them have a history of drug and alcohol abuse.

'Our teams go out and deal with their problems. If crimes are being committed they do law enforcement as well. But there's only so much you can do. Just because they are homeless doesn't mean they can't be in the park.'

The sergeants and others have been passing around the picture I took of Mary Ann, but not surprisingly nobody recognises her. 'It's a pity you haven't got her last name,' they say.

But the sergeant in charge of the homeless unit has dug out a 20-year-old black and white calendar showing the young men and women of the force striking poses. They reminisce as they go through the pages: one is now very rich, one has come out as gay, and a third has committed suicide. But many are still working for the force, some in senior positions. The continuity is impressive.

While I am in Pasadena I have one more story to revisit: having my hair cut.

Men's hair was still an issue in 1969 America. My BUNAC guidebook advised: 'Long hair is still regarded as eccentric in North America, so be prepared for endless boring jokes on the subject.' Mine wasn't particularly long, nor was I the butt of endless boring jokes on the subject, but it was untidy enough for my increasingly mischievous editors to send me out for a trim.

Nobody at the police station could remember Mary Ann, the officer who arranged for my 1969 police car tour, here pictured at the Arboretum.

The resulting story appeared under the headline 'Despite British Propriety, Englishman Lets Hair Down'. There were before and after pictures of my head, with a caption saying I had changed from a 'semi-hippy type' to a 'disconsolate and shorn lad'.

So now I ask at the police station for a recommendation and am told that several members of the force use a barber on the ground floor of my old lodgings, the YMCA. I take their advice and find myself stepping down a few stairs into an old-fashioned barber's shop with black and white squares on the floor, and chrome and plastic chairs for the cutting.

It is presided over by 77-year-old Joe, who tells me that he came with his family by Greyhound bus to California in 1947. He seems well informed about the UK and talks about Brexit and Boris Johnson.

'But I like that other one. What's his name? Oh yes, Nigel Farage.'

I am moderately pleased with the haircut, though I come out with the suspicion that the left side has been treated more harshly than the right.

My Uber driver is a young man from mainland China in a huge white car with teddy bear upholstery (which he says was chosen by his daughters). Today's papers report that thousands of protesters in Hong Kong have held hands in a long chain. The driver is cross with Trump for whipping up these 'terrorists' and says he expects China to send in the army and 'restore order to part of China'.

I wonder what the Chief would have made of that.

6. San Jose: from oranges to Apple

Saturday 24 August

As I creep downstairs at 8 am with my case, a figure rises from the sofa. It is my host, and yes, she has been sleeping there. She quizzes me about my stay, which is not something I want to get engaged in at that time in the morning. I mention that a chair and a table would have enhanced my experience. Further pressed I say that I found everything downstairs rather dark.

'You could have opened the curtains,' she says. How was I to know?

Our host has told me that she is often away on business, which is why she lets out all three bedrooms. With what I hear about the cost of housing I suspect there might be a financial imperative at the back of all this. But I wonder what quality of life this has left her with? As for me, Airbnb may be cheap and fashionable but at the places I've stayed in so far I'm missing the hospitality.

My Uber driver today comes from Honduras. He has been in the US for 24 years and has a 22-year-old son who has just got a mechanical engineering degree, and a daughter studying performance art. He is now a US citizen.

'There are a lot of people – illegals – who are trying to damage this country,' he says. They come here to be criminals. I agree that we should not have them. But there are a lot of poor countries. One solution would be for the United States to help these countries so their people wouldn't have to come here.'

Unprompted, he adds: 'We have ten years to fix the planet. Otherwise it will be too late.'

Today I celebrate my return to the buses with a seven-hour journey north to San Jose, the third largest city in California (after Los Angeles and San Diego) and the heart of Silicon Valley – home to Cisco, eBay, Adobe, PayPal, Acer, Hewlett Packard and many more. The city has the most millionaires and billionaires in the world, the third highest GDP per capita

Back on the buses and the scenery kicks in: on the road from Los Angeles to San Jose.

in the world (after Zurich and Oslo), and the most expensive housing market in the USA. My 1969 BUNAC Guide makes no mention of the place, nor does my 1969 diary.

I have booked into an interesting-looking hotel, the Hayes Mansion, a sprawling 214-room resort built around the country house of a once-prominent local family. The two brothers – Jay O and Everis A Hayes, who were newspaper proprietors and politicians – lived, with their families, in separate wings. The mansion was bought by the city of San Jose in 1985 and the resort built around it.

As I am driven up, I see the front lawn filled with lines of chairs and multi-coloured saris. An Indian wedding is being celebrated. Later I learn that there were two that day – one dry, and the other (as I can tell from my seat in the bar) with guests drinking tray-loads of Black Label and vodka-with-Sprite. I corner one of the guests from the dry party: their families had migrated to America decades before and yes, most of them are working in high-tech businesses.

I start to talk to the man on the stool next to me, a soft-spoken salesman of protective packaging in his late 60s. He was born and bred in San Jose. 'This used to be the "valley of heart's delight" – oranges, berries, apricots,' he says. 'All the farms have gone now. When I was a kid we used to pick string beans for two and a half cents a pound; now the farm is Apple.

'In the old days you knew everyone on the block. Now you don't know anyone any more; everyone's a stranger. You can't find a parking space outside your own home. People drive in and park their cars, and then ride 4 miles to work on their scooters.

'The pace of life has got so much faster. Before there was no congestion on the freeway. Now I sometimes won't take appointments at certain times because of the traffic.'

'Where will it end?' I ask.

He laughs. 'There seems to be no stopping it.'

He is here checking out the hotel for a friend who is thinking of booking it for his parents' anniversary. I say I think there is a shortage of staff. The barman joins in.

'It's not just here, it's everywhere,' he says. 'I went to a restaurant in the city with my girlfriend the other day and there was only one server. I ended up helping her out. There are restaurants that don't open for lunch any more because they can't find the staff. The trouble is people can't afford to live here.'

Sunday 25 August

On my way back from breakfast I chat with another man checking the place out, this time with his wife, two daughters and future son-in-law, and they are thinking of having the wedding here next spring. He is also from India originally, and is in computers, as is one of the daughters.

'What do you think of the current state of America?' I ask.

'The younger generation is above all that,' says the one about to be married. 'If you are a good person you are a good person.'

Her sister follows quickly: 'With all the turbulence life goes on. People get married, have kids …'

My 22-year-old self would have had great difficulty understanding what goes on in Silicon Valley, and my 72-year-old self fears he won't fare much better. So my first call is at the Tech Interactive, a science and technology museum that started in 1990 and moved to a new site in 1998. Like the library in Orlando, it has a National Medal for Museum and Library Service, this one awarded in 2015. On the website I see a visitor's comment that they hadn't realised it was for children; that's going to be the right place for me.

On the outside the building is mango and azure; inside it is bright and spacious, stuffed full of gadgets, displays, precocious children and baffled adults. As I start wandering around the floor l am rescued by a chirpy volunteer called Kay who turns out to be a science writer. I tell her about the book I am researching, which she dismisses as a 'non-rechargeable paper thingy'. She then tries to introduce me to biomimicry – 'using patterns of a coral reef skeleton as inspiration for cardiac stents'. I concentrate hard.

I see a colourful wall with stylised pictures of animals in various poses. In front of it small children are rushing around little tables piled with Lego. I tell Kay that I think it's time for me to have some hands-on experience and that I wish to build a Lego turtle.

I try to rein in my enthusiasm – I seem to be the only unaccompanied adult in this area – but can't stop myself raiding my three-year-old neighbour's tray for the special brick I need to complete the task. I place the finished article – the kind of thing that only a mother would praise – on a revolving tray and switch on a scanner. But technology recognises my talent and translates it into a much nicer picture of a turtle projected onto the wall. I rotate the picture so the turtle is on its tail, and leave.

I have been using the Animaker – a 'curious robot powered by artificial intelligence' that will 'build your favourite animal … recognise it and bring it to life'. Kay patiently explains what I have been doing: 'It's your first foray into machine learning and image processing – teaching the machine to see.'

'But what's the point?' I ask.

She gives two uses that go over my head – first, to help geneticists with their protein maps and, second, to help astronomers with their star charts. The third, though, I can understand. Basically – and 'if you don't mind the adult language', as Kay puts it – Google can use it to identify pornography.

Kay leaves me for another bemused visitor and I spend a happy hour wandering around the rest of the museum. I compose some music by putting dots on lines on a screen. It turns itself into a pleasant little tune. As I go off to the bathroom I can hear it chiming away, and when I come back it's still chiming away. Slightly embarrassed by now, I notice a tiny icon in the bottom left hand corner and stop the chime. I'm learning.

Whether it is enough is another matter. Down in the café I have to be shown how to get water out of the lemonade tap in the drinks dispenser.

Outside the museum a lively street party is going on, though blocked from public view. I walk right round the perimeter before I find the entrance. This is Silicon Valley Pride – not one but two concepts that I wasn't aware of in 1969.

In fact the event's roots go back nearly half a century, to a gay rights rally in 1975 that became San Jose Pride Festival in 1976 and Silicon Valley Pride in 2014. This year, it says on its website, it 'is important, now more than ever, to make our voices heard and to celebrate our diversity'.

I look in the official programme. 'Out and proud' local politicians have written letters of support: they include a state assembly member, two mayors and a county superintendent of schools. Sponsors include corporate giants such as Kaiser Permanente, Google, Volkswagen, Jack Daniels, Texas Instruments, Adobe, Microsoft and NBC.

This is my first slice of Pride so I approach it cautiously, along an avenue of stalls. All kinds of groups are represented, from main (and not-so-main) political parties to police departments, from the AARP (American Association of Retired Persons) to Princess Cruises and the Silicon Valley Gay Men's Chorus. Everyone seems happy, a few people are in outrageous outfits, and several wish me 'Happy Pride' as they go past. Rainbow flags are everywhere and the water bottles are on brand. I go through to the main stage, which is featuring Macy Gray (1999 breakout hit, 'I Try').

One busy stall sports the banner 'Faith Communities who Love'. It turns out to be a group of supportive churches, and I speak to a Lutheran pastor, Cristina Beauchemin.

'This is something that didn't exist in 1969,' I say, indicating the scene around me.

'It was there. But they weren't allowed to be that open. The turning point was the Stonewall Riots. That was the first time that they revolted. And things changed.

'There is more acceptance nowadays. This is a process. When I look around and see all the people that are here I see a world that is open. I know we have been told we are sinners but that's not true. I've been coming here for ten years. I love coming here. I love being part of a big community …'

'And are things still getting better?' I ask.

'I think some people would say that things are really nasty. We have a shift of power, and when there is a shift the people in power work very hard to maintain it …

'As a woman I find it a power issue. Women are gaining power. How do you keep them from having power? That's why abortion and birth control

Celebrating diversity at Silicon Valley Pride 2019: 'There is more acceptance nowadays'.

are once again part of the struggle. It's a patriarchal thing. We've had a white-male-dominated system since the first settlers.'

That evening I have supper in the hotel bar again. On the TV I watch a clip of a man playing golf in Orlando. He is at the top of his swing when an alligator saunters across in front of him. He finishes the shot. The presenter says the golfer's name must be 'Steel, as in nerves of'.

Not long after, when football has replaced golf on the television, I am telling my barstool neighbour about my trip when he suddenly stiffens.

'Oh my God!' he says. 'Oh my God!'

I follow his gaze to the screen. The game has gone and there is a newsflash. My neighbour whips out his phone to find out more.

'It's a possible shooting at the Great Mall,' he says, looking at the local news report.

The woman behind the bar looks up and deflates.

'Not again!' she says. 'Not after Gilroy ... These shooters are deliberately doing malls because you can't escape from them.' (Gilroy, they remind me, is a nearby town where there was a shooting incident last month, of which more later.)

My neighbour, a former faculty member at Berkeley, is more measured. 'The trouble is it stops people from going out. In my opinion, and you can put this in your book, it stops people from being able to connect.'

He starts to gather statistics from his phone. 'So far this year at least 17 deadly mass shootings; 2,185 deadly mass shootings since Sandy Hook. So far this year 255 people killed in mass shootings – defined as those of four or more people, excluding the shooter. And we are only in the 215th day of the year. It's crazy.'

He texts his girlfriend, who is driving to meet him: 'Stay away from the Great Mall area.' He turns to me: 'People are scared. But they're shrugging their shoulders. If it becomes the norm ... that's scary.'

Another newsflash. The shootings are still unconfirmed: 'Out of an abundance of caution' people caught up in it are being 'sheltered in place.'

A younger couple come into the bar and immediately catch the drama.

'Oh boy!' he says. 'It's a becoming a regular occurrence.'

'Like every day,' his girlfriend adds.

After a short while regular programming resumes but the violence seems to linger. I go to my room to pack and keep the television on in case of an update. There isn't.

One of the first things I do in the morning is check my phone for news of the incident. What happened is now clear: there had been an attempted robbery, and some glass was smashed. This was mistakenly thought to be gunfire. Police are still investigating. There were no casualties.

By the evening the story has disappeared, but the damage has been done. It's a jumpy country these days, and with good reason.

THE BIT IN THE MIDDLE

1. Eastward ho!: the rocky road to Vegas

Monday 26 August

Crossing America is still one of the great adventures – the huge distances, the beauty and variety of the landscapes, and the ambition and skill of the man-made enterprises. In 1969, anxious to get back to New York, I rushed through, leaving San Francisco at 1 am on a Friday morning and arriving in Chicago two days and six hours later, at 7 am on the Sunday.

My diary does not dwell on the trip. The first day took me through 'dry, flat land … long straight roads'; the second was 'boring all day – vast fields of corn with little ridges parallel to the road … nothing stimulating'. For the first few hours I'd sat next to a man going home with a new leg; towards the end of the journey a couple of young men behind me played music and smoked pot. My bottom ached.

This year I plan to proceed at a more sedate pace, which will allow me to spend more time in what are now dubbed the flyover states – and reduce the chances of an aching bum. Over 11 days my planned route from San Jose to Chicago will take me through Nevada, Utah, Wyoming, Nebraska, Iowa and Illinois. That still leaves me with a couple of 12-hour journeys, starting with today's trip to Las Vegas. This is a bit of a detour south, but more northern routes seemed thin, and would have meant departing and arriving at highly unsocial times.

Our first stop today is Gilroy, a pleasant-looking country town of nearly 50,000 people, known for growing garlic and holding an annual garlic festival (speciality: garlic ice cream). I would have passed through the place without a second glance had I not been reminded in the bar last night of the tragedy that took place there just four weeks ago.

As the last day of this year's festival was drawing to a close, a young man from the town opened fire with a semi-automatic rifle. He killed three and wounded seventeen before turning the gun on himself. His motives remain unclear, though inflammatory pamphlets from both left-wing and right-wing extremists were found in his belongings. I am finding out that in America these days you are never far from a place of shooting.

We change drivers at Fresno: the replacement is a bossy little man who (unlike most of the drivers I have met so far) wears his peaked cap. He won't let me off the bus 'because we're leaving', then doesn't for about ten minutes. Just before starting up, he struts up and down the aisle telling us to turn off our ring tones and just vibrate. However, he is the only driver so far who tells us to use our seatbelts.

The Greyhound WiFi and my T-Mobile coverage start flitting in and out. In a connected moment I try to look up today's itinerary on Morris to see where we will be taking our breaks. My search is wasted: the details of this trip – plus tickets and details for two others – have disappeared. Before I can get them back the connection goes again.

Around lunchtime we have a half-hour stop at Bakersfield, which gives me enough time to confirm its description in my *Rough Guide* as a 'flat, colourless oil town'. By the middle of the afternoon we are chugging up into the mountains: on the left a wave of flaxen hills, dotted with trees and merging into the huge blue sky; on the right a sharper incline covered with more trees. I should be writing my journal but can't stop looking out of the window. I see a train snaking under our road. This is America the bold and beautiful.

After some time we stop chugging and are on the way down. I see a railway tunnel to the right: freeway and railway are clearly intertwined. What a feat it must have been to build them. Another interminable freight train meanders past: there must be something in these hills that someone is extracting.

Out onto a plain at Tehachapi, where we have a brief stop. The town looks well cared for and is ringed with mountains. From the bus stop I can see a library and a theatre. I wish I knew more about the place, but the internet is down again.

As we leave, I see a small airport and a huge windfarm. We turn another corner and I see the side of a mountain that looks defaced by extraction. We continue to twist and turn, past regiments of wind turbines, some turning, some at rest. They look magnificent, and clean. I reach for Morris so that I can take a photo.

'Speak to me,' says Morris. I don't want a bloody conversation with an inanimate object; I want to take a picture. By the time I've shut Morris up, the windmills are well behind and waving goodbye.

Suddenly we are out of the mountains and in a desert, with sandy soil and little tufts of vegetation. I see some curious cactus-like plants And not much else. We go through the small town of Mojave, which looks depressed. As we draw away I look back and see a crowd of planes, grouped together as if they are in storage. Many of these planes were probably in the planning stage when I was here in 1969; now they're sitting in the sun, superannuated old-timers like me.

The desert seems endless. I see a sign for the turning for Edwards Air Force Base, which sounds familiar but I still can't get a signal to find out why. Next stop is Boron where I get enough signal for someone to send me an advert: 'Cheap Senior Dental Transplants'. How did they find me?

We stop for supper at Barstow, where the WiFi comes back. I stopped here in 1969, *en route* from the Grand Canyon to Pasadena. I remember sipping coffee in a Howard Johnson restaurant; now we are debouched into an emporium filled with outlets selling food and a range of tourist tat – though not the model Greyhound bus I am looking for. Our driver is still grumpy: as we are about to leave he refuses to let me get off the bus to get rid of a bag of rubbish.

There's a glorious sunset over the mountains, and we are about to enter Las Vegas as one should – at night. The desert starts to make way to signs of habitation, and billboards begin to bloom: MGM Resorts, then World Class Cannabis. Lights appear, but these are outliers, and dark reclaims us.

Soon it's the real thing and we are driving on a motorway parallel to the Strip – Mandalay Bay, a Magic Kingdom, a New York skyline, a pencil-thin laser probing up into the sky, a colonnaded Caesar's Palace. Then, inevitably, a building reaching up to the sky, unadorned apart from a golden sign: TRUMP. Neon continues to follow neon, then suddenly the glitz diminishes as we move away from the heart of the action and into the bus station, where we stop and the bus lights come on. We are in Las Vegas, a mere half an hour late. It's been a long day, but this afternoon the scenery was more than enough compensation.

In 1969 I arrived at Las Vegas at 6 am and was surprised to see people gambling on slot machines and at the tables so early in the morning. I was equally surprised to see marriage 'chapels' garlanded with flowers and dotted with Coca Cola machines. I particularly like the look of the Olde Highland Kirk.

I had teamed up with two sisters at the Grand Canyon and we stayed at a small hotel with a swimming pool and free coffee, as recommended in my BUNAC guide. In the evening I went with one of them to see the Strip. (The other sister was under 21 and had to stay and watch television.) 'Very plush, like an extended clean Piccadilly Circus in the middle of the desert', I wrote.

After some time walking around and nursing drinks, I braved the roulette table, using a technique I had read about in a James Bond book. This involved playing on the reds and blacks, and doubling up each time you lost: 'My gambling career lasts about one minute because of a run of seven blacks. $5 gone. Try a few cents on the slots but no good!'

This time I am booked at the Plaza, near the bus station and away from the Strip. I am paying what I think is an extremely low price of $58 for the night (other nights can be three times that, but this is Monday). The hotel has sent me a welcoming email telling me that the Greyhound station is next to the hotel. That seems a nice touch.

The lobby offers automated check-in desks but after 12 hours on a bus I opt for a real person. There's only one, and she's taking her time dealing with the couple in front of me asking endless questions. Eventually it's my turn. I give her my name, she looks at her screen, and frowns. She can't find my details, even though – as I am quick to tell her – they sent me an email of welcome only a few hours ago. She calls her manager. He takes my reservation printout and disappears into a back office.

I keep asking what the problem is, and no-one can give me a straight answer. This goes on for about ten minutes. I note some scurrying around in the back office, but no-one gives me eye contact. I start to feel alone and vulnerable. Are my papers not in order? Am I on a blacklist? Is Big Brother looking at me from behind the two-way mirror and pointing?

Eventually the receptionist gives me a room and a key card. I ask if the delay has something to do with the low price I am paying. She gives me no meaningful explanation though she mutters variously about allocating the room to someone else and 'a problem with the app'. When I walk away I notice that I am shaking, whether from anger or fear I am not sure.

I have been given a de luxe room, which is needlessly grand for a stay of 12 hours. I have approximately 325 square feet with a kingsize bed, a 32-inch flat-screen TV with premium cable channels, a table, a desk, a settee, and a bathroom with a little lobby. However, I do notice that the toilet paper here – and in many other places in America – is by British standards remarkably thin.

I take a walk through the hotel casino. It's a Monday night. This hotel is a little way away from the main action, but people are still clustering around the tables and the slot machines. Smoking is allowed. Fifty years ago we wouldn't have given it a second sniff, but today it makes the place seem seedy. The croupiers are a mixed lot: some young men, some women of my generation or thereabouts, some matronly and some unnaturally skinny. I wonder if the glamorous figures I remember in 1969 have gone elsewhere, and then it occurs to me that it's the exact opposite: they haven't.

A sequence of whoops comes flying out from a roulette table: they originate from a happy gambler wearing shorts and a straw hat whose number has just come up. Elsewhere a group of Chinese men cluster around a slot machine (bets $1 to $1,000) laughing and clapping each other on the shoulder. They are some of the few I see looking as if they are having a good time.

I had intended to replicate my 1969 experience and see whether I could last longer with a $35 stake (the equivalent of $5 in 1969 prices). But I am tired, and reluctant to give the hotel any more money than I have to.

I am approached by a young man. He saw me waiting at the front desk and now asks if I have sorted things out. He agrees that the staff behaved oddly. He comes from Denmark, and, as this is only a few days after Trump asked the Danes if he could buy Greenland from them, I ask him if they have decided to sell. He laughs, then tells me the joke going around Denmark that Trump wants to buy the North Pole next – and is furious with Poland for refusing to sell it. It can't be good for a nation, particularly one with ambitions to be Great Again, when foreign visitors start mocking their president within a few minutes of starting a conversation.

I go through a side door and find myself in the Greyhound bus station. I talk to a staff member about my trip on the buses. 'They're dangerous,' he says. 'I've only travelled on them twice – once when I was a baby and once when I came out of jail.' He was the station's night security guard.

I go back to my room and go to sleep in my oversized bed in my oversized room. I do not sleep well.

For the record I have since googled some of the places I passed today. The curious cacti-like plants may have been Joshua trees. Tehachapi is known for the Tehachapi loop, an 1874 engineering triumph which allows trains to climb a particularly steep gradient. There are nearly 5,000 wind turbines in the area, and this year a Walmart store has opened. The Mojave Air and Space Port is used for testing commercial space rockets as well as storing superannuated planes. Edwards Air Force Base is where the space shuttle used to take off and land. Boron is the site of the California's largest open pit mine, the largest borax mine in the world.

I am not sure whether knowing all this would have improved my enjoyment of today's trip. By forcing me to direct my eyes at what was flowing past my window rather than at a tiny screen, the skittishness of the signal probably did me a service.

2. Salt Lake City: the Mormon stronghold

Tuesday 27 August

It's a dream start today: all I have to do is go out of a side door and I am in the Greyhound bus station. On my way I notice that the gambler wearing shorts and a straw hat is back on the tables – or has he been up all night? I have an eight-hour journey in front of me, heading north-east to Salt Lake City. When I stopped there for two hours in 1969 I concluded: 'Very pretty Temple Square … clean and modern town.' This time I will have two nights and a day to check it out again.

The bus is particularly noisy today, with a couple of bag-rustling munchers, someone playing an electronic game with the sound on, and another phoning in a job application. The bus soon asserts itself, moving into the now-familiar climbing rhythm as we go through rocky terrain, then back onto dusty plains. Man's imprint is everywhere: cliffs gouged for their minerals, mountains crowned with electronic installations, golf courses with startlingly incongruous patches of green and beckoning pools. As the Americans wrote all over Europe in the Second World War, Kilroy has been here.

During the lunch break at Parowan I talk to a fellow passenger who is a Greyhound bus driver in plain clothes. He tells me he has been 'deadheading' (driving an empty bus) to El Paso and he's now 'on a cushion' (riding on a bus from one job to another) to Salt Lake City. I tell him what the security guard told me last night and he agrees that sometimes there is trouble on the buses.

'Does it come from people coming up from across the border?' I ask.

'No. They are very quiet, very well behaved,' he replies. 'And they don't get off at the stops – they are frightened of missing the bus.'

Back on the road the man behind me who has been talking for most of the journey continues his monologues. My neighbour across the aisle leans over and offers me a small plastic envelope containing several small packages. I wonder whether he has managed to get to the marijuana superstore, but they are ear plugs. I take a packet gratefully, noting that they will be more useful than the pillow and inflatable cushion I've brought with me but have not yet used.

We arrive at Salt Lake City just after 5 o'clock. I revert to my old, bad habit, and leave Morris in the Uber. But my phone recovery skills are improving. I use the hotel's phone to call, and the driver hears it and brings him back, beaming. I take out my wallet to give him a generous tip.

'No. No. No,' he says.

Even though my record for losing things was as bad (or worse) 50 years ago, I am still upset: this is the third time that I have left my mobile phone behind. I come up with a plan, based on the assumption that I take too much clutter with me into the back of the car. From now on I will put my rucksack in the boot/trunk, leaving me only four things to worry about – wallet, notebook, phone, self. It works. This is the last time, on this trip at least, that I leave Morris behind.

I have booked at the Carlton Hotel just off Temple Square in the centre of Salt Lake City. It is well situated, not a chain, and reasonably priced with 45 rooms and plenty of wooden furnishings. As I settle in, I open the Salt Lake City entry in my 1969 BUNAC Guide, and realise I am staying in a hotel that they recommended half a century ago. Then the cost was $3.00 single, $4.50 with bath; I am paying $107 per night – and I have a bath.

Later I meet James Wright III, casually dressed in blue jeans, and discover that the hotel is owned and run by a dynasty. His grandfather James Wright I bought the hotel in 1964; his father James Wright II ran the hotel after him; he himself has been working here since he was 15. He would like his son James Wright IV to take over, but he would rather be an airline pilot. His daughter is in the business scholar programme at the University of Utah, and he thinks she might take over the family business. I neglect to ask if she is called Jane.

The building started out as apartments in 1929 and now is squashed incongruously between bigger modern buildings. 'We like to think we have old English charm. I don't want to change it. We have to keep up with things like the internet, but I don't want to lose that charm. Those who want a big hotel with a restaurant or a bar – they just have to go somewhere else.'

He has had many offers to buy the site but he won't sell it. 'First, I wouldn't know what to do if I didn't run it, and second, if they turned it into something else it would break my heart.'

The city has changed dramatically, he says. 'There was a building frenzy for the 2002 Winter Olympics. But it's still one of the safest cities you can come across.' He remembers the Olympics fondly. 'We had *Sports Illustrated* staying here – reporters, photographers. It was one of those things I never forget. I wished it would never end.'

Wednesday 28 August

After two long days on the buses I am relaxing by taking a four-hour bus tour of the city. As we assemble, our guide/ driver tells us that the city is particularly crowded because a major UN conference is in town. The topic is civil society.

'That's nice,' comments one of our group. 'We can do with being more civil with each other.' She is a director of a health care organisation, and she warms to her theme: 'We have to teach young people how to put down their phones, and smile and talk to people.'

'Cell phones,' the tour guide chips in. 'They are the biggest change in 50 years.'

We turn to the matter in hand: visiting the city. It is ringed with mountains. Some of them are badly scarred by mines and we are told that one open-cast mine is three miles across, with one of its holes three quarters of a mile deep. Before I can make a snarky comment about irresponsible Americans ravaging their own land, he adds that it is owned by the British company RTZ.

On the streets the dress code differs from that in California. Many men still wear suits, jackets and ties – and perspire accordingly. We are in a desert, as our guide reminds us.

At the This Is the Place Heritage Park we learn of the city's foundation by the Mormons, or as we are frequently reminded the Church of Latter-day Saints (commonly abbreviated to LDS). The story is stirring: a long and gruelling trek from persecution into an arid land, now transformed into a modern, diverse industrial city and the world headquarters of a thriving church. It is on this spot in 1847 that Brigham Young is said to have been propped up on the bed in his wagon, then peered out and declared that this was the chosen site revealed to him in a dream.

At the Capitol, a huge domed building in the Corinthian style that dominates the town, we go inside. No-one searches our bags, though a single bored cop is standing by. Inside, the building is immense, impressive, empty – full of marble. Our little group wanders around; the only others in the building seem to be five Asian boys sitting on the grand staircase posing for a group selfie.

When I hear talk of capitols I think of the one in Washington, and usually forget there are another 50 of these awe-inspiring edifices scattered around the country. Legislators may constantly snipe at the perils of 'big government', but that doesn't seem to have stopped them enjoying the opulent buildings constructed for their use.

And it's not as if they are a representative bunch. On one wall is a picture of the state senators. I count them: I make 23 white men, and six women, one of whom is of Japanese descent. I wonder if the proportion has changed much in 50 years.

The marble theme carries on into the public washrooms, which are so impressive that I tweet a view. The soap dispenser is an independent spirit and ensures that the soap it dispenses bypasses my outstretched hands and lands on my trousers; that I don't tweet.

Finally to Temple Square, the spiritual centre of the city. After an organ recital in the magnificent Mormon Tabernacle, we have a cafeteria lunch in the former house of Brigham Young himself. We leave the tour with our guide's superlatives ringing in our ears: the Conference Centre is the biggest concert hall in the world; the capitol is the second biggest after (inevitably) Texas; the pillars are the largest pillars on the American continent; the city has the third most centenarians in the USA (or was that the world?).

Just down the road from my hotel is Harmon's Grocery, a huge supermarket where I look for something to buy for dinner. The range of food is extraordinarily broad, but I am told that wine is only available at a state-controlled liquor store.

On my way out I pass a notice advertising the services of a dietitian. She is not in her office but her colleagues next door in the demonstration kitchen tell me that her job is to give classes on healthier cooking, and to advise customers and employees.

'She will take a shopping trip with you or give personal advice. It keeps her pretty busy,' I am told. This seems a great idea.

I walk, slowly in the heat, to the City Creek Center, a huge shopping complex that I found myself in last night. It is a $1.5 billion redevelopment by the LDS Church, which involved dismantling two malls, a skyscraper and other buildings. It has the usual selection of modern shops, a brace of department stores, a waterfall and a wandering rivulet. It doesn't seem to have a lot of people in it, though.

On the corner in a prime position is a shop called Deseret Publishing, which is clearly part of the LDS activities. (Deseret is the name of the short-lived state that the original LDS settlers wanted to set up.) The airy space is interspersed with cheery staff wearing aprons. They sell books, rather cheesy religious paintings, handbags, bibles, ties. In a separate room are racks full of white dresses which I assume are for some religious purpose. They make me think of the Handmaid's Tale images – and then I remember the picture I still have of myself at my first holy communion in the Catholic Church, surrounded by young girls in white dresses.

I start chatting with one of the salesmen. He is a charming young man, just out of college and soon to start postgraduate studies in dentistry. I tell him about my book and ask him what he thinks of America at the moment.

'It is pretty divided, which is a shame. If you look at politics, people are divided 50:50. But as a whole, apart from politics, I think we are doing well. There are a lot of things we are united on still.'

'But not abortion or gay rights,' I say.

'I believe we should have equal rights, but we don't support them when we believe it's a sin. I have a lot of friends who are gay. They are great and I love them, but it wouldn't be for me.'

'And abortion?'

'I believe you don't have the right to take a life.'

We get onto gun control.

'I have a few rifles,' he says. 'They're fun. I just have to keep them in a safe spot in my house. It does need to be controlled, but I don't know how we do it.'

I worry that these issues seem to be dominating public discourse, while inequality and poverty, justice and honesty remain largely undiscussed. I keep my views to myself.

3. Into the Rockies: a dose of health care

Thursday 29 August

My rash has returned with a vengeance and I itch horribly, particularly on that part of the back that only a partner can reach. I toss and turn and try not to scratch all night. Luckily it's not a long night: I have been told that rush hour traffic in Salt Lake City is terrible, so I am up at 5.30 for a 7.10 bus.

My Uber driver today is a retired medical products salesman. I say I found this a pleasant city to be in.

'People are pretty civilised round here,' he says.

'Are they not at a national level?'

'We have way too many power-hungry people and they will do anything to achieve what they want – lie, steal, kill,' he says.

He says he used to look at the candidates and work out which one to vote for. No longer.

'I watched some of the Kavanaugh hearings [for the Supreme Court], and the things those Democrats did to him were ridiculous. I wouldn't vote for them now. They're just trashing everybody.'

Salt Lake City has a scary side after all. As soon as I get into the bus station I am led to a little cart in the middle of the booking hall, where two security guards go through my rucksack, then scan me with their magic wand. They find nothing. I ask what they are looking for – drugs, guns?

'Concealed items,' I am told. 'Sometimes the police come down with their dogs and carry out searches as well.'

I ask the guard if he has ever found anything, and he says no. I need to go to the restroom, which is down a corridor with admission by ticket only. He calls another guard, who comes with me to unlock it.

'There's a shelter across the road and they keep trying to get in,' the second guard explains. 'They take drugs in there. And they have a skin disease.'

I am puzzled by the high level of security. I am told that last year the police had Operation Rio Grande to 'clean things up' near the bus station, but the homeless just moved elsewhere. This may be a prosperous, well-kept and largely religious city – but it has not escaped the current wave of homelessness.

As we set off in our bus the sun is rising over the mountains; as I did several times in 1969, I am experiencing a dawn breaking over America. We are only three passengers: one talks loudly to the driver; the second talks into his phone in Punjabi (I check this with him later); the third – me – is trying to write.

The bus is subsidised by the states of Utah and Colorado and has 12 scheduled stops on the mountain roads. Our first stop is Park City, a ski resort 7,000 feet high which hosted some of the Olympics events. We are in the Wasatch range, the western edge of the Rockies. Our driver is an old-timer, born, like me, in 1947, and he first drove for Greyhound 50 years ago; in theory he could have driven me when I first did this trip. After a strike at Greyhound he joined the army, then the marines, serving in Vietnam and Teheran, which he left only a matter of days before the hostages were taken in 1979. He went back to the buses.

Over the years the company has cut routes and buses, but he stays. 'It's a love–hate thing. I like the driving. I don't like the passengers. They are much more demanding than they used to be. They used to be polite. They used to wear suits. Now they come because they're barred from airline travel.'

He shows me a picture of his daughter. He is working to help her through college. She graduates this year and is thinking of going to medical school. He is hoping to retire and says she will have to fund herself from now on. Our conversation gets political. For once I find the tables turned and I am having to do the answering.

'I hear you're all socialist over there in England,' he asks me. 'What's it like?'

'I wouldn't call it socialism, but it's fine.'

'Socialism.' He pauses on the word. 'I wouldn't want that. I want to be free, to pay my way. I wouldn't want the state looking after me from cradle to grave.'

Earlier he has told me about his brother, who ran a business with contracts worth $1 million; now he has a bad back and lives off benefit. I remind him of that.

'Yes, but he hates it. We want to pay our own way, and not have handouts.'

Later he comes up and asks if I was offended. I assure him I was not.

We are now driving through farming country, horses in their enclosures, tree-lined hills, a lake with more hills behind. And just when I am thinking how beautiful and unspoilt it all is, a heavily-loaded lorry trundles across the landscape, leaving a trail of dust, or worse. I wonder whether it is taking out or dumping.

We drive into a town called Duchesne, a pleasant-looking place surrounded by unusual rock formations. A sign flashes by: STOP THE LAND GRAB. Connections are good today so l google the town to see if I can find out more. I don't get any answers to my query, but Morris volunteers the information that there are 14 registered sex offenders in the vicinity.

I google 'land grabs' instead. I start off assuming that the phrase refers to stopping big businesses coming in and slicing out a chunk of the countryside for a quarry, factory farm or housing estate. But the slogan has been annexed by the other side as well: it also refers to stopping pesky lawmakers who want to stop big business building quarries, factory farms or housing estates on 'areas of beauty and cultural significance'.

Shortly after, Morris the mobile decides to show me a picture of five dead mice, artfully arranged around a mousetrap. It is an ad for a device that kills mice sonically. I instinctively look under the seat. Who says you don't notice ads on Google?

The drive continues, with more spectacular views. I have asked the driver and one of the passengers whether they know anything about the land grab sign. The passenger comes back and looks around him as if to check that no-one else is listening.

'I can tell you what it's all about,' he says. 'It's the Mormon church selling land. There is no separation here between church and state. They are very rich, they make Bill Gates look like a pauper.' He puts his fingers to his lips.

I never found a conclusive explanation.

We arrive suddenly at the resort town of Steamboat Springs, my destination today. I walk over to the bus station before I realise that I haven't taken my case out of the bus. The driver hasn't taken it out either; it doesn't seem to be on his manifest. Since our combined age is 144, I think we can be excused the occasional near-miss.

Zach arrives in his pick-up truck. He is in his early thirties and the son of our New York friends Wolf and Rita. I first met him in 2001 when the family came on a brief holiday to Europe. He is now a qualified and experienced chef, who works as a salesman for a specialty food company supplying restaurants in northern and central Colorado. On Thursdays he stays overnight at Steamboat Springs and tomorrow I will join him on his rounds before going back with him to his apartment in Avon, a couple of mountain passes away.

I decide to seek advice on my rash, and Zach drives me to a medical centre. Steamboat Medical is on the ground floor of an office building, clean and bright, with friendly receptionists and a copy of the day's local paper. A handful of people are waiting, mainly large men with serious beards.

I have forms to fill – and a $174 initial payment. I ask if there is likely to be any more to pay and the receptionist says only if there are more procedures. I ask if I will be told of extra costs before I incur them, and she says I will.

After about an hour I see a nurse, who checks me out thoroughly. A few minutes later the doctor arrives. Our talk quickly gets on to our 'socialist' health system, which she thinks is terrible.

'How many Americans go to Britain for health care?' she asks,

I struggle for an answer.

'We get lots of British people coming *here* for treatment,' she adds.

I still struggle for an answer. And then I hit on it: 'Socialism is merely the economic application of Christianity.'

We have a truce after that, and she is helpful about my rash and we end on good terms. She writes me out a prescription and advises me to avoid heat – as in sun, hot tubs and showers. As I leave, a new receptionist has come on duty and she stops me.

'Did you pay the extra?' she asks. 'That will be $84.'

Luckily the doctor comes in. She quotes some procedure or other and tells the receptionist not to charge me the extra. We go to a pharmacist and they give me the cream: $16.24. They haven't got the lotion I have been prescribed, but I can get it at another pharmacist. We go there. The list price is $75 for two tubes; they give me a discount so I pay £31.25.

That makes a total of $221.49. But it could have been $349.24, had it not been for (I like to think) my unique brand of British charm. Or perhaps they just took pity on a struggling victim of socialism.

I have booked into another small independent hotel, this time with coffee and iced water in the lounge plus a large modern table with built-in plugs for visitors' devices. The receptionist tells me the town's name comes from some local springs that early settlers thought sounded like a steamboat coming down the river.

'If you have any time here you should try Strawberry Park. The hot springs there are awesome,' he says.

Zach knows the hot springs well: 'In the winter it's fantastic. You go in and it's snowing and dark. It's super-cold out and you can't see a damn thing, but once you get into the pool it's a mysterious place. The steam is so thick that you can't see people around you.'

Here I am in a mecca for hot springs – and I have to stick to cold showers.

That night we go to a restaurant and order small plates, which thankfully are now fashionable in some US restaurants. Colorado peaches are the food in season and are well represented in all parts of the menu. Zach is well known here, and we sit at the bar. The barman is a well-built man, quick with tongue and cocktails, and he comperes a discussion about politics that stops just short of a fight. A man to the right of me is eye-poppingly adamant in his hatred of Hillary Clinton.

'Evil conniving bitch,' he says. 'The Clinton administration was all lies, all deceit and all bullshit.'

Several of us challenge him for substance; he comes up with none. I still have not worked out why in certain quarters Hillary provokes such visceral hatred.

Friday 30 August

Zach and I have breakfast at a client's restaurant before getting on the road. We go to Breckenridge, another well-known ski resort, stopping off first at a brewery and then to see a cheerful chef with a generous white moustache and a generous white chef's hat. There's plenty of joshing but the work is serious. The staff I meet in the kitchens are worried at what Trump is doing.

'He's a jackass,' says one. 'He's destroying our country, let alone our integrity.'

In another restaurant the staff, who are busy prepping, say that they have one colleague who comes in once a week who is a Trump supporter, but they don't discuss politics with him. Here, as elsewhere in the country, discourse seems to be dying, and families and workmates are divided.

We drive amid magnificent mountains, some topped with pockets of snow even though it's August. Zach points out a bison in a field, but I miss it. As we sweep round mountain bends we talk about a wide range of topics, from chlorinated chicken to Latter Day Saints. He says that if you do computer dating in Utah one of the questions will be 'LDS or non-LDS?'.

That evening I go to Zach's apartment and meet his girlfriend Sarah, a skier, climber and cyclist whose daytime job is as a biomechanical engineer working on anterior cruciate ligament tears. We go out for some more small plates, many also featuring peaches. Zach knows his local restaurants and they know him.

It has been a great day, travelling the way America is configured to be travelled – by car, free from the tyranny of bus schedules. The expensive unguents I was prescribed are doing their work. Tonight I have the best sleep of this leg so far.

Would it be dangerous to say that I am beginning to get the hang of this trip?

4. Avon: levels of fun

Saturday 31 August

When I rise, Zach and Sarah are talking about a news story: the Cherokee Nation is applying to send a delegate to Congress under an 1835 treaty. The position would be non-voting, as for Guam and Puerto Rico, but the delegate could speak, introduce legislation and sit on committees. An attorney for the Native American Rights Fund said that a Cherokee Nation delegate would be welcomed across tribes, but should not be seen by the public as a Native American Delegate at Large.

Also in the news today is the stabbing in prison of Sirhan Sirhan, who shot and killed Robert Kennedy in 1968. When I was in the US the following year, Sirhan had already been found guilty and sentenced to death, though this was later commuted to life imprisonment. I had long since forgotten about him, but this resurrects my memories.

Most of the people I talk to today – at least a generation younger – have no idea who he is; one asks if he was in a band. Yet had Robert Kennedy lived he might have beaten Nixon. How quickly we forget those who, like Sirhan Sirhan, may have single-handedly changed the course of history.

Zach and I go into Vail, some ten miles away, to visit a food festival called Gourmet on Gore, named after the river and the mountain range, not the former vice-president. It has been an annual event for about 14 years and many of the local restaurants have stalls out in the baking-hot streets. Zach knows many of the owners and tries their wares; he also knows the organiser and I talk to her briefly.

She tells me that last night they held a food trailer event for the first time. 'Food tastes are changing,' she says. 'People want clean food. They want to know where it comes from, they want it to be local.'

She repeats what I heard constantly yesterday: the rising cost of accommodation is making it harder to find staff. Zach agrees, saying he is often being asked to do some freelance cooking to fill a gap.

'What about immigration?' I ask.

'That door is getting shut in Washington, not here,' she says.

Zach runs into another colleague, a seafood company salesman. They start comparing notes on the economy.

'We are going to hit the earth hard,' says the friend.

'If tariffs are imposed on European cheeses they could go up 100 per cent,' says Zach. 'Hopefully it will get negotiated out. There's a big threat on the line. But this guy [he is referring to the President] makes threats that he never carries out.'

'It's trickle-down economics,' says the friend. 'The restaurant has to pay more, the customer has to pay more. When our costs go up, everything else will get hit. We are planning for a down-gear next year.'

When Zach and I talked about chlorinated chickens during our ride yesterday, he told me about a particularly tasty piece of meat he had recently eaten that had come from a nearby smallholding. He used to buy vegetables from them when he worked as a chef. I said I would be interested in visiting the place, and we do.

It is a small house and farm in a neighbourhood called the Horse Pasture. It is run by Chris and Tom, who own a picture-framing business in town, and Tom, an engineer, inspects ski lifts and gondolas. They also work the five acres I am standing on, packed with vegetables and herbs, some in a greenhouse that Tom built. They have a horse, two cows and some twenty chickens. The chickens are mainly black, the roosters are white: I make the obvious joke – more dominant white males. They laugh politely.

Chris has a degree in horticulture and it is she who lovingly tends the vegetable beds. Their animals are a good source of manure and – a key to the farm's viability – Chris and Tom have water rights. Water these days sells for more than land.

We move on to talking about how America has changed.

'We are all so polarised,' says Tom. 'You can't have a conversation any more. Remember back when all we needed was love?'

'I am amazed that all the hippies I grew up with are now voting for Trump,' says Chris. 'I think they're scared of immigrants, which is really sad. Here we see them as good labour.'

As we drive back I take a look at Morris. There has been a shooting in Texas.

At dinner I hear about Sarah's remarkable achievements, which make my sedentary expedition look like lacking ambition. In 2015 she was having what she calls a 'quarter life crisis' (relationship and career difficulties, she adds), so she decided to cycle to Alaska. She did just over 3,000 miles in 62 days. Two years later she did 1,700 miles, this time with her brother. For 2020 she is planning to cycle from Juneau to Tuktoyaktuk on the Arctic Ocean, a distance of about 1,000 miles.

'The first time I was running away from my problems,' she says. 'The second was because I hadn't finished the first one. Now I'm addicted. Twelve miles an hour is the right way to see the world. In a car you pass the little old towns so quickly you don't stop to see them – or the scenic views. On a bicycle you do that, and every town becomes more meaningful.'

'I was really afraid of camping alone and I found it really really challenging. But the human brain's capacity to forget suffering is amazing.' And she goes on to explain that those in the 'outdoor industries' talk of three categories of Fun.

- Type 1 – Genuinely enjoyable, and nobody cares when you try to brag about it at the bar later. Good food, scenic bike rides and beautiful day hikes, warm/sunny camping trips, powder skiing, drinking cocktails on a boat …

- Type 2 – Mostly miserable when you are doing it but fun in retrospect. After a few hours (or days – or weeks) you want to go through it again. Biking across the country, most forms of mountaineering, the grand adventures when something goes wrong but you manage to salvage everything and come out the other end victorious. Good stories at the bar and opportunities for 'character building'.

- Type 3 – The stuff you set out with the intention of being Type 2 fun, but it was so horrific it's not even fun in retrospect. These can involve extreme and unexpected weather, running out of food, getting lost or stranded, requiring search and rescue, losing fingers or toes to frostbite. Some of these types of fun make for really exciting books or IMAX films.

She tells me that the originator of the Fun Scale is climber and writer Kelly Cordes, and on his website he concludes: 'Maybe the whole goal, the path of the enlightened, is to turn Type 3 situations into Type 1 fun.'

Later that evening I have a little burst of Type 2 fun myself. I look on Morris to see if any of my Greyhound tickets have returned. They haven't. I get one back, though this disappears when I greedily try for a second. I decide to

dig out the paper backups I had thoughtfully printed and forget about the
e-tickets.

Sunday 1 September

It's now two calendar months since my adventure began. I wake up after a
second sound night's sleep to see a clear blue sky and mountains beyond.
Life is beginning to feel good.

Then I read the paper and discover that yesterday's shooting in Odessa,
Texas, has claimed 7 lives with another 22 injured. It started when a man
in his thirties, sacked from his job that morning, was pulled over for a
traffic violation. It brings the number of people killed in public shootings
this month to 51. A pundit on CNN says this time it will be different and
there will be changes in the law. We have heard that before.

'It's so routine now we can't react,' says Sarah. 'If we gave it the emotion
it deserved, we'd be exhausted by now.'

Zach takes me and his dog Dakota for a morning stroll in the stunning
landscape, then shows me his allotment and the house that Sarah has
bought, and finally drops me off at the bus station. I learn that although I
am booked on Greyhound the route is run by Bustang. I am advised to get
in the queue early because it's a busy service and seats are limited. My Pre-
Embarkation Anxiety Syndrome returns.

I make sure I am one of the first on, and as the bus fills up a young man
sits next to me. He is of Russian extraction, a chef in Vail who is going
to Fort Collins where he has some belongings in storage. He says that
he meditates for an hour a day and then has cold shock therapy – 15–30
minutes of sauna followed by 2–3 minutes plunging in a cold bath. He
urges me to try it. He also asks if I take weed and/or magic mushrooms,
both of which he commends as broadening the mind. He then clamps on
his earphones and ignores me, and then fist-bumps me when he gets off.

The bus station at Denver is more depressing than most, with benches
filled with what I have been calling 'homeless', though 'dispossessed' might
be more suitable. Some look pitiful – ill-dressed, emaciated, clutching
a bundle of belongings, and almost certainly using the bus station for
shelter, not travel. They sit on the benches or stand around in little groups.
The atmosphere is not helped by a large sign saying that passengers
needing the washrooms will need to show their tickets to get a key. I see
no security guard.

Colorado splendours: Zach and Dakota take a morning stroll near their home in Vail.

As I wait outside the terminal doors for my Uber, I feel more vulnerable than I have in other places. I move away from people down the street and I notice, incongruously, a large and opulent Ritz Carlton Hotel just opposite. I think of sheltering there, but my ride comes before I have time to cross the street.

By contrast, my Uber driver comes with an uplifting story. He is originally from Afghanistan, and is now an American citizen. Of his four children, all American citizens, one is a Boeing engineer, one is in HR, and the third a teacher; the fourth is still in school. 'America gave me freedom,' he says. 'The opportunity to raise my kids.'

That evening I go out with Zach's brother Ben and his girlfriend Shelby. They take me to an upmarket restaurant. They are a delightful couple, full of plans for themselves, their two dogs and two cats.

It is not until the end of the meal that we start talking about America, and in particular the latest shooting. 'There are lots of stories in the news about people who are overwhelmed by life and go out and get a gun and do harm,' says Ben. They both think something urgently needs to be done to stop powerful armaments being used by 'people who are sick'.

And then the conversation takes an unexpected turn.

'I have a gun myself,' says Ben. It is a pistol. He says it is strictly for personal protection and he has taken safety courses. He takes it to the range for target practice but otherwise keeps it in a safe. 'It seems to me that I am a level-headed person and will only use it if I have to, But better safe than sorry.'

I have now heard the other side of the story.

As we leave the restaurant there is a volley of bangs. Heads turn in alarm. Another shooting? It turns out to be a Labor Day firework display.

5. Denver to Omaha: the long, slow road with vomiting

Monday 2 September – Labor Day

The bus station at Denver seems calmer this morning and I feel safe enough to look – in vain – for the elusive toy Greyhound bus. The full-size Greyhounds are a bit thin on the ground also: my bus today is an Arrow: not so comfortable, and the WiFi isn't working.

Soon we are out of the city on a long straight road, presumably quite empty because it is a public holiday. I am on my way to Nebraska, the only state that's triply landlocked, which means I will be separated from a sea by three US states, or two US states and a Canadian province. I have roughly 12 hours of travel ahead of me and I hope I will enjoy Omaha more than I did last time: 'very dull city with nothing going on', I wrote in my diary.

Seated just across the aisle is a young man with dyed blond hair and a trilby perched on top of it, sitting with his girlfriend. I'd noticed him earlier darting around the waiting room when we were waiting to board. A couple of hours into the trip he lies down in the aisle and starts doing stretching exercises. He then lies across his girlfriend's knees while she massages his back.

As this is going on, our bus grinds to a halt. It edges forward agonisingly slowly while we can see ahead of us a long file of traffic. A rumour goes around the bus that there has been an accident – 56 miles ahead. I overhear the young man in the trilby tell his girlfriend that he has been sick. I try to ignore both pieces of news.

The information about a 56-mile tailback turns out to be fake: a couple of miles later we pass a section of road littered with crushed apples, and an overturned burnt-out trailer lying on the verge. It is the second roadside fire I have seen on my trip. A fellow passenger, a lorry driver, says that drivers forget to check the oil and they suddenly burst into flames. We pull into our next stop about an hour behind schedule.

When the break is over our driver, a man with a crisp shirt and crisper

Out of the mountains: one of the long straight roads between Denver and Omaha.

demeanour, realises that one of our passengers is missing – the man sitting behind me. He waits five minutes, honks his horn, drives over to the restaurant across the road, honks his horn again. No sign of the missing person. We leave. His bag of rubbish swings as a memorial alongside his seat but I can't see any other sign of left-behind luggage. Has he disappeared deliberately?

As we drive on, the young man in the trilby keeps going to the back of the bus to stretch or to be sick in the washroom. I doze, only to be woken by some strange sounds. The young man is now at the front of the bus, lying on the floor by the driver – and he is moaning. The man in the front passenger seat is an off-duty driver and he calls an ambulance.

We are approaching the next stop, and when we pull up an ambulance is waiting and a police car arrives shortly afterwards. The young man is taken to the ambulance and his girlfriend goes with him, but he is soon discharged. The police talk to the two of them but lose interest. Meanwhile our driver has offloaded their baggage from the hold.

As the emergency services drive off, the two rejected passengers try to get back into the coach but the driver leaves them standing on the roadside, luggage around them, looking lost, as in a sense they now are. That makes three passengers down so far, and we still have another four hours to go. My lorry driver friend expresses the hope that the young man didn't have anything infectious. I would be lying to say that the thought hadn't crossed my mind also, though I suspect the sickness has been self-inflicted.

The rest of the trip is gloriously uneventful. We get to Omaha a mere 45 minutes late, though at the cost of our scheduled 30-minute supper break. A fresh driver arrives for the last leg, perhaps because the previous one has run out of hours (or patience?).

I have not seen the last of police officers today. At my hotel a youngish African American is asking for a room. He has a credit card but no ID, so under company rules the receptionist cannot allow him in. He refuses to go. This standoff has been going on for half an hour, with an escalating series of requests to leave. As I sign in, the police arrive and he is ejected.

The receptionist, who has handled this well, is upset: 'I felt really sorry for him, but what could I do?'

Tuesday 3 September
I don't have to be at Omaha bus station until 11.50 am, so this morning I walk towards the old market. I pass an information centre and dive in to talk to the staff. 'This city has really transitioned from stock yards to modern businesses,' says one.

She and her colleague then sing Omaha's praises: consistently rated as one of the top ten places to raise a family: plenty of employers, riverside walk, plenty of historic buildings (I later learn my hotel is a recycled creamery), a symphony orchestra, top sporting events, above average number of millionaires, and 'plenty of philanthropy'. The billionaire Warren Buffett has a connection here, which must help.

I tell them of the homeless people I saw in Denver.

'Fifty years ago we had mental health facilities; we don't any more,' one says. 'Most of them have closed. They were moving towards community-based services – I agree with the concept but they don't meet everybody's needs.'

His colleague chips in: 'I had a student who went to a mental health facility. After 20 days he was released. They said he was cured, but his insurance had run out.'

I walk on to the old market. I have seen several developments of this type before on this trip, with restaurants, bars and small boutiques inhabiting a former marketplace. In the middle distance loom skyscrapers that weren't built when I was last around.

I see a policeman on a horse; sadly he is wearing a helmet and not a cowboy hat, and he has no star. He tells me the horse is called Maximus and is one of eight horses and six riders (plus a boss) in a unit which started in 1857 – and was revived in 1989.

'It's mostly PR,' he tells me. 'The police don't get a good name, so if we are able to connect to the public through a horse, then it's a good tool.'

The hotel has a shuttle bus, and the driver is happy to take me to the bus station, though he says it is not a destination he is often asked to go to. He detours to show me the river front, the 'wide Missouri', disappointingly not wide at this point – and a grand convention centre sponsored by a local health care organisation.

My bus today is operated by Burlington Trailways. As we wait for the driver I talk to 77-year-old Twyla from North Dakota, who is dressed in what looks like a pinafore. She is resting her feet on what I call a vanity case, and what her father called a train case. She is using her phone, which is even older than the one I used until only a few months ago, and she has to tap out the letters – once for A, two for B, three for C, and so on.

'I have had it for a long time. Verizon has told me that after January it won't be serviced, so I might want to start thinking about what to do. But I won't yet. I have more important things to do.' I like her attitude.

On the bus I am seated next to a lady who tells me she is a native American. Her tribal name is Beggehtayah, which she says means the first grand-daughter from 12 sons. Her American name is Dana-Lee. She was born on a reservation in Macy/Winnebago, Nebraska.

Her tribe is the Omaha (that should be Umaha, she says) and she has been a nurse, Headstart teacher and cook – and is now a college student studying early childhood. She has children: one a police officer in Winnebago, one a homemaker and one in prison (for domestic issues, she says, and I do not press her on an open bus).

She has three grandchildren: 'They know their Indian names. I teach them the traditions. I was raised in the country on a farm. We hunted and fished. All our food was wild game. Then we moved to white man's stores. I went to a boarding school in Utah for a year, but didn't care for it. They tried to change me; I never went back.'

She says life is good for her. Her husband inherited 2,000 acres of tribal land from his mother, and she has now inherited it from him. She rents it out to farmers: last year she received in rent $8,000 in October and $10,000 last March.

Politics? 'I'm not very much involved.'

Changes over 50 years? 'Too much war.'

Race? 'There is prejudice here, as there is everywhere else. But we stay in our own way. We're all right.'

We stop at Des Moines. I look in vain for a statue to commemorate the author Bill Bryson who memorably starts one of his books: 'I come from Des Moines. Somebody had to.' (*The Lost Continent: travels in small-town America*, Bill Bryson, 1989).

The place doesn't look too bad to me: we pass an imposing building with a golden roof that I assume is the state capitol. I look around the bus station for a copy of the *Des Moines Register*, the paper that employed Bryson's father as a sports writer. I couldn't find one, but then this time around I rarely find newspapers on sale at bus stations – and certainly none left on buses for others to read, as there were in 1969.

The autocorrect function on my computer makes its own contribution to my trip, and one that Bryson would have appreciated. When I try to capitalise 'headstart', it flashes up a message asking whether I want to substitute 'head's tart' instead.

6. Grinnell, Iowa: an offer refused

It is early afternoon and we are passing cattle, corn and wind farms. The wind farms must be calling up reinforcements: on the highway we now pass a long procession of elongated lorries each carrying a huge wind farm component, such as a single blade. A swarm of little cars, lights twinkling, buzz in and out of lanes, shepherding them along with as little disruption to other road users as humanly possible. Who says coal is king? Other than those who own coalfields.

I am heading for Grinnell, a small agricultural town in Iowa with a liberal arts college and some 9,000 residents, one of whom is my wife's cousin's wife's sister, Susan.

Earlier in the year I had become aware of the painful destruction of traditional rural Midwestern farming communities – a major development since I was last here. I went to a photographic lecture by Tony and Eva Worobiek, who showed beautiful but disturbing images of rotting wooden homes, abandoned churches and tractors, even fading photographs from a long-disbanded family.

Then I read a book by Pulitzer prize-winning journalist Art Cullen that described the upheavals in his home town of Storm Lake, Iowa, as small farmers were replaced by agribusiness and migrant labour: 'an unsentimental ode to America's heartland' says the blurb. 'A story of invention and resilience, environmental and economic struggle, and surprising diversity of hope.' (Art Cullen, *Storm Lake*, Penguin Random House, 2018)

Grinnell is the same kind of town – and Susan used to be married to a local farmer. I want to find out more.

As our bus leaves the highway and takes the road into Grinnell, we pass a trio of mid-market hotels, an insurance office, a John Deere tractor franchise and a large corn store. As we move into a residential area our driver inexplicably stops the bus and bounds off towards a group of houses for ten minutes; we have no idea why. When he comes back he drives a short distance before turning into the middle of the well-tended grounds of Grinnell College, where Susan is waiting to greet me.

Later that evening we talk about her work: she is an assistant director of a public library in a nearby town. 'Public libraries are social places,' she says. 'Some of the older patrons come in for the whole day: they just want to be in a place with other people. But the kids don't hang out at the library, because they are connected on their social networks.'

A big concern is public safety. She digs into her bag and shows me a curly piece of what looks like plastic, with a point on the end. It is a Kubaton and she bought it recently after attending a security course for library staff. She describes it as a 'non-lethal stabbing weapon'.

She reluctantly tells me about the course. It was run by a senior law enforcement officer, and the take-home acronym was ALICE – Alert, Lockdown, Inform, Counter, Evacuate. One of the first exercises he set was for participants to find a hiding place. He went out of the room and Susan hid under her desk. When he came back, she was first in view. He came to within five feet of her – and fired his gun (presumably a blank).

'It was a huge shock. I couldn't concentrate on the rest of the course. I was upset for days. The overall message was 'Don't be a hero. Don't worry about the people around you, just run.' But we are librarians. What if we are in the library with a group of small children? Are we just going to leave them there?

'This was so different from other training we have had. In tornado training, for example, we are the last to leave the building. But with ALICE we are just supposed to get out.'

Wednesday 4 September

Not long after breakfast the phone rings. Susan thinks it's a political call and I ask if I can answer. She hands me the phone. An impersonal voice tells me he is calling on behalf of the Republican National Committee and President Trump. He asks for Susan and I say she is not available.

He asks if I am in favour of what President Trump is doing, I say not. He says, 'Thank you and goodbye.'

'Before you go,' I say, 'I have a question.'

'Yes,' he says.

'I am visiting from England and writing a book about how America has changed in the past 50 years. Could you tell me why anyone should vote for President Trump?'

'I don't have a scripted response to that,' he says. 'Please ring the

Barney on his farm in Grinnell, Iowa: 'It's pretty darn hard right now'.

Republican National Committee Headquarters.' He reels off a phone number.

As I hang up, I wonder whether I have been speaking to a person or a robot. Then I start to wonder whether these days, when it comes to American politics, it's a meaningful distinction.

That evening Susan takes me to see Barney, her former husband and the latest in a line of farmers who have been on the land here since the 1860s. We drive down a track, leaving a trail of dust, and arrive at a cluster of buildings and farm machinery, some of them derelict. Barney arrives in a battered pickup, with Duchess his dog. He is a small, bearded man in weathered jeans and the inevitable cap. She is a small German shepherd, particularly amenable if you are willing to throw pieces of wood for her entertainment.

Barney is in partnership with his wife Suzanne and together they tend 500 acres. Whereas most Iowan farmers grow corn and soya beans, they grow only organic soya beans plus whatever they need to feed their 3 sows, 45 ewes, 75 cows – and 75 broiler chickens that live in a moveable cage so that they constantly feed on fresh grass. In the area, he says, they are considered 'farming freaks'.

'It's pretty darn hard right now,' he says. 'If the government was not helping corn and soya bean farmers they would be in terrible trouble. Prices are not covering the cost of production.' Of the government subsidy he says: 'A lot of the farmers, who are mostly Republican, are against that, but if they weren't getting cheques from the government things just wouldn't happen for them …'

He worries about a return to the 1980s, when interest rates rocketed. Many farmers couldn't make a living and some committed suicide. 'Now suicide rates are going up again among farmers. I worry that things are going to get a lot worse. It seems to me that already we are having more farm evictions listed in the paper.'

'Are you positive or negative about the future?' I ask. There is a pause.

'Ahhhmmm … That depends on the day, I guess. The people we interact with are Practical Farmers. [He is referring to Practical Farmers of Iowa, whose mission is to 'equip farmers to build resilient farms and communities'.] When I see what they are doing I am positive. But when I look at the middle-of-the-road agriculture it's pretty negative. Things are changing, but not nearly fast enough.'

As dusk closes in, his wife/business partner Suzanne comes up with their son Gabriel and two pizzas. I ask if he would like any of his three boys to take over the farm, as he has done.

'I would be excited if any one of them wanted to. That's one reason why I am transitioning to organic – to make it more viable.'

We take the food down to the bottom of a nearby field, watching the cattle chew steadily and the sun go down and the mist rise. It's very peaceful.

On the way home we stop at Walmart. I think the shop is huge but Susan says there are plenty bigger. I have heard there are guns for sale on the shelves and I find them easily – a couple of shelves in the outdoor pursuit section, not far from the gym equipment. I discreetly take a couple of pictures on Morris, and leave.

We go back to Susan's and I take Morris out again and start grazing. After a few minutes an ad comes up: it's for a website called Palmettostate. armory.com, and they are offering me AK-47s on mail order. They're on special offer, with the cheapest I see for $629.99 (but without a cleaning rod, which may matter). For another $20 I could have a touch of wood panelling on the gun as well. Dozens more pages offer dozens more ways of killing.

'Why is it on my mobile?' I ask Susan.

'Where have you just been?' she replies.

'Oh shit,' I say. Susan the librarian says this has been a 'fuck-me moment'.

I sleep a little uneasily that night. Someone is tracking me and trying to sell me weapons. I premiere a new anxiety dream in which I am in a driverless car, only nobody has a clue how to control it – or where we're going.

7. Chicago: the Daley legacies

Thursday 5 September

Barney the farmer taught me a new acronym last night: CAFO – Confined Animal Feeding Operation. 'In Iowa Falls there is a spot where you can see 10-15 CAFOs. If you go east of Grinnell you'll drive past the chicken factory – huge buildings with egg-processing operations. There are probably millions of them. They smell as you pass by.'

Today Susan is driving me into the countryside so I can see at first hand what he was talking about. The landscape is idyllic: picture-book red-roofed farms, fields of corn, trees and livestock, silos and barns, here and there a little pool. And then we pass our first large industrial building, square and white with a scattering of windows. There are no signs outside the facility, so we can't identify what it is or who owns it. But we don't have to open the car windows to smell it.

The two faces of the countryside around Grinnell.

We go back to town then take another road out, this time to the west, past some handsome two-storey houses, most likely the homes of college professors. A few miles out, another set of white buildings comes into view: bigger, still no signs, same smell. I get out of the car to take a few pictures and then jump back in quickly: after last night I worry about who might be taking pictures of me.

There are plenty of fields and fresh air around, so do these installations matter? Barney thinks it does. Water quality is being affected by the runoff from industrial quantities of manure as well as by the increasing use of nitrogen fertiliser. In his lifetime, he says, the hilltops have become lighter in colour: the soil is disappearing, and what's left is being contaminated by chemicals and overgrazing.

Later that afternoon Susan takes me to the college campus to wait for the bus that the Greyhound schedules do not recognise. When it turns up, it is (as I expected) the continuation of the Burlington Trailways route I'd come in on two days before. I ask the driver why it's not listed on the Greyhound site; he has no idea.

The bus is half-empty, the six-and-a-half-hour trip to Chicago uneventful, and I arrive in Chicago just after 10 pm.

The bar is set low for my visit: 'Chicago and I don't really hit it off,' I had written in my letter home in 1969. 'It's not too clean and not too safe and the tall skyscrapers and elevated tramways [sic] make even the city centre look dark and dismal.' One of my fellow British students said it was a bit like Birmingham.

I had arrived just after dawn: 'Awaken to find myself passing railway yards under a dismal grey sky – this must be Chicago.' I had hoped to link up with a friend from home but though I made some enquiries I was unable to do so. (This was clearly an occasion when mobile phones would have come in handy.) Instead I wandered alone along the windy Lake Michigan shore, went to a Franciscan church (impressed by the uniformed ushers), visited two art galleries, sat through a double bill of British whodunits in a small cinema, and ate three portions of fish and chips in an all-you-can-eat restaurant.

I also booked myself for one night into the Hotel Astor for $5. Here I shared the bathroom with a cockroach and my bedroom with fleas. 'Noisy and bad value, $7' warned the BUNAC guide. I don't know why I'd ignored the advice; perhaps it was the $2 discount.

The one bright spot was when an American student/waitress took pity on me as I was eating my dinner at the counter, and after her shift had ended she took me on a guided tour of her city. She showed me the marina ('slight whiff of urban renewal,' I wrote) and the old town ('trendy in a commercial way'). We also looked into Grant Park, scene of the notorious protests at the Democratic Convention the previous year (of which more later).

Now, 50 years later, I have a full day to revise my opinion.

Friday 6 September
This time I have booked in at the Dewitt Rooms and Suites, a 1921 building with a spacious Art Nouveau lobby, situated one block and a busy highway away from the North Shore. The reception is more of a cubby hole than a desk, with just one bored person on duty. The lift is eccentrically old, and clunks and wheezes as it rises and falls. If it does get into difficulty I will find out if the 1930s emergency phone is more than decorative.

1969 diary: 'Awaken to find myself passing railway yards under a dismal grey sky – this must be Chicago.'

My large room has sharp corners on the bed to crack my shins, a glass-topped coffee table in the middle of the living area to knock my knees, a hidden step into the bathroom to trip me up, and a slithering toilet mat poised to land me flat on my back. I tread carefully.

Having avoided damaging myself overnight, I set forth in the morning along Michigan Avenue towards the centre of Chicago. I pass a store with denim-wearing dummies in the window and think how good they look. Then I notice the sign in the window: this is a branch of GAP and they too are celebrating a golden jubilee – 50 years since their first store was opened in San Francisco. The window display features clothes from that era, though they still look contemporary to me.

I have a 9 am appointment with Howard Bauchner, editor of the *Journal of the American Medical Association* (*JAMA*). I know him from my earlier professional life when I ran courses for medical journal editors, and I hope he will give me some balanced opinions on some of the matters that have been troubling me.

He works from a glass-fronted office way up in the sky in what used to be the IBM Building. It is the last American building designed by Mies van der Rohe and is on the National Register of Historic Places. Its website boasts of 'timeless design and trophy quality attributes'.

We look out over an elegant – and taller – building just next door: the Trump International Hotel and Spa. It's a cue for me to ask Howard what he thinks of the eponymous owner.

'He occupies so much intellectual and scientific space,' he says. 'In our house we've just had a Trump-free weekend. It's been interesting to see your Parliament where you have people who actually have scruples. It seems in the USA that some politicians don't have a moral compass.'

I go on to tell him about the attempt to sell me AK-47s via my mobile. He is not surprised: 'They know all about you. They're following you around. Google could probably write my Wikipedia entry better than I could.'

I tell him I have been reading and hearing how opioids have caused major problems in the United States. 'It was a conspiracy of everyone,' he says. 'The drug companies behaved abysmally, but physicians wrote out the prescriptions. It was easy to do, and it made patients happy. It's a complicated issue and there are many lessons to be learned.

'The entire focus has been on the drug companies, but we need to think long and hard about everything that has contributed to this epidemic. There has been a huge personal cost, and it will take a decade to unravel it.'

Next on my agenda: US health care. I tell him of my encounter with the doctor in Colorado who was terrified of 'socialist' medicine.

'A handful of people,' he says, 'want a Canadian or British single payment system, but that's a minority. Others want to keep insurance, but believe they can extend it … I would expect the Democratic platform will say health care is a right not a privilege, and will talk about different approaches to get coverage for 90–95 per cent. Currently roughly 85 per cent are covered, and 15 per cent not.'

He makes the point – one that often gets lost in the health debates – that the USA has made great advances in health care. 'Our level of innovation for drugs and devices is still extraordinary.'

He takes me round the building to look at the views, introduces me to the publisher, and offers me the choice of a branded cap or mug. I take the cap.

I resist the temptation to wear the cap to help me blend in while I make an unscheduled diversion into the lobby of the Trump Hotel. I expect security but there is none. The inside has a pleasant feel to it, with good views over the river it borders. The lobby is quite busy, mainly with older white Americans, but also quite a few foreigners. I wander around the ground floor expecting to be challenged, but nobody gives me a second glance.

It's a beautiful building, soaring 98 storeys above the Chicago River in three diminishing steps, each step lining up with the top of a nearby building. The hotel website says it is the fourth-tallest building in the United States, with 339 guest rooms and 486 luxury condominiums.

It has been controversial. Some lengthy litigation over loan repayment between Trump and the Deutsche Bank was settled out of court. There were protests when the original award-winning planting was replaced with plants that took less watering. And when the huge TRUMP sign went up, the architect distanced himself from the project and the mayor's spokesperson said it was now 'an architecturally tasteful building scarred by an architecturally tasteless sign'.

Half the people I meet think Trump is a buffoon or worse, yet the building he has created is a significant achievement.

Next stop is the Chicago History Museum and, seasoned traveller that I now am, I go to the cafeteria for lunch. As I queue, I notice an elegant woman of about my age in a long black coat with a stylish and colourful cloth brooch. I approach her with my usual schtick: I am writing a book about America and can I talk to her? I am hoping for a Trump supporter.

She is happy to talk and moves across to my table. She has strong connections with the museum and I start with an easy question: What's changed in Chicago over the past half-century? She answers that there are more people in the city and that 'culture' has expanded. She recommends that I visit Millennium Park.

We get on to politics and I have misread her. 'I think it will take years to undo Trump's damage,' she says. 'It's so embarrassing. It's the worst thing that has happened to this country. Please don't think badly of us.'

We talk about politics in the USA and the UK, about lies and divisions. Suddenly the woman at the next table leans over.

'I couldn't help hearing your conversation,' she says, looking at my new friend. 'I am 87. I didn't have the same privileges as you.' She then reels off a list of what I presume are prestigious schools and colleges in Chicago that she clearly was unable to attend. She concludes: 'We were divided then also. Only no-one talked about it.'

It's a fair point and my new friend is gracious about the criticism. I haven't the heart (or is it courage?) to ask the standard 'Can you tell me about yourself' question, but she hands me a card and afterwards I look her up on Google. I find a picture of her from the *Classic Chicago Magazine*, taken just under a year ago at a gala dinner to celebrate the 70-year anniversary of the Guild of the Chicago History Museum. She is standing at a table being applauded. She is clearly a museum insider.

Lunch over, I look for exhibits on Chicago's history over the past half-century, and find a list of key events. The Union Stock Yard, where at one time more meat was packed than anywhere else in the world, closed in 1971. The city's first African American mayor, Harold Washington, was elected in 1983, the same year as the Federal Communications Commission approved the first mobile phone, produced by Motorola. In 1995 a five-day heatwave led to 739 deaths, mostly elderly poor. The Democratic Convention returned in 1996, and 2004 saw the opening of Millennium Park.

I am particularly interested in two events that took place in 1968, a year before my visit. The first, in April, was the riots sparked by the assassination of Martin Luther King and they lasted three days. By the end 11 citizens were dead, 48 wounded by police gunfire, 90 policemen injured and 2,150 people arrested. Damage to buildings was estimated at $10 million.

Four months later the Democratic Party assembled for their party's convention, procured for the city by the powerful mayor, Richard J Daley. This was at the height of the Vietnam War, and students gathered to protest. The result was mayhem. According to the narrative in the museum: 'As the Democrats clashed inside the convention, police battled with demonstrators, the press and innocent bystanders in front of television cameras while the whole world was watching.'

The museum records a spirited defence by Daley: no-one was killed; it was all the fault of the television. 'The American public was defrauded by the coverage.' The fake news defence, it seems, is long-running and bipartisan.

I decide to get out into the fresh air and walk by the lake, as I did before. This time I have a goal: Millennium Park, about two miles away. An

A walk by the lake in Chicago: 'an overcast and windy September day'.

underpass and a bridge take me over several lanes of steaming traffic and then I am on the shore. A sign tells me that 60 million people a year visit the 18 miles of shorefront track that provide 'easy access to the rich fabric that is Chicago'. The 5.5 mile section I am about to walk on has been renovated with support from Coca-Cola, which seems an interesting piece of product placement.

It is an overcast and windy September day. Red flags are fluttering in case anyone is foolish enough to want to go into the water, and the lifeguard's high chair is tipped over on its side, perhaps redundant until next spring. A shorefront restaurant looks as if it is packing up for the season.

The people of Chicago aren't daunted, though. As I get nearer to the centre of the city, more and more people are on the trackways: young men jogging and bravely stripped to the waist; tourists speaking in strange tongues; mothers and fathers pushing prams; elderly men pushing themselves. Cyclists of assorted shapes and sizes push into the wind, for the most part keeping in their designated lane.

Half-way along I stop to admire the view, which is spectacular: a beach piled with golden sand (which I assume is imported) in the foreground with a flurry of skyscrapers reaching up towards the clouds. I carry on past the Columbia Yacht Club, established 1892. I must have walked past it in 1969, when its clubhouse was a 'superannuated excursion steamer'; now it's a superannuated Canadian Railways icebreaker.

The going gets complicated, with paths intertwined with roads and interrupted by building projects. I have to ask fellow pedestrians where to go, but make it through to Millennium Park, where I find myself face to face with what looks like a giant balloon, shiny and reflecting. It is a sculpture by Anish Kapoor, called Cloud Gate by him and The Bean by everyone else, and made up of 168 highly polished stainless-steel plates welded together with no visible seams. It was planned to cost $6 million but the actual cost soared to $23 million. I take a picture of the art work reflecting the world around it, including my distorted self.

The oom-pah-pah of a brass ensemble draws me to the next landmark – the Jay Pritzker Pavilion, a huge, stainless-steel band pavilion. This has been designed by Frank Gehry and named after a major sponsor, a member of the family that founded Hyatt Hotels. It has 4,000 fixed seats and room for 7,000 more on the lawn. A brass ensemble is warming up the gathering audience, most wearing several layers of clothes, for tonight's free concert. It will be given by the Lyric Opera of Chicago, conductor Andrew Davis, formerly of the BBC Symphony Orchestra and Last Night of the Proms.

The park is another Mayor Daley legacy, but this time it is from his son, Richard J, who was mayor from 1989 until 2011. This hugely ambitious project had a mixed reception. On the one hand the project massively overran its $150 million budget: the final bill was reckoned to be $475 million. It also attracted accusations of over-commercialisation (hence the Boeing Galleries, McDonald's Cycle Centre and BP Pedestrian Bridge) and cronyism.

On the other hand, the city now has an extraordinary space, filled with major art pieces and a popular tourist attraction, particularly in winter when the ice rink is installed. It has covered the mess of car parks and railway lines – perhaps the very ones that depressed me so in 1969.

I am too tired to walk the mile back to my hotel, so call an Uber. The driver is not pleased with me because I'm not standing on the exact spot the computer has designated. I have had this problem before, but I tell him it's not easy to stand on the designated spot if you can't see any street numbers.

He mellows. He is an African American who works in an occupational health/welfare position in the NBC building. He talks about a different Chicago from the one I have been visiting, in which low-income housing has been torn down and/or converted into high-income homes. 'The people who lived there are now spread out all over the city. That's why there's so much crime.'

Later that evening I walk to a Cheesecake Factory restaurant, one of a large and apparently successful chain. My appetite has not been good on this trip, but today I decide I should have a proper meal, and order chicken breast escalope, breaded, with mash and asparagus spears and lemon sauce. I'm expecting something modest – a slice of chicken, a scoop of potato, four or five asparagus spears, a little sauce. I've forgotten I'm in America, or that last time in Chicago I guzzled three portions of fish and chips.

What appears (after a bowl filled with sizeable chunks of bread has been dropped onto my table) is not one but three chicken breasts on a plate the size of our best serving dish at home. Around it are eight pieces of asparagus and a mound of potato (I am later told it is 10 ounces) with indeterminate bits in it, all swimming in a glutinous lemony sauce. My appetite deserts me, though I manage to eat all the asparagus and part of one of the escalopes.

I count the dishes on the menu. There are 17 small plates and snacks, 28 appetisers, 7 pizzas, 15 superfoods, 12 glamburgers, 61 specialties, 9 sides, 8 salads, 10 sandwiches. If that's not enough there are 33 cheesecakes and 9 speciality desserts. Oh, and there's a special menu for the calorie-conscious, but I have lost the will to count those as well.

I am offered dessert and I ask for one scoop of ice cream. It is later described on the bill as a child's portion.

My waiter, who comes from Spain, is sympathetic when I say there was too much food. He calls his supervisor, who looks as though he could cope easily with three escalopes. He says that customers often complain they are not given enough food.

I appear to be the smallest adult in the room.

8. Detroit: Barbara and a beach

Saturday 7 September

'All politicians are arseholes,' says today's Uber driver as he takes me to the Chicago bus station. Then his rant takes an unexpected turn. He points to the Trump Hotel: 'But this guy says what he thinks. He won't hide anything. We can believe him.'

'I'm not saying he's a good guy,' he adds. 'But he does have lots of money.'

I am on my way to Detroit, Michigan. So is Barbara. As I board my bus, she is high in the sky, flying out from London. We will spend 12 of the next 18 days together, and I get that end-of-term feeling. I have enjoyed my solo adventures, but I am hoping that having someone to share them with will increase the frequency of my Type 1 fun.

I have enjoyed Chicago this time. I was prepared for the biting wind and the towering skyscrapers. I had some informative encounters, rekindled some memories and took a brisk shorefront walk. I avoided falling over my hotel furniture and so far have no reason to believe I was sharing with bed bugs. And now the sun is shining.

It's a straightforward run to Kalamazoo, a town of about 75,000, known for goods as diverse as windmills, taxicabs, mandolins, paper, peppermint oil and celery. The name comes from an Indian American word and is popular with lyricists (sample title: 'I've Got a Gal in Kalamazoo'). It has a historic train station, now also a bus station, which is listed on the Great American Stations website.

I go inside and step back a century. Unlike the utilitarian, slightly dingy bus stations I have been frequenting, this one has wooden panelling, ornate metalwork over and around the counters, Art Nouveau signage and Art Deco benches. It is not a well-kept hangover from the past, however, but the result of a prize-winning $13 million restoration project completed in 2006.

My pleasure is short-lived. The lavatories are as neglected as the front office is well tended. Then, as we are sitting back in the bus just before leaving, a policeman in baseball cap and shorts walks up and down the aisle looking closely at each of us. He has a gun of course. There is no explanation and no action taken. I find it disconcerting.

There is little to see out of the bus windows today, which is fine because I'm trying to get my journal up-to-date before my reunion with Barbara. Writing on a small keyboard on a moving bus is hard, and particularly so today. It may be that my excitement has rubbed off on Geoffrey, but whatever the reason my cursor keeps jumping back a paragraph or two when I'm not looking, and the text inexplicably decides to re-form itself with a series of hanging indents.

Suddenly a header appears on all my pages: I have been writing about last night's chicken dinner and the word selected for the header is 'breast'. I delete it quickly, grateful that there is no-one in the next seat snatching covert glances at my writings. Or a policeman in shorts making a spot check.

Then I notice that all the margins and page breaks have disappeared. I look for the WTF key.

Our last but one stop is Ann Arbor, which I remember fondly from 1969. At that time, bored with Detroit, I left my luggage in a locker and took the mid-morning bus to what my BUNAC guide told me was the home of the University of Michigan. Earlier on in my trip I had met someone studying there, and so I left a message in his pigeonhole before talking my way into a visit around the student newspaper offices and being impressed: 'A daily!' I wrote in my diary. 'On UPI [the news agency tapes]!!! Offices almost as large as Floor 3 of the Star-News. Jealousy.' The *Michigan Daily* still earns my respect, publishing daily in term time since 1890. Since the *Ann Arbor News* closed ten years ago, it is the only daily printed newspaper in the area.

I take a good look at the bus stop and wonder whether it's in the same place as where my friend caught up with me in 1969 as I was waiting for the bus back to Detroit. He persuaded me to spend the night, which I did on a foam rubber bed in his fraternity house. I wrote in my diary that the food was good but insufficient, and that everyone sang a 'school song'. Afterwards we went for pizza.

With this tenuous link to the university I am pleased when, 50 years later, a young student takes the seat next to mine for the last leg of the day. We start chatting.

'How do you see the future of this country?' I ask.

'I think we're going to be the best. We might bounce back. We have had bad presidents before, but so far nothing momentous has changed. Most people think Trump is a joke at this point, and that he's going to lose. But we need someone not just to beat Trump but to build up hope again.'

He then tells me he is studying neuroscience and politics – and wants to go into politics.

'How do we build up that hope you're talking about?' I ask.

'The thing to change is the way this country measures how we're doing. Now we base everything on GDP. It's economically accurate, but we need to find a way of looking at how the average American is doing. If the richest people get another $1 billion it shows up on GDP – but everyone else is still screwed.

'If we get people involved in democracy they will realise that they can benefit. We need to redefine the terms of conversation, then things will start to change.'

He drifts off into his own electronic world and we don't speak again. When we part at Detroit he doesn't make eye contact or say goodbye. It seems curious behaviour from an aspiring politician.

In 1969, Detroit was the thriving centre of the car industry. My BUNAC guide recommended tours of the Cadillac, Chrysler or Ford assembly lines. It said that the city 'could not make any claim to scenic or civic beauty', adding that the skyscrapers suggested 'nothing but the robust affluence of industrial America'.

The city has, however, turned out to be not as robust as we then thought. Over the last half-century it has gone in and out of bankruptcy and seen one of its mayors sentenced to 28 years in prison for fraud. The big car companies still have their headquarters in or near the city, but all but two of the assembly lines have closed. The population has fallen from 1.85 million in 1950 to just over 700,000 in 2015.

'Vast swathes of the city lie abandoned in scenes more reminiscent of Chernobyl than the Midwest,' says my 2019 *Lonely Planet* guide. The remains have become a tourist destination in what is now called 'ruin tourism' (or 'ruins porn'). Yet not all is urban wasteland, says the guide: more recently a new city has been emerging 'from artists reclaiming abandoned factories and organic farming on empty lots, to the billion-dollar rejuvenation of downtown.'

My first impressions are favourable enough, as I am driven from the bus station to the downtown chain hotel I have booked. For the first time

Detroit on a Saturday evening: a trip to the city-centre 'beach'.

in this trip I go into a bedroom that is already populated, and it's a good experience: Barbara is there and has brought me supplies, such as smart trousers for an upcoming family gathering and some extra notebooks.

We go out on the town to celebrate our reunion. Directly opposite our hotel is a handsome six-storey office block, simple, well-proportioned and clean. But it is empty: the upper floor windows have been stripped of glass and the ground floor windows – presumably once shop fronts parading their wares to affluent car-workers – are covered with pictures of faces, in colour and black and white alternately. On the pavement outside is a small tree; I am pleased to see it looks healthy.

Following advice from the front desk, we head down a few blocks to Campus Martius Park where a sign welcomes us to The Beach. Water does not lap onto the pavement, but there is a thick covering of golden sand, blue chairs and yellow awnings, a busy restaurant, a fair crowd and a small band. On the street outside, a bar on wheels glides past with about a dozen people drinking, carousing – and pedalling. None of these activities seem particularly well co-ordinated, and one of the men is wearing a grass skirt.

We are drawn to a 40-storey neo-Gothic skyscraper with Cadillac written along it, though whether it is named for the founder of the city or the motor manufacturer I am not sure. Two young men are on security duty. The building is now largely empty, one tells me, though people are trying to find more tenants, perhaps a new owner. I tell him that I was here 50 years ago and he can't believe it. He summons his mate.

'Fifty years ago,' he says, pointing at me. 'He was here fifty years ago. Fifty years!' I feel a bit of a relic.

I feel even more of a relic back in the hotel, which is seething with younger people. I am told that the Jonas Brothers are in town, giving a concert. I haven't the slightest idea who they are, but clearly things are happening in Detroit these days.

Sunday 8 September

As we eat our breakfast, groups of runners – and some walkers – go past our window. There is clearly a race on of some kind, yet another sign that Detroit is trying hard to be an active city, or at least a city of activities. We have an hour to learn more.

I want to see some of the ruins, particularly Michigan Central Station which has been empty since 1988, or perhaps one of the neighbourhoods that are underpopulated and in bad shape. We enlist the help of a doorman to see if he can find a driver to give us an hour's tour. He comes back with a price of $150 for two hours minimum: I assume they aren't keen to take us. We next consider a ride on the People Mover, Detroit's light railway, but apparently on Sundays it doesn't start moving people until lunchtime, which would be too late for us.

So we start walking back past the beach, which is not empty but quieter, and then down to Hart Plaza, on the waterfront and opened in 1975. Something is going on here. We see a cluster of stalls, dozens of American flags, and several hundred people, some in military uniforms. Someone is winding up a speech and the crowd applauds and breaks into 'The Star-Spangled Banner', hand on hearts. We are not sure what it is all about: some but not all of those present are in uniform, most are in disciplined columns, some carry flags and all carry backpacks. They start filing out of the square and march along the riverbank.

We ask a bystander, well dressed in suit and tie. We have happened upon the third annual Patriot Ruck, organised by the Wins for Warriors Foundation. The foundation was founded in 2016 by baseball pitcher Justin Verlander and the purpose of the ruck is to commemorate the first responders to 9/11. Participants walk a three- or six-mile route with a rucksack (weight not specified) on their backs.

Our informant is a former veteran, teacher and now social worker supporting veterans: 'We are able to offer a lot more to support veterans – and their families.' He says their work is funded by the state, and I ask how that fits in with the common cry I hear of 'no socialism'?

'I'm a former history teacher and know all about the -isms. People just don't understand. But we need to work from the inside out.'

The man on the Red Cross stand is wearing a Vietnam Veteran pin. Now aged 70, he was in a family of ten children, four of whom went into the military. He was one of them. But because two brothers were already in Vietnam he was assigned to be a cook in a military hospital in America. 'When I came out I was branded a baby killer because of the war. I am glad that this country has finally stood up for what we have done.'

I ask how Detroit has changed. 'All my family were raised to be colour-blind. But I think a lot of people have been influenced by the media. We need to be more homogeneous. We need to get along and stop taking sides. A lot of people are tired of playing the race game.'

We go to the bus station for the four-hour journey to Cleveland. With Barbara about to take her second bus trip I am relieved that the station is much nicer than the one in Newark we travelled from in July. It is Art Deco on the outside and bright and spacious on the inside. But I see no model Greyhound buses on sale.

The bus driver starts with a prayer to Jesus (though is distinctly un-Christian later on when he refuses to let anyone off his bus for the scheduled ten-minute break). The journey is better than some I have taken on this trip: no packet scrunchers, no twitchers, no monologists and no young men with trilby hats stretching and vomiting in the aisle. Barbara is having it lucky – or bringing me luck.

9. Cleveland: a river on fire and a landmark shooting

I call an Uber to take us to our Airbnb in Cleveland Heights. The quote seems expensive: $35 for a 10-15 minute drive. When the car arrives I ask the driver what's going on.

'The football game has just finished,' he says. 'So they've raised the prices.'

As he drives us past the Cleveland Clinic, one of the top-rated hospitals in the US, we start talking about health care. 'To say we are this great country – but at the same time people are dying because they can't get treatment – is crazy,' says the driver.

Our Airbnb is part of a 1902 coach house and we breach the keypad defences without fuss. It is a comfortable conversion, the nicest of my trip so far. It even has two separate sets of patio table and chairs in different parts of the garden for our personal use. Once settled in, we stroll down the street to have dinner together at a local restaurant. I am no longer a lonesome traveller.

Monday 9 September

We meet our friend Darice for breakfast at a café over the road. She is the niece of my 1969 co-sponsor Maria, and an artist with a growing reputation. Afterwards she drives us to Kent State University, where she is an associate professor.

To my generation the university is linked with the horrific shooting of 49 years ago. It took place just a few months after my US trip, as I was revising for my final exams. We were appalled that protesting university students could be killed by 'forces of law and order'.

An iconic photograph, widely circulated at the time, showed one student lying dead while a bystander – not a fellow student but a 14-year-old runaway who happened to be passing – screams her anguish.

So far on my travels I have seen the picture prominently displayed twice – once in the Washington Newseum and last night in the small neighbourhood restaurant where we ate.

'It was a game changer,' says Darice. 'It really mobilised the youth. It's been interesting teaching on the Kent campus adjacent to where the shooting occurred. There are still people working at Kent who were here when the shootings happened. It's still very much part of the conversation.'

For many years the university authorities downplayed the tragedy. Now, under a new university president, they are acknowledging it. One result is a learning centre/museum, which we visit. And the story unfolds ...

It took place in early May 1970, a few days after President Nixon had ordered the invasion of Cambodia. All over the country students were protesting, and at Kent State the ROTC (Reserve Officers' Training Corps) headquarters was burnt to the ground. As a response, a detachment of National Guard was sent to the university and set up camp in the grounds. General Canterbury, their commander, did not come in peace: 'These students will have to learn what law and order is all about,' he is quoted as saying.

On the morning of 4 May the students and the National Guard confronted each other. The demonstrating students retreated to a car park. The guards advanced, and 29 of them opened fire. Now, in a film running on a loop in the centre's small cinema, we hear the crackle of gunfire. The narrator tells us there are 676 shots and they last 13 seconds. This is followed by muffled shouts: 'Someone has been shot!' then 'Call an ambulance!' Their voices shake with shock. Four students were killed, two aged 19 and two aged 20; nine others were wounded. I notice that a box of tissues has been left on the cinema seats and that it has been well used.

Four days later Nixon promised to withdraw troops from Cambodia.

He also set up a commission which concluded in September that the killings were 'unnecessary, unwarranted and inexcusable'.

A little shaken, we walk across to the car park, past a sculpture still disfigured by a bullet hole, next to which someone has chalked an arrow. The car park is full, apart from four empty spaces each marked off with pillars on top of which have been

Kent State University: blocked off car-park spaces commemorate where the four students were shot in 1970.

piled little stones of mourning. Each space marks where a student was killed, and they are now part of a national monument.

I walk across a hockey pitch and talk to two young women students. I ask about the shootings.

'I don't know a lot about it,' one says. 'I don't have a lot to add ...'

'I think you just did,' I retort. Her friend and I laugh.

'I understand it should be meaningful,' she continues. 'But there are mass shootings every other day and they all blur together. This was the first big one, but it was pretty small, actually.'

Her friend takes over: 'My father and brother were a block away from the Dayton shooting [36 days ago a gunman killed nine people before being killed himself]. They didn't make a big deal of it; they just sent me a text.'

'How do you feel about the future?' I ask.

'Yikes!' There's a pause: 'Optimistic, I guess, but I wouldn't be surprised if I were proved very wrong.'

I find it hard today to share their optimism. In the museum I have read an extract from the Nixon commission on the Kent State Shootings: 'Public statements can either heal or divide. Harsh and bitter rhetoric has set citizen against citizen, exacerbated tension and encouraged violence.' From what I've seen on my trip, we're back where we were.

Next, Darice drives us to Oberlin, a little town with a well-known liberal arts college. We head for a retirement community, and as we enter a notice on the door reminds us to leave our gun outside. In a room off the main corridor a small group is square dancing, and one of the dancers peels off to ask if we can make up the numbers. We decline. We are here to look at the exhibition of Darice's work in the main corridor.

On show are drawings taken from family photographs of her grandparents and of frames from family home movies showing the family in front of the Statue of

Welcoming sign to retirement community, Oberlin.

Liberty. Her intention is to show an often stigmatised culture – that of Puerto Rico.

I detour into a well-equipped library where I see a newspaper article about a current court case: Gibson's Bakery vs. Oberlin College. It's a disturbing story, involving a fight that broke out after a shoplifter (black) was chased and caught by the owner's son (white). The shoplifter and two friends were charged with assault and arrested. The following day – 10 November, two days after the 2016 US presidential election – college students started to protest that the store was racist.

The protest gathered steam, allegedly backed by the Dean of Students, and the college cancelled their contract with the bakery. The bakery sued for libel and won the case, with the college ordered to pay £31.6 million in damages. At the time of writing, the college is appealing.

We return to Cleveland via the edge of Lake Erie. Darice talks about her latest project, a film essay on Puerto Rico. It is inspired by a letter her grandfather co-wrote in 1940 in response to a magazine article describing Puerto Rican immigrants coming through Ellis Island as 'paupers and criminals'.

'My grandfather was hearing derogatory comments made about Mexicans and other Latin Americans coming to this country – nearly a century ago. His article suggests that Puerto Ricans were coming to the United States for the same reason that they are today – they are being exploited.'

Tuesday 10 September

Today we are off to a national park. It's a relatively quiet country valley, not one of the well-known parks. But its story shows the progress made in environmental issues over the last half-century – and highlights the dangers ahead.

The spark that quite literally started this chain of events came from a railway train on a bridge over the heavily polluted Cuyahoga River in Cleveland on 22 June 1969 – another event celebrating its golden anniversary this year. The spark ignited a patch of oil and a part of the river was set ablaze. The fire did not last long, but it was long enough to make the local papers and then national magazines. These stories were illustrated by a dramatic picture of the blazing river, though (and it pains me to say this) the photograph came from a previous Cuyahoga River fire and was therefore fake news.

The incident set off a national debate: how could something as clean and pure as water have become a fire hazard? Amid the ensuing public concern, the Clean Water Act was passed, the Environmental Protection Agency was established, and the movement to increase the number of protected areas picked up support.

One beneficiary was the Cuyahoga Valley. At the end of 1974, after some ferocious cross-party lobbying, President Ford finally signed the bill that would make the valley a national recreation area; in 2000 it was designated a national park.

One of the people closely involved with the national park is John P Debo, the superintendent for 21 years and then chief development officer for the park's Conservancy (which in British terms would make him the chief fundraiser for the Friends). He is also a friend of one of Barbara's cousins, and he has agreed to see us today.

'Over the course of the past 50 years the valley has been transformed into a really beautiful place,' says John. It had a 'remarkable resource' – the remains of the Ohio & Erie Canal which had been destroyed by floods in 1913. Along the canal the towpath has been revived, opening up 100 miles of trail for hiking and cycling.

But the park's success has been taking place against a background of what John calls an 'ever-declining flight path' of funding: 'Since 2002 (during the George H W Bush administration) there has been a slow and quiet strangulation of national park funding,' he says. 'Nothing precipitous, but year after year after year there has been a belt-tightening of federal budgets. And it was Republicans and Democrats alike. There is progressively less money and we have had to work under the mantra "Tax cut! Tax cut! Tax cut!" I can see the day when the federal government will cease to own these places and responsibility shifts to the non-profit or private sector.'

One response has been a rapid rise in the importance of 'non-profit' groups. The Conservancy for Cuyahoga Valley National Park has gone from having no employees in 1988 to employing nearly 90 people with a $6.2 million operating budget. It now raises funds, runs a retail store, co-ordinates some 6,000 volunteers and is developing a new visitor centre. 'Friends groups started out as a small movement but has grown to being a tremendously successful factor in funding, operation and protection of national parks,' he says.

'Will it distort the work in the parks?' I ask.

'There are plenty of controls, like donor vetting and a ban on putting donor names on public buildings. Any involvement would be consistent with the National Park Service mission.'

So presumably no Coca-Cola-branded trails here, as there were on the Chicago shore. But other threats exist: 'President Trump is trying to dismantle all the things that happened since the fire to make America a better, cleaner place. It's been a shocking reversal of progress and environmental stewardship, but I think it will eventually be turned around. This park will survive – and I guess our country will too.'

That afternoon Barbara and I walk two miles along the towpath. It's a glorious September day – in the 90s with a cloudless sky – and it's busy. We see several species of walkers: fast, slow, in pairs, single, in T-shirts, sweating with headbands. Cyclists whizz past us several times a minute, and they come sitting up, lying down, lying down in tandem, single file and two abreast; those swooping up on us from behind shout a warning: 'Cyclist to your left!' They are loud, but friendly.

We don't meet much other wildlife, though the land is said to support all kinds of creatures, including skunks, which I have never seen but once unmistakeably smelt. Back in the shop a volunteer waxes lyrical: he talks of blue herons, bald eagles, coyotes. 'We are standing on land now that will be protected for ever.' Let's hope he's right.

John and his wife Cyndee have invited us to their home, and after a pleasant evening (which included our introduction to chicken cooked on a barbecue with a can of beer stuck up its bottom), I log into Uber to book a ride back to Cleveland. There is bad news. My Uber app tells me that it cannot accept my calls, though it continues to urge me to order some Uber Eats. I have no idea what is wrong.

Our host kindly offers to drive us back – a round trip of one and a half hours. As he drives I search for solutions, and eventually unearth a notice saying that there has been trouble with a payment. That's news to me.

Back in our Airbnb I continue searching for another hour. Eventually I receive a notification saying that they have refunded $0 to my card and the app appears to be working again.

In the morning I continue my enquiries. Someone in Uber sends me an email saying it looks as if my account has been blocked, which is what I spent nearly two hours trying to tell them yesterday. They ask for details and I write what I consider is a remarkably restrained email. I am not hopeful of a reply.

A day with such good hospitality deserved a better ending.

Wednesday 11 September
Today is 9/11. Flags are at half-mast. I see few other outward signs of remembrance, though I do read an article in the *New York Times* about the ceremony at the memorial we visited in New York:

> The families assembled at ground zero again, the place where nearly 3,000 people died on that bright September morning. There was grief again, and the mournful sound of bagpipes echoed again. And there was the rhythm of names of the dead being recited again.

> (James Barron, *NYT*, 'Remembering Those Lost 18 Years Ago', 11 September 2019, revised 12 September)

While I'd been bussing around in the south in July, Barbara had gone away on her own adventure – with her cousin Jim to Minsk, Belarus, visiting the places where their Jewish ancestors had lived. The guide on the trip lives in Cleveland and he has invited us for lunch; before we eat he takes us to the Maltz Museum of Jewish Heritage.

'Stop the Hate' says a sign as we approach. Then: 'The Museum of Diversity and Tolerance'.

One of the first exhibits allows us to test our knowledge of America – and to see whether we would have qualified for citizenship. Barbara gets nine out of ten, which she should. I get seven out of ten, which would have been good enough to let me in. One of the questions that foxed me was the number of original states.

Other exhibits tell of those who arrived penniless, worked hard, and ended up running businesses of their own: 'Beginning in 1880 a flood of nearly 600,000 mainly eastern European immigrants – including some 70,000 Jews – fuelled the region's growth as an industrial powerhouse.' But that brought what we now call pushback: 'Even members of the educated classes saw nothing wrong in callow jokes and mean-spirited caricatures, as long as they were directed to people different from themselves.'

But it wasn't uniformly bad. I take a picture of an election poster, judging from the clothes, from sometime early in the 20th century: 'Vote Goldman for council against the Ku Klux Klan.' Goldman won after winning the endorsement of the *Cleveland News* and the Republican Executive Committee.

A map in the museum shows the current existence of current hate groups in the USA and is accompanied by the comment: 'Nothing seems to slow the persistent power of malice.'

Our bus to Buffalo is due to leave at 6 pm. We are dropped at the station. I am delighted to see that our luck is still holding (perhaps it's Barbara's influence). The place is clean and bright and relaxed, with a little café off to one side. As I check out the crisps and croissants I see a welcome sight: on top of the counter are a couple of boxes containing toy Greyhound buses. Finally, my search is over. The fact that I am not allowed to open a box to see what's inside is not enough to stop me buying one. Later, when I open it, I see that it doubles as a money box; I hope that Nicole will like it.

Soon we are being driven along Lake Erie, not that we see much of it. The forecast of thunderstorms fulfils its promise and much of the journey is accompanied by clashing thunder, rain clattering on the roof, and lightning flashing brief visions of the landscape. It's not the most pleasant of journeys, but at least the danger is outside the bus.

I have booked two nights at the Hotel Delavan, some 11 miles out of town near the airport, run by a dynasty of Italian restaurateurs who promise spacious bedrooms, fine food and a celebrated wine list. I think we deserve a treat and we're looking forward to it.

The hotel is grand, with chandeliers and a pool table in the hall, a posse of Wild West statuettes in the corridor and chimes in the lift. We go to the bar for a celebratory drink and some supper. It is staffed by well-built young men in dinner jackets and is particularly noisy: it's a birthday celebration for one of the staff.

Our celebration is more muted: it is 10 pm and we are told that food is no longer available. On request they bring us four sticks of olives. We have a glass of Prosecco each and go to bed. We may be tired and hungry, but tomorrow we will visit one of the great sights of America.

BACK EAST

1. Upstate New York: Kermit the Frog is 50 and other celebrations

Thursday 12 September

I loved Niagara Falls in 1969 even though I was short-changed. One of the three waterfalls – the American Falls – had been turned off for the summer or, in the official parlance, 'dewatered'. It didn't seem to make much difference: I had a great time and wrote in my diary:

> Arrive at sunrise and walk down to the park. Sky very blue. No-one around, except for a middle-aged couple from Wales. The American Falls is empty … Then walk along the side of the gorge … Leaves just beginning to turn. Walk towards Horseshoe Falls; very noisy and soon very wet – lots of water!

I was amused by the tacky hotels and amusements catering for the honeymooner trade, and then took the first Maid of the Mist boat trip of the day out towards the base of the falls. We chugged out to what seemed recklessly close. I still have the photos I took on board, with my fellow passengers togged up in black rubber coats. One of them looks uncannily like Barbara, though she swears that the only time she went to Niagara was earlier than 1969.

I took the noon bus to New York City: another world-famous landmark to tick off my list and boast about.

Fifty years on we have settled on a form of sightseeing more suited to our advancing years than wandering around at sun-up: a Gray Line bus tour. After breakfast a small shuttle bus picks us up from our hotel. With last night's storm the temperature has dropped from mid-80s to mid-60s (from about 30°C to about 18°C) and, unlike my previous visit, the day is damp and dull.

We are driven through grey streets past a grey river to Niagara where we stop in the lee of the extravagant casino owned by the Seneca Nation of New York, built where the Shredded Wheat factory used to be. We are merged into a larger bus with 14 other tourists and a laconic driver-guide called John. Now we have made up the numbers he gives us the basics: three falls; 750 thousand gallons of water a second going over them; heights of up to 167 feet (51 metres); half the water being taken out for power generation.

The falls were dewatered in 1969 so that engineers could inspect the base and decide whether or not to remove some rocks. 'They turned it off, stared at it for a little while then turned it on again,' says John. The rocks stayed. There is a plan to do some more dewatering and take another look at the rocks next year.

We are taken to a 'multi-media experience' at The World Changed Here pavilion. It tells how the falls were being ruined by 'carnival hucksters and dilapidated mills' in the mid-19th century. In 1885, after a massive clean-up, the American side was turned into a state park. Later, Nikola Tesla (yet another immigrant who made his mark in America) changed the world (as in the pavilion's title) by using its water to generate electricity. The film ends with a snappy soundbite: 'By working together we can ensure that beauty and power can work together.' If only.

We are given 'souvenir sandals' and plastic yellow ponchos, and file past a sign for those who haven't quite understood what lies in store: 'Be advised that conditions are wet and can result in damp clothing.' A lift takes us down 174 feet into the gorge and onto a series of wooden walkways that will take us within feet of one of the falls.

I take a tentative step or two out, and then turn back. The thought of walking out in the mist over the river on steep (and slippery?) wooden steps does not appeal. Am I more cowardly than my younger self, or more sensible? Or both?

Back in the minibus John drives us through Main Street. 'If you like boarded-up buildings this could be the highlight of your tour,' he says.

It's a timely warning. Just a short distance from one of the great natural wonders of the world is another run-down shell of a town. Buildings that once housed grocers and ironmongers now have boarded-up doors and windows stripped of merchandise. Hardly anyone walks the pavements. The few enterprises still functioning, behind tight security, are social not commercial: Family Center, Community Action Program, Municipal Corporation, Police Station. And this in the country that abhors socialism.

John says the city used to have up to 60,000 factory jobs; now there are

1,700. He blames it on money being siphoned off from the town into the park, plus corrupt politicians and bad developments.

'On the Canadian side the Niagara Park Commission controls everything within the park – every tourist shop, every golf course, every parking lot. On this side everything is controlled by the state of New York and goes through Albany. And they are thieves – I'm not making that up, because two have been convicted and are waiting for sentencing.'

As for bad developments, he suggests that I look up the activities of Robert Moses. He explains that he was a powerful but unelected public official who built the pioneering power stations that harnessed the power of Niagara Falls. But at the same time he pushed through the construction of motorways which divided communities and destroyed natural environments: one was built so near the edge of the cliff that within a few years it was considered unsafe and downgraded to a bicycle path. A lot of what he did is now being torn up, says John.

(I later take his advice and look up Robert Moses. From the 1920s until the 1970s he was a major influence on public projects, pushing through roads, bridges, parks, playgrounds and public housing. He secured large amounts of federal funding but also pioneered the introduction of independent authorities that raised their own funds, for instance by levying tolls. Some described him as a 'master builder' while others criticised him for destroying viable communities with his mission to build highways and high-rise housing. In 1973 a Pulitzer prize-winning book, *The Power Broker* by Robert Caro, added the charge of racism. Caro accused Moses of keeping the bridges over the parkways deliberately low to stop coaches (which could be full of non-whites) getting through to the parks and beaches, and keeping temperatures low in swimming pools (because he believed this would deter non-whites from using them).

We walk along the cliff and see a whirlpool far below. A jetboat with a cargo of well-wrapped tourists teeters on the edge of foaming water. We talk of accidents – and suicides. A couple in our group say that they were staying last night in a hotel overlooking the falls and police officers came in to ask them if they had seen anyone going over; they hadn't.

John says there used to be 20–25 suicides in the falls a year, though they became less common after the mainstream media were prohibited from covering them. But social media has made this sensible rule obsolete: a recent suicide carried out in full view of thousands of tourists was captured on thousands of mobile phones and then circulated.

At this point I walk away from the edge.

And now to the climax I have been looking forward to – a repeat trip on the Maid of the Mist. We get suited up, but in blue plastic ponchos, not the rubber outfits I remember. 'This is real progress,' says John. 'As soon as you got off the lift you could smell the old costumes – they smelt like dead fish. They were wet the first time the boats went out and stayed wet for the rest of the season.'

Our boat edges out from the bank and towards the falls. Then this happens:

> Suddenly the sky is blotted out by the cliffs above and we are surrounded by water pouring down from above. The river becomes turbulent and the boat shakes and we have to hold tight and protect our cameras and still we look up, incredulous, at all the gushing water and wonder how on earth we are going to describe it. And just when you think that the boat has gone too far, it turns around, leaving you still wondering how to describe it.

That's how I described it for the *Pasadena Star-News* as a 22-year-old, and as a 72-year-old I find it hard to improve on it. The only comments I have is that the words didn't do justice to just how wet, wet, wet it is. And cold, cold, cold. I feel sure we have ventured into the world of Type 3 fun, except that once we are back in the car park we start giggling about how great it has been. Definitely Type 2, then.

I also have a new set of photos of Niagara Falls, with pictures of Barbara – definitely her this time – gazing at columns of water which look remarkably close, encased not in black rubber but in blue plastic.

Friday 13 September

Our alarms are not needed this morning. We have been awakened long before the appointed hour by what sounds like a herd of bison (or should that be buffalo? *See 24 September*) trampling through the room above, or a group of swingers having imaginative sex. It continues for some time. When we have breakfast there is a family with two small children at the next table. The children stamp a lot and we think our mystery has been solved.

We are collected by Barbara's cousins Sue and Andy. They are taking us in their car to their home in Rochester, about an hour away, where we will help them to celebrate another 1969 event – their wedding.

I tell Andy about my adventures with Geoffrey and Morris, and particularly the near-impossibility of finding help when things go wrong:

The water still falls: edging close to Niagara on a Maid of the Mist boat, 50 years apart.

'There's no customer service these days,' he says. 'It's like sending mail into a black hole.' Andy has spent most of his life working in and around computers, including representing Apple.

This is a restful day, catching up with family, journal and laundry. In the evening we have an extended family supper. I hear that schools are now beginning to teach 'cursive writing' – what we would call handwriting – again. I am shocked that they'd stopped.

Saturday 14 September

I have access to secure WiFi, so this morning I am going to book my last remaining ticket: from Boston to New York next Saturday. I log onto the website where I am told that I have earned a free ticket to anywhere. A just reward for all my efforts, I think, but my happy thoughts are short-lived. As I put in the final details of the trip I want to take, the screen goes blank – a sure sign of trouble ahead.

Then a notice comes up, in that mock-chummy tone that confirms that trouble is around the corner: 'Well. This is rare. We don't have a schedule that matches your selected date and destinations.'

Phooey. Or should that be Bullshit? As I am about to prove.

I log on again and repeat my details, this time with no mention of the free trip I have been promised. And yes, you may have guessed: I am instantly offered a ticket from Boston to New York – for $20.90. I am sure there is a piece of small print languishing in some corner of the website saying 'subject to availability', but that's the computer equivalent of protesting the truth with your fingers crossed behind your back. And anyway the ticket is available – they just don't want to give it to me for free. It was a porky pie, a lie.

I no longer have the heart to pursue with Greyhound a windmill-tilting quest that is unlikely to end in my favour. So I buy the ticket. And then I am told that I have another $2 to pay for a service charge. So that's two lies then. This is corporate gaslighting.

Andy takes me on a calming walk around the district, past the local high school. The sports facilities are amazing: a hard-surface running track, lacrosse and football fields, a little stadium, a large scoreboard. Some of the homes we pass sport American flags, others a list of Democratic candidates for an upcoming election. These are the suburbs, and all feels safe and comfortable.

Later I talk to a fellow house-guest about the misgivings I have about

Google Maps: they direct you to where you want to go, but it's harder to find out the context of where you are. She agrees: 'What's happening is that electronic media doesn't allow curiosity to go off the path. But when we're told where to go all day, then we're developing a dictatorship.'

That evening we have a slap-up dinner for 17 people at a restaurant in the centre of town. Andy and Sue's grand-daughter entertains us with Irish dancing as we drink fine French wines. We hear that Andy had proposed to Sue in the back of his parents' car – and they married a week later. I expect people said it wouldn't last.

Their golden jubilee qualified them for a greetings card from the White House. No-one was inclined to apply.

Sunday 15 September

This weekend has been about family – and appropriately we visit a reputed Museum of Play in the city of Rochester. It's the Strong Museum, and it opened in 1982 based on the collection of a wealthy resident. It is now a huge space – and still expanding. I want to find toys that will show how times have changed since 1969 and it's not difficult.

In a prominent place on the first floor yet another golden anniversary is being celebrated: Sesame Street. Exhibits include a glass case showing several different Kermits (and who knew that the first version had eyes made of ping-pong balls?). But this is a museum and there is a serious point to be made: 'The once nutritionally reckless Cookie Monster now considers cookies a "sometimes food", Oscar the Grouch splits his time between his trash can and a nearby recycling bin, Elmo consults his cell phone which he calls "Smartie". (It's encouraging to know that naming my phone puts me in such good company.)

I raise a silent prayer for those unsung heroes and heroines who write the words that accompany museum exhibits. They have entertained and enlightened me along my trip, usually with a blend of information and wry humour. They have not been afraid – and I think of the Katrina exhibit in New Orleans – to grasp some political nettles.

Next I find a display cabinet stuffed with seven Greyhound buses: unlike the one I bought they are made of metal and have clearly been played with. All but one look prewar, and three of the older ones are trucks and trailers. Nearby another cabinet is filled with board games. One that catches my eye is Electronic Mall Madness, a shopping themed game released in 1988.

'We played that!' says the lady standing next to me. I ask how. 'There was a bunch of stores around the board. You had to hit them all. The one who hit them all first was the winner.'

A little further on are some classic electronic games: Pong, Grand Theft Auto, Super Mario Bros, Zaxxon, Assault, Kung Fu Master, Sunset Rider, Teenage Mutant Ninja Turtles, Smash, Aliens. I haven't played any of them. I have however, played on pinball machines – and here one is, but I have been beaten to the buttons.

Downstairs is a train, a roundabout, a taxi and a little theatre which allows children to dress up and appear on a television screen. Most popular of all is a miniature Wegman's food store with plastic produce (from chops to sushi) and tins (empty) which children are pulling off the shelves and taking to a miniature check-out counter.

As I go out I see some quotes writ large on the wall: 'To play is to create' and 'Play is training for the unexpected'. I would be happy to donate another one: 'Play is training for the consumer society.'

Andy drives us through downtown Rochester. I did not visit the city in 1969; if I had I would have encountered a self-assured, prosperous place – exemplified by a line of mansions just off the city centre. Half a century ago it boasted major state-of-the-art companies, a pioneering downtown inner mall and a sunken inner ring road to accommodate all those cars that were being produced not far away in Detroit.

'The biggest changes have been the shrinking of Kodak and Xerox and the growth of the University of Rochester,' says Andy. 'Kodak employed more than 60,000 in Rochester in 1982. I believe that it's something like 2,000 today.'

The mall, Midtown Plaza, was a great success when it opened in 1962 to an award-winning design. It contained major department stores, a Greyhound bus station, and a celebrated Clock of Nations with little figurines from 12 different countries that would come out and jiggle about every hour on the hour. At Christmas a monorail would take shoppers around the mall. But shoppers dwindled, the major shops closed, and the clock was transferred to the airport terminal and is now in storage. In 2008 Midtown Plaza closed its doors and most of the buildings were demolished and replaced with offices and homes.

One portion of land, known as Parcel 5, still lies flat and empty. There's an ongoing dispute over what to do with it. More apartments and offices? An open space? A performing arts centre? A casino?

Elsewhere a sizeable chunk of what was a ring road has been closed and

Rochester: this is where once proudly stood the award-winning Midtown Plaza shopping centre (1962-2008).

filled in – and is being developed. The traffic solution once seen as the way of the future has lost its appeal. Critics argue that they discouraged the development of public transport, and caused habitable houses to be destroyed and their residents transplanted to high-rise apartments. They also separated the city centre from residential areas, isolating communities and creating ghettoes.

On the way home we go to the kind of place that displaced the mall – a huge out-of-town shopping complex, straggling along the highway. It is dominated by an adult version of Wegmans, with every kind of food you could think of in many different varieties. As if that was not enough, it is about to be joined just down the road by an equally huge Whole Foods store. For that they have knocked down an Italian restaurant and a bowling alley.

But now, with the growth of online shopping, are these giant emporiums, like the city centre mall, also destined for extinction?

That evening we talk about family life. 'In some ways the 1950s and 1960s were "fat city" for Americans,' says Andy. 'The USA was the dominant industrial player. Super efficiency was not critical then. Profitability was not a difficulty. Incomes were growing.

'But by the 1970s there was serious competition – and a drive for efficiency and profitability at the expense of health, family and culture. Today families not only need two incomes but, more and more, both parents are working at multiple jobs. The whole Uber business – this is the only way they can get by. And a huge percentage are at a level where they are one disaster away from poverty and even homelessness.

'But more than the economy and the job market I worry about the climate and what we are going to do about that. As for what life will be like for my grand-daughter … I worry about that too.'

2. Unadilla, New York: the centre holds, just

Monday 16 September

Over the last three days I have got used to treading on soft carpets, taking leisurely showers after breakfast, eating food that hasn't been deep fried, and travelling from door to door in private cars. Now I have to go back on the road for one last solo trip, east to Boston then south to New York. Barbara is staying behind: she will spend a few days with her cousins before flying down to meet me in New York. The separation should be easier than the last two times: we will be in the same time zone.

Greyhound have sent me a Trailways bus again, and our first stop is Geneva, a little town on the shores of Lake Seneca, surrounded by vineyards, and with no sign of boarded-up properties on Main Street. It calls itself the Lake Trout Capital of the World.

We continue from the top of Lake Seneca to the bottom of Lake Cayuga, which takes us to Ithaca, home to Cornell University, the Dalai Lama and Ithaca Guns (Annie Oakley's weapon of choice). The guns were tested by firing them into the base of the Ithaca Falls, which required a major clean-up early in the 20th century to get rid of all the accumulated lead.

I catch up on writing my journal as we go, until Morris the mobile whimpers for my attention. Google wants me to do something or other so that my voice can be recognised. I reject the proposition, though I am tempted by the thought that I could speak abuse to Google instead of just thinking it. Then Morris whimpers again. This time it is T-Mobile thinking I owe them money for the coming month; they are not quite sure but please could I get in touch on the attached number.

We roar past the exit to Unadilla, New York. This is where I will visit tomorrow, but it has a shortage of accommodation and no bus stop so I have arranged to stay in Oneonta, a few miles further on. It is another college town, and I realise that some of the smaller bus routes I have travelled have been kept open because of student populations.

The bus station is a cosy one-room affair at the side of a multi-storey car park. My hotel is a little way out of town, with a great view of the mountains and next to a shopping centre where Google Maps tell me there is a T-Mobile store.

Google is wrong: it is an AT&T store. So I go outside and ring the T-Mobile number I have been given. After the usual duet with robots I get through to a human (I can tell because I find the English difficult to understand). She tells me I owe $6 ($7.20 with tax) for an overseas call or text. I am puzzled: I don't remember making any overseas calls or sending an overseas text. And no, she can't give me any details.

As the sun begins to set I stand in the middle of the shopping centre and unleash my frustrations with modern commerce. I tell the T-Mobile lady that I am going back to England in a week and won't need my American number, but that I was forced to buy a month at a time so I have another three weeks I have paid for but won't use, and now I am being asked to pay more for running up extra charges but they can't tell me what they were.

The Voice sounds a little startled and lets me off with a warning. I never found out what the $6 ($7.20 with tax) was for.

Later that evening I take an Uber back into town. The driver tells me he has three jobs: one in a museum, one driving an Uber and one working in a shop in the mall. 'The economy's changing. Jobs are changing.'

But why so many jobs?

'I like to travel.'

He drops me at an Italian restaurant filled with plastic flowers but bereft of anyone prepared to serve me, though they are hardly overwhelmed with other diners. I go next door to a cheerful Chinese restaurant instead. The driver who takes me back to my hotel tells me he was brought up in Unadilla and then lived for some time in Los Angeles, working as an actor. He gives me his card.

Tuesday 17 September

Today I have a second chance to meet a mayor of Unadilla. I have prepared with some care, writing in advance to Clarissa the village clerk who referred me to the local history society. I have been in touch with their president and he has offered to pick me up at my hotel and show me around. It looks as if this time I won't have to walk alone along deserted streets, fretting about guns and escaped prisoners.

I have briefed myself. Unadilla, NY, is the name of a town and a village. Confusingly the town is what in the UK we would call a district council, and the village, which is where I'm headed, is what we would call a small town. Its population is about 1,700, about half that of Unadilla GA. The population is nearly 100 per cent white, compared with Unadilla, GA, which is about one third white and two thirds black. The median household income is nearly $35,000, compared with $22,500 in Unadilla, GA. The county pivoted to Trump in 2016, as did Unadilla GA, but whereas in Georgia the margin was tight (51 to 49 per cent) here there was a much larger swing, with Trump winning by 53 to 40 per cent.

As I hang about in the hotel lobby, a presenter on Fox News is angrily attacking the *New York Times* for a story they have written about the latest (and controversial) supreme court judge, Brett Kavanaugh. The story has an 'egregious omission', he says, and accuses his fellow journalists of being 'masters of insinuation and innuendo'. This item is followed by an interview with a Republican congressman from Ohio who opposes a mild attempt to curb the shooting epidemic. Referring to the millions who own guns, he says: 'We don't want to criminalize law-abiding citizens.'

My guide turns up and we have breakfast together. Donald Tuttle was born 74 years ago in the neighbouring (and slightly larger) town of Sidney, and has lived in Unadilla for the last 35 years. He has been a teacher, a Baptist missionary in Lesotho, and a Scouting District Commissioner. He is President of the Unadilla Historical Association and the town historian: 'Under New York state law each municipality has to employ one,' he says.

As we drive into Unadilla, NY, Donald stokes my fears: 'It's a beautiful place but kind of hollowed out,' he says. I see what he means. We pass a school that is closed and up for sale, then a long low building that was a bowling alley but is now an apartment block. We also pass a drive-in cinema (one of the last still open in upstate New York) and a succession of handsome houses with two floors and more, surrounded with balconies and standing in well-tended grounds. There is clearly money around.

We stop at a haughty colonnaded building: the Masonic Hall. In 2010 the three remaining freemasons closed the lodge and transferred the building to the Historical Association. It now houses the Rotary Club in winter and the Scouts all year round.

And they are not just any scouts – they are Troop 1 Boy Scouts of America, the oldest continually operating troop in the country. It was formed in 1910 by the Revd Yale Lyon, minister in charge of St Matthew's Episcopalian Church next door. He was fresh back from training in Oxford, England, where he had learnt about Baden-Powell and the fledgling movement he had founded two years before. Cabinets around the walls hold books, photos, camping equipment, trophies, badges and even

Donald's old uniform. I take a picture of him standing by it, and he tells me where to best catch the light. He has done this before.

As we tour St Matthew's he tells me that before the Second World War Catholic boys were only allowed to take part in the troop 'as long as they saw the light'. This led to the formation of Troop 2 for boys with non-Episcopalian views. The worship of God has not been a unifying force in America.

We go to the centre of town, where the mixed messages continue. There is a little parade: a bank, a furniture shop, a coffee shop (closed today), a lawyer's office and a photographer. Across the street is what looks like an attractive diner that has been empty for some years but is being restored.

Further down, surrounded by an empty car park, is the Family Dollar store, with windows screaming: '$1 WOW!' 'CLEARANCE!' 'Every Day LOW Prices', We Accept Food Stamp Benefits'. It used to be a proper grocery, says Donald, but they lost business to the two big stores six miles away in Sidney. They sold to a large chain of what he says used to be called 'five and dime' stores.

But this means that the village no longer has a shop selling fresh food, so a group of residents has been working to set up a co-operative to do so. They have been given a $4,000 grant from a yoghurt company and hope to get started before the end of the year. 'I don't know whether it will work,' says Donald. 'We'll have to wait and see. The state of the economy in upstate New York is a pervasive problem that very small communities can't solve on their own.'

He leaves me to wander while he goes off home to collect some papers for a meeting. Morris rings out. It is the 'escalation department' at Uber. They have taken my comment seriously because the woman speaking to me is American. She tells me that they have looked carefully into my problem last week: my suspension was caused by a glitch, but she can offer no explanation as to how or why I was suddenly reinstated. After more apologies and assurances that they are trying to do better she offers me $10 credit – plus a written explanation on how to use it. Mmmm.

When Donald comes back he presents me with a Unadilla pennant and a 1992 reprint of two books about the village published by the Halsey brothers in 1902 to raise funds for St Matthew's.

I ask him about the President and get the Trump sigh, followed by a pause; I am getting used to it by now. 'Four years ago it was Trump country here,' he says. 'But I think most of my circle have got fed up with him. He doesn't have a moral centre. I read his book *The Art of the Deal*. The gist was that any negotiation is not successful until the other guy is gouged.

'I wish Trump had grown up as a Scout,' he adds. 'That might have made a difference.'

We are into mid-afternoon and I still haven't met my mayor. Donald has been trying without success to phone him all morning, so we decide to drop in anyway. The village hall is in a timbered building, with a veranda and a splendid wooden staircase. The mayor and the clerk share a room on the ground floor. They are in, and so, finally, are we.

David Welch, Mayor of Unadilla, is an affable bearded man and a stalwart of the local volunteer fire service. He sits at his desk signing a sheaf of papers and wearing a cap (which I persuade him to keep on while I take a photograph). I ask him about the issues he faces.

'A lot of them are not caused by the village or the area. Everybody likes the area and would love it if there were more manufacturing jobs. But this is a bedroom community. People go into Sidney to work.

'This is a nice place to live and we keep trying to improve things – but they are always in a constant state of flux.'

David Welch, the mayor of Unadilla New York: 'Here the biggest danger is being run over by a cow'.

As I am about to leave I tell him about my experiences in Unadilla, GA. 'At one stage I was walking down a street pulling my luggage in 90-degree heat thinking every house had a gun in it – and knowing there was a prison less than a mile away,' I say.

'Here the biggest danger is being run over by a cow,' he replies.

That evening I walk into Oneonta and find a good Italian restaurant. Afterwards I call an Uber and get the same driver as last night. We greet each other like long-lost friends and for the first time on this trip I sit in the front of the car.

Steve Quimby grew up in Unadilla, NY, and went away to train as an actor and try his luck in Hollywood. He came back to look after his ailing parents, but plans to go back to Hollywood and try his luck at acting again. He shows me on his phone a clip of him being killed in a film that went down well in Bangladesh. He also tells me he was the mad pizza man in *Power Rangers Turbo* episode 22, but he wasn't killed in that one.

I throw him the usual questions.

'I think we have to moderate things. I don't think the next president is going to get in if they say we must do away with all the aeroplanes and cows.'

'What's changed?'

'It would seem that some people have lost their sense of humour,' he answers.

We part as best mates. 'I hope you have some more good killings,' I say.

When I browse through the books that Donald gave me, my eye is caught by a passage at the end of one – the memoirs of a doctor – under the heading: 'A look into the future'.

> Who would have called a man sane 50 years ago that should have sincerely said we would ever talk with another living thousands of miles away? Or that one's voice could be stirred up and again given to another's auditory sense years after?
>
> In view of this and other equally incredible developments, how long before the air will be as safely navigable as the earth or water? It is but a question of time when principles of economy will secure us against extravagant waste of fuel.
>
> (*Reminiscences*, Dr Gaius Leonard Halsey, 1902, reprinted 1991)

That evening I watch CNN, where political discussion is interspersed with advertisements for treatments for ulcerative colitis, asthma, heart failure and memory loss. I wonder what the doctor would have made of that.

Wednesday 18 September

Another long journey – this time 12 hours with two connections. The first bus leaves at 6.15 am: all three alarms go off at once and my taxi arrives on the dot. As the bus leaves Oneonta in the early morning mist I am the only passenger. I sit in the front seat next to Peter the driver, originally from Poland. As we bump along he tells me that the road is a lot better than it was last year. I wait for the sun to rise but it is obscured by the mountain mist. By the time we get a clear view it is already well risen. As we go Peter looks after my interests.

'Get your phone ready! Round the next corner. Some wooden chickens …

'Watch for the crossroads coming up! You'll see the statue of an eagle that was taken from Grand Central Station in New York City.'

We cross over a little stream, pass by a little church. Travel can be great in an empty coach on a small road when the sun is starting to unwrap the views and the trees are tinged with early autumn colours. When people ask me (as they will) to describe the best bits of my trip, this will be a contender.

I don't have a monopoly on Peter for long, because this is a community bus. We stop in a succession of small towns whose names reflect the melting pot that is America: Delhi, Andes, Indian Wilderness, Kingston. We also stop between them to pick up passengers who have been waiting patiently by the side of the road. Some are going shopping or going to work in the next town. Some are elderly, leaning on sticks – or have a walking frame that has to be bundled into the hold. Some are dressed in business clothes, carrying not the usual rucksack but a leather briefcase primed for a day of meetings in New York City, which is where the bus should end up just after 11 o'clock this morning.

At Kingston the bus station is gentle and suburban with an ace diner next door. The next leg takes me to Albany where I go for my lunch in a little store doing sandwiches and soup. Behind me in the queue is a man with jeans, a T-shirt – and a flak jacket with POLICE written on it. On his right hip is a gun in a holster. This is the first time – I think – I have eaten my lunch next to someone packing a gun. It's a good thing I have worked up an appetite.

The final ride into Boston is uneventful, boring even. There are only so many tinged autumnal leaves and still pools of water that a chap can take.

Today's Uber driver comes from Sierra Leone. He has been in America for three years. His main job is working at one of the car rental companies out at the airport. I ask him how he is treated. 'Some of them know that immigrants are not bad people. A lot of them appreciate us.' The implication hangs in the air: others do not.

The Catskills, New York: 'Travel can be great in an empty coach when the sun is starting to unwrap the views'.

3. Boston: hope for the future

I find the doorway I am looking for between a micro-brewery and a wig shop. I have just been decanted from an Uber onto a street described as being in a historic area in the heart of Boston. It is on the fringe of the theatre district and, historic area notwithstanding, is a daunting mixture of office workers, tourists, street vendors, shoppers, opera-lovers, street musicians, hustlers and maybe worse. As my car was pulling up, I saw what looked like a drug deal, but I may have seen too many films.

I have booked a 'micro-room', which is a first for me. The company running the property has made it clear that it is not a hotel, which means no staff is on site. The control centre (whatever that comprises – a single person with a computer, perhaps?) has sent me via Morris a series of codes that will let me into first the front door, then the floor I am on, and finally my room. The control centre has also sent me an email address in case things go wrong.

I surprise myself by making the numbers work first time. However, I worry what I would do if the codes follow the example of my Greyhound tickets and disappear from Morris. I note them down on a piece of paper and stick it in my wallet. I then write down a second set to keep in my trouser pocket.

My room is not like the overprovided hotel chain rooms I have been staying in, with two double beds and a smorgasbord of pillows to suit each traveller's neck. This is a smaller space, U-shaped around an inner well, out of which emerge two large white ventilation tubes, looking like oversize Slinkies creeping in from the window. Unlike in my Pasadena Airbnb, I have all the furniture I need but it is well-worn and utilitarian. And though there are two beds, they have metal frames and one is on top of the other. On the lower bunk, along with the towels, is a packet of ear plugs, which does not augur well.

Thursday 19 September
I never needed the earplugs. I assume there have been some complaints

My micro-room in Boston: ventilation tubes creep in 'like oversize Slinkies'.

about the many air conditioners snaking out into the common well, but I must be immune to background noise by now. Also, I have another early start because I want to reprise my first experience of Boston 50 years ago.

That year I arrived on an overnight bus at 5.30 am. I wrote:

> Unusual for me to see a city so early in the morning. Weather fine. Take a walk in the park and on edge of common. Very beautiful in the early sunlight and more squirrels than men [*sic*]. Get talking to a policeman (about violence, hippies, London etc) and flatter him by taking his photo.

I have set the alarm for 6 o'clock, and since my micro-room is just a few shops away from Boston Common, I am there by ten past. The sky is brightening in the east, but little else stirs. It is cold – only 48 degrees (9°C). A park employee sets up a pressure washer to clean a fountain terrace. An early jogger jogs through. One homeless man tidies up his small package of belongings while another is fast asleep tucked behind a park bench and under a plaid blanket. I see no squirrels and wonder whether they have been evicted. I see no policemen either. (Though I do manage to track one down and photograph him later).

Sunrise is at 6.28, and soon afterwards I see the first rays lighting up the tops of the taller buildings. More joggers turn up. A play group of dogs bound with their owners on one of the swards of grass.

I find someone to speak to. He is standing outside a small pickup truck parked on one of the larger paths and his name is Norm. Since 2012 he has been in charge of the trees, many of which are elms and used to be in a bad state. His predecessor wanted to give them massive injections, he says, but he has taken a gentler approach, trying to improve tree health generally and control bark beetles specifically. The elms are much improved.

Boston Cops 1969 (above) and 2019 (right).

It's now half an hour after sunrise and while the tops of office blocks are gleaming we remain in shadow.

'This will be a change since you were last here,' says Norm. 'All those tall buildings … and there's another one on the way. We don't get the morning light now until about 9 o'clock.'

As I try to take photos Morris keeps flashing up a message: 'Hi, I'm your Google Assistant. Speak to me.' This is harassment. I ignore him.

At around 7 am I head back towards my micro-room. Norm is inspecting trees. The dog party is dispersing. The squirrels have woken up and are leaping in and out of the rubbish bins, tails high. The paving by the fountain is sparkling clean, waiting for the day's onslaught of tourists. I still haven't seen a policeman.

Of the many museums in Boston one has caught my eye: the Edward M Kennedy Institute for the United States Senate, opened in April 2015 and funded by public and private donations.

I had followed Senator Kennedy's career since my 1969 trip, when our lives had briefly touched. One of the good friends of my sponsor Maria Goldwater had been on Kennedy's staff, and the original plan had been for me to stay with her when I was in Washington. But she had to cancel that in order to cover for her friend, Mary Jo Kopechne, who was going up to a Kennedy party in Chappaquiddick.

It was after this party that Mary Jo was found drowned in Kennedy's car after it had skidded off a bridge. He had fled the scene, which almost certainly ended his chances of becoming President. Instead he carved out a long and distinguished career as a senator, pushing for improved educational standards, LGBTQ and women's rights, universal health care and more.

His memorial institute is a square, white building which nestles up against his brother's much larger Presidential Library on land fronting the sea and redeveloped as a University of Massachusetts campus. In the centre of the building is the heart of the museum: a copy of the Washington Senate.

When I look in, a man with a South African accent is making an impassioned speech: 'We should be improving the world of our citizens, not those people who have just come across the border. I don't see how paying people to shortcut the system is going to work.'

He is part of a group of army officers from all over the world on a year-long Master's Program at the National Defense University, an elite educational institution for senior members of the armed forces. They are taking part in an exercise which has them role playing as senators arguing over a bill to increase funding to process backlogged immigration applicants.

As they break for lunch I catch a quick word from a British colonel. 'A brilliant opportunity,' he says. 'One of the things we are trying to do is understand how America operates.'

Back in the chamber the next scheduled activity is another role play, this one for ordinary visitors like myself. The scenario this time is the introduction of a bill to impose extra taxes on employers who are not paying their workers the minimum wage. There is only one other visitor apart from me who wants to take part, but the staff decide to go ahead anyway, and we both become 'trainee senators'.

My new colleague opts to be leader of the Democrats, so I become a Republican and move to the majority leader's seat. Three members of the institute team start the proceedings, one as presiding officer with the other two each giving a party line.

Then we are invited to speak. When my turn comes, I bluster for a bit and then attack the iniquity of fining brave employers who are trying hard to give people work. I end with a flourish: 'The proposed bill is pernicious, ineffective and lazy.' The audience slam their desks in approval. It's a pity there are only four of them, but I remember that when I attended the real Senate in 1969 it was similarly sparse.

We vote along party lines (this is 2019 America) and the motion is tied. Our facilitator/chairman votes against the bill, and I win. It's been good fun. It also made me realise how easy it is to wax eloquent on a point of view that you don't really hold, particularly if the surroundings are impressive.

The institute staff facilitate at least five of these role plays a week in term time, and last year 22,000 school children visited the institute. 'We want to get kids from a very early age to know what negotiation is,' says Nate Gundy, manager of educational programmes. 'We want to give them a personal memory of wrestling with a particular issue. And we want to be part of a wave of a civic revival so that people feel invested in the institutions that run this country, and have an influence over them.'

I have scheduled a treat for tonight: a return to the Durgin Park Dining Rooms at the Faneuil Hall Marketplace. They came highly recommended in my 1969 BUNAC handbook – 'definitely a must' – and I enjoyed my lunch there so much I kept a copy of the menu.

On the front cover is a line drawing of the 1827 marketplace, and on the back a sentimental poem about the joys of sons. The centrefold offers long lists of food: Frankfort (*sic*) and beans, Yankee pot roast, New England boiled dinner, clams, broiled schrod (*sic*), fresh lobster stew. I

My treasured 50-year-old menu from the Durgin Park Dining Rooms.

particularly like the warning to beef-eaters: 'We are not responsible for any steak ordered well done.'

In my diary I wrote:

> Long queue. Had 95 cent meal: clam chowder (ugh!), chicken and coffee. Atmosphere extraordinary and waitress rude (gave me back my 5 cent tip as insulting). Dropped my cigarette in the sauce which led to me chatting with my neighbours on the long table. Two nurses and one large friend ... They took me round Boston in their Volkswagen.

Fired up with these memories, the Dining Rooms were one of the first places I'd googled when planning the 2019 trip, and I was delighted to find the place was still going strong. But that was a year ago. When I googled the restaurant yesterday from my micro-room in Boston I discovered that it had closed down in January. It was a major blow. I saw that a branded restaurant is still going strong out at the airport, but I didn't think that would be the same experience.

I decide to make a pilgrimage to the site anyway. I find the building empty, with scars where the awnings used to be attached. I am used to seeing abandoned buildings by now, but this seems personal. I go into the Irish pub next door to try to find out why it closed.

'It's gone,' says the barman. shrugging. 'It changed a lot over the last few years. A new company came in and ran it into the ground.'

So I never got the chance to review my 'ugh!' ranking of the clam chowder, or insult a waitress with a derisory tip, or step into a car with a couple of nurses to be driven around Boston. Mind you, these days I would probably have felt inclined to decline the invitation.

Friday 20 September

On my 1969 trip to Boston I went to stay with a former neighbour who had married an American teacher who had become a housemaster at a school called Phillips Academy at Andover, some 21 miles from the city. It meant nothing to me. I did not realise until I got there that it was one of the most prestigious schools in America. I made friends with some of the teaching assistants, watched the film *Tom Jones* with an enthusiastic audience in a communal hall, and took my meals at an upmarket self-service eatery called Commons. I was very impressed:

> Phillips Academy is *the* prep [school] in the USA. The students are hand-picked and the snippets of conversation I hear are frightfully intellectual. The grounds are really beautiful. The facilities are

incredible – vast number of residences and suites rather than rooms, gymnasium, cage [sic], hotel, chapel and an Infirmary which is a registered hospital.

The school's reputation has not dimmed, not least because since I was there two of its alumni have become presidents of the United States – George H W Bush and his son George W Bush. It has also in half a century turned out a co-founder of Facebook, the head of the FBI (at the time of writing), at least three winners apiece of the Nobel and Pulitzer prizes – and offspring of Rupert Murdoch, President Kennedy and the Aga Khan.

I am keen to ask some questions, such as how the school is helping students to prepare for the changes anticipated in the 21st century. I sent emails and phoned, and finally got diverted by the publicity office to the archivist, who will be in a meeting for most of the day. I have decided to go anyway and see what happens.

I take the suburban train to Andover, but first I have a small diversion to make. Today is the Global Climate Strike and I have seen on the web that a demonstration is planned for the town.

The designated square is quiet when I get there. As I stand looking lost, a woman detaches herself from a small group huddled by a car and asks if I am looking for the demonstration. There has been a mistake in the listing, she says; the protest is planned for tomorrow, Saturday. Most local schoolchildren have not been given time off. 'School administrators are nervy about letting kids off campus,' she says.

I call an Uber. The driver scolds me for not standing in the right place. When she drops me off at Phillips Academy she comments: 'This place is terrible. Broken chairs lying around, rubbish … And with what their parents are paying!'

I find no rubbish and no broken chairs. What I do find is an impeccable campus with enviable facilities, as before: sturdy red-brick school blocks, a church, and a museum; plenty of signs to various sports facilities – and all quiet and apparently well regulated.

There must have been a signal (do schools still have bells?) because suddenly students start to pour out of the buildings. I had expected the campus to be filled, as before, with white boys, but I'm glad to see there are now many students from other groups, particularly of Asian and Indian origin, and lots of girls.

I manage to find Commons: there is a plaque on the wall saying it was refurbished in 1981. I walk in unchallenged. But I am conscious of my vulnerable position as an outsider among minors, and wander back through the little town to the railway station. I am sorry I never got to speak to anyone, and yes, I do feel a bit of a failure. Perhaps my younger self would have had more bluster and greater success.

Waiting on the station platform for the train back to Boston, I start talking to a well-dressed man of roughly my age. (I mention the age because it may explain why we started talking to each other, as opposed to our phones.)

I tell him about the changes I have seen in small town America and he points to a large industrial-looking building just outside the station. When he was growing up it was the Tyer rubber factory (named after the founders, not a misspelling) that made boots and raincoats. Now it has been turned into condominiums, and they aren't cheap. The cost of housing has rocketed: 20 years ago, rental for a two-bedroom apartment was $500 a month; now it's $1500.

We talk our way back to Boston. When he says he is a criminal lawyer I ask if he's the person that gets all the villains off. He launches into a plausible defence (as he should): his role is to make sure that the institutions don't over-reach themselves. Besides, most of the people he defends are not out-and-out villains, but have problems with drugs, poverty, lack of education – and other issues.

He is dismissive of Trump, and thinks the Democrats will come up with a plausible candidate. He likes Elizabeth Warren's ideas, but does not feel she is electable. 'She says some things that need to be said. But business and companies will never do something against their own interests.'

My day improves some more. Back in Boston I head for the common and another climate strike demonstration. As I turn the corner by the Massachusetts State House I run into a crowd of several hundred young people, mainly school students. They have come with wit and placards.

There is no Planet B

I'll show up for school when you grow up

What I stand for is what I stand on

A young woman is taking advantage of an open mic: 'I want everyone of the age of 24 and up to look around and see these young people. We have only one chance. This is it. I'm proud of you all.'

Another takes over: 'The government doesn't give a fuck about our world. Stop putting profits before people!'

A chant starts: 'No more lies or corporate ties!'

The commitment and intensity are infective, and I begin to feel a bit emotional. It must be showing, because an adult turns to me and asks if I'm OK. We start to talk. He teaches at a school in New Hampshire and has driven here this morning with a group of 31 students. I mention how the schools in Andover didn't allow their students to take part.

'This has all been student-run. They put the paperwork together. This is seen as a field trip, so they have to write about why they think this is important. The school was very happy to let them take part.'

I ask the usual question: Are you optimistic?

Usual pause.

'Sometimes.'

Suddenly attention shifts to the end of the street. Those who took part in the rally in City Hall are arriving – thousands of them, with two bands and a group of drummers. I ask a marshal to estimate the numbers: about 10,000 he reckons.

A young man strains to shout: 'What does democracy look like?'

'This is what democracy looks like!' comes the response.

It is a stonking hot September day. Another chant goes up: 'We're

Boston climate strike: 'Have I found an optimistic ending?'

fucking melting!' Are they referring to themselves, or to the environment, or both?

'Don't forget to hydrate!' somebody shouts.

People chat to each other, support each other, shout with each other, hug each other. Despite the expletives, this is a friendly crowd. I have seen only a handful of police officers, and the majority of these were on bicycles bringing up the end of the procession. The young people I speak to say this is the first time they have done something like this, and they plan to come again for the next protest, scheduled for the day after Thanksgiving – Black Friday, the feast of shopping.

I have now spent eight weeks touring this country, hearing endless tales of division, incivility and impending ecological disaster. My book has been heading for a gloomy view. Have I found an optimistic ending?

And then I think back to the peaceful campus at Phillips Academy, a short train ride and a world away. I wonder if the students there are getting involved in the day's activities. It is from them that the next generation of leaders is likely to emerge.

There is another hopeful postscript to the day. A few weeks after my return, the Bill and Melinda Gates Foundation announced that it was giving the Kennedy Institute a $500,000 donation. The money will fund an 'immersive and interactive visitor experience that draws upon stories of youth movements'. Students will serve as advisors on the project.

4. Last Greyhound bus: only it isn't

Saturday 21 September

I'm not sorry to leave my gloomy apartment. It has been a strange place, stark and unwelcoming, with the bunk bed above me reminding me that I'm on my own. I have managed not to lock myself out (or lose Morris and the entry codes), but I have had my fill of hospitality by numbers.

I am into the home straight now. I don't want to leave anything to chance so arrive at the bus station in plenty of time. The five-storey building, with an impressive dome, was opened in 1995, just south of South Station, and the passenger facilities and bus platforms are up on the third floor, accessible via a long escalator or a glass-sided lift. It's busy today, with a broader selection of bus queues and a more upmarket clientele than I am used to, including tourists from Argentina, France, Japan and many more whose suitcase labels I can't get close enough to read.

The bus to New York fills up quickly. As it pulls out I realise that I am one of only two people who have an empty seat beside them. I put it down to a combination of good luck and subconscious learning. I haven't travelled 6,000 miles without acquiring the traits that make me unattractive to any passenger who might want to sit next to me: being untidy and disorganised (not difficult), spreading my food and my spare clothing out onto the other seat, plugging in devices to the power plugs – and avoiding eye contact.

We are soon out of Boston, with trees on either side, lining our route in their early autumn colours. There is not a cloud in the sky,

As the wheels roll me through Massachusetts I reflect on my 6,000-mile journey – and the Greyhound bus company that, with a couple of exceptions and some code shares, has brought me thus far. I had set off nervously, unsettled by some unwise meandering on social media and by the nervous laughter of Barbara's friends and family when I told them of my proposed adventure. But the trip has worked well and, with the two exceptions at the start of my solo travels, the buses have delivered me to my destination pretty much on time.

And safely: I still have a few more miles to go but it looks as if I'll make it in one piece. At times I have felt that some of the people around might have been a danger to me (or to themselves), but these encounters took place generally in and around bus stations, not in the buses. Once inside the buses, the rules – no undue noise, no drugs, no smoking, no violence – were strict, and strictly applied. My most fearful moment was when the young man in the trilby had started being sick and I started to worry I would catch whatever it was he might have had.

Most buses were surprisingly pleasant: comfortable seats, good leg room, WiFi, and power points that usually worked. Unlike last time I did not suffer from an aching posterior, and I never once had to blow up my cushion.

But the rides were not nearly as much fun as I remember them. The vibrant social scene my diary records in 1969 – when we students made up a critical mass of those travelling, and we mingled inside and outside the buses – has gone. Now, we have become wary of talking to others, and public discourse is diminished. We ride in our own bubbles, and our relationships are with our little devices, not our fellow travellers.

Those little devices have been great for bringing me the world beyond the bus, but not so good in helping me with my journey. I yearned for the 1969 days when we had month-long passes and real people to advise

us where to go and when. This time I have found planning and booking tedious, unsatisfying and – when things went wrong – infuriating.

The heroes of my trip, without doubt, have been the real live people working on the ground for Greyhound and other

On the buses 2019: 'Our relationships are with our little devices, not our fellow travellers'.

companies. There were far too few counter staff but they coped with delays, diversions and drunks. The security men and women, apparently without guns, maintained orderly lines, defused disputes and kept the buildings safe. The drivers were (with a few exceptions) courteous, helpful and reassuring, with skills ranging from persuading stroppy passengers not to shout into their mobile phone to steering their bus safely through horrendous traffic and tropical storms. I would like to think they get paid more than the people who designed the Greyhound website – but I'm sure they don't.

It's clearly not a crumbling, dangerous institution but a workable network and in some places an invaluable social service. It would be good to know that whoever buys Greyhound buses understands that.

As I muse I realise that something unexpected is happening. We are coming off the motorway and heading into Hartford, Connecticut. We leave the countryside and go through city streets to stop at the bus station. This is not in the schedule.

The driver stands to make an announcement. He has bad news and good, he says. The bus's indicators are not working and therefore the bus is unsafe. On the other hand there is another bus to New York due in an hour or two. The good news is diluted by the fact that, under questioning, he can't say if there will be enough seats for all.

This is the kind of situation for quick thinking and skilful use of the apps. I have enough self-awareness to realise I certainly haven't the latter, and adhere myself to a young Brit studying at Harvard and his girlfriend. They are already busy at work on their mobiles, and have come up with a choice of options: a train in half an hour or a Peter Pan bus about to leave. We opt for the bus and pay $18.50 each: I have stopped caring about spending money. So, it seems, have others: the queue behind us has lengthened considerably.

Within a few minutes we are boarding the rival bus. It seems comfortable enough, with all the usual facilities (though the WiFi isn't working today) – plus little pull-down tables on the seat in front; they would have come in useful for typing on Geoffrey. We get the usual homily about using phones responsibly and respecting the other passengers. And we're back on the road again.

I sleep first, then play with Morris. When I look up we are crossing an expanse of water, clear and still with small sailing ships in the middle distance and wooded hills on either side. I google and discover we are crossing the Hudson River. What a beautiful country this is, and what sights the buses have delivered over the past three months.

We approach the city where my trip started a week short of three months ago. I see high-rise buildings approaching fast. We turn into the Lincoln Tunnel, past a large hoarding advertising the services of some five-star injury lawyers called Lynch. (Who awards lawyers their stars? A panel of bankers, perhaps?) We pass into the tunnel and seem to be there for an unreasonably long time. Finally we burst out of the gloom and into the glare of New York City on a late summer Saturday afternoon, bursting with colour and noise and hundreds of little cameos playing out on the pavements as we pass.

I have completed my Greyhound bus trip as I started: not on a Greyhound bus. But only an hour late.

That night Barbara and I have dinner with Paula and Robert, as we did at the start of the trip. We talk about the world I have been travelling through, and Robert says that everybody is brought up these days to be important. I reckon the corollary is that everyone is brought up to think others are unimportant. I add to this that few people seem to value the big picture – as the Uber app showed me, for example, decision making has become a series of binary choices.

Tonight's Uber driver is an angry Indian. He had a good job back home working for the state pharmaceutical company, then came to the US for an arranged marriage. He has not been able to get a good job in America and is bitter about it.

'The economy is going down. Trump has no economic policy. The only thing he's interested in is his own economy.

'But he'll get re-elected.'

That's been a regular, if at times reluctant, refrain.

5. New York: full circle

Sunday 22 September

I wake up in the Stewart Hotel, New York City, where my adventure started: a soft bed (without another stacked on top), crisp sheets, Barbara beside me – and the pleasant thought that I don't have to worry about missing a bus ever again.

Today's plan is to recreate a photo that I think I took from the top of the Empire State Building in 1969. It shows a uniformed security guard in profile and beyond him a sea of tall buildings. Our friend Rita has introduced me to Hardy Phippen, a New York guide, and he has agreed to help me.

We meet early at the foot of the skyscraper: he is a man of the same vintage as myself and in an earlier life he was an actor. I show him my photo from 1969. He gently points out that it is not taken *from* the Empire State Building; it is *of* the Empire State Building and was taken from the Rockefeller Center. We go there.

Tickets for 'Top of the Rock' cost just over $100 for the three of us, roughly the same as we would have paid for the Empire State visit. We could have spent much more: an escorted tour would have set us back $460 per person.

Our lift whisks us up to the 70th floor. NBC is a major tenant in the building and, as we rise, extracts of notable NBC television productions flash across the ceiling. Show over, we walk out of the lift and towards the view. Since I was last here, my fear of heights has, well, heightened, so I stay as far away from the huge glass panels as I reasonably can.

Hardy shepherds us to the north side, towards Central Park. Between us and the park are a handful of tall, slender blocks, so new they aren't featured in the official guides that were handed out when we came in. He points to one towering building, summit still waiting to be clad: 'It's going to be the tallest apartment block in the western hemisphere.'

He points to another tower. 'Sting bought an apartment there for $65 million,' he says. 'And there's another apartment in that building

New York: from the top of the Rockefeller Centre half a century apart.

going for £238 million. If you're a billionaire you have to park your money somewhere. Manhattan property is better than a bank. These apartments may or may not be used, but they're where they hang their $50 million Andy Warhols. They're like safe deposit boxes.'

We climb higher still and out onto the open-air viewing platform where I find a uniformed security guard; unlike his 1969 predecessor he is not in a jacket but in shirtsleeves. I show him my 1969 picture and he readily agrees to pose. I take a series of pictures and as I am taking the last one I realise that a couple have moved into the middle ground and are posing with their selfie stick. It is very 21st century.

I realise that the term 'viewing platform' has become a misnomer. It is more of an outdoor photographic studio with the stunning view the background, not the focus. Visitors line up their shots: some point, some pout, some raise their arms, some cuddle each other. They don't do much viewing.

When we come down in the lift we get that reassuring sight of queues that have grown considerably since we were queuing. We walk through the

Rockefeller Centre, towards the skating rink that attracts the Christmas crowds. Hardy points to the restaurant beside it.

'That's closing,' he says. 'It's greed, greed, greed. Whenever a lease is finished they'll kick you out.'

We sit down over a coffee and Hardy tells us more about his city. 'New Yorkers had a lot of fun. They had a reputation for being rude but they weren't being rude – they were running at a different speed. Since 9/11 people are much more patient: if one person starts helping you another will join in, and then a third. You'll end up having to be the referee.

'9/11 made a huge difference. More than 2,750 people died here. In many ways it's a small town. Whether it was first, second or at most third hand, anyone who lived here knew somebody who was killed.'

The problem today is lack of affordable housing. 'Smart people from China are buying houses over here. The value of apartments is going up and up. Eventually the laws of supply and demand will catch up. New buildings are having a hard time selling. We've overbuilt. I think there's another, bigger, crash coming in the next few years.'

We walk over to East 51st and Park Avenue, which is where I had taken another picture in 1969. Judging on the exteriors alone, nothing much has changed. But it has. The luxurious hotel nearby, bristling with police guarding visiting heads of state attending the UN General Assembly, is owned by the Sultan of Brunei. Down the road is the Waldorf Astoria, which is closed for renovation by its new owners, a Chinese company.

On our way back I tell Hardy about my time in Boston, and ask him if he has heard of Phillips Academy.

'Heard of it?' he says. 'I went there.'

He loved it. 'It's much more international and much more diverse than many schools. There are major endowments, and if you need a scholarship you can get one.

'Being a boarding school it's well organised, with lots of extra-curricular activities. Things like music and art are disappearing from the public schools. It's an extraordinarily broad-based student body, and that's not always true of schools in the suburbs.'

That evening we return to Barbara's cousin Jim and his wife Barbara in West Orange. They have gone to some trouble to devise a 1969 menu so they can cook me a celebration meal. The first course is iceberg lettuce and diced tomatoes. Dessert is Jell-O Mold, a circle of fruit in a jelly mould with some cream whipped up in something that looks like an oversize jam jar.

The main course is turkey tetrazzini – the most popular American dish of 1969 according to the *Daily Meal* website: turkey in white sauce with pasta, breadcrumbs and frozen peas (which apparently are also celebrating their golden jubilee this year; they seem to have been with us for ever). Researching the dish uncovers a coincidence. it was named after the coloratura soprano Luisa Tetrazzini, who is believed to have made the first broadcast from a New York hotel in 1920 and was honoured with several dishes by its executive chef, Louis Paquet. The hotel in question was the McAlpin, where I stayed for my first two nights in New York in 1969.

I talk with cousin Jim about my experiences at the climate strike and wonder how it compares with the protests of 1969. Jim says: 'When the kids were shot at Kent State – and bear in mind I was living in Princeton – a lot of the students were out like a shot. We went on strike for several days. No-one was angry with the school, but we were angry with what had happened.

'All the kids whose parents worked at the university walked out of school. The others who were on the football team – we called them the "swifties" – were in the minority. They did not participate. Some of them went on to serve in Vietnam – they were the ones enlisting.

'These were kids who believed in the war and that it was their duty to serve. A lot of our cohort gave them a really hard time. We were white, liberal, intellectual kids: we had no sensitivity. Four or five of those who went to Vietnam never came back.

'But the tenor of the march last Friday was different. The Vietnam War rallies were larger. The unrest was really profound – vicious and brutal. People blew up buildings. There was violence at the National Convention.

'We now give respect to the military; people are careful to separate those who fight from the government. This time there was a peacefulness and dignity that was rather nice.'

Monday 23 September

I spent a lot of time in 1969 visiting courtrooms – they were free and dry, and I had just taken a criminology course. Some imaginative sentencing caught my eye: a group of young men found trespassing on forestry land were ordered to do 'voluntary' work for the forestry authority; a man with a drink problem yearning to go home to Oklahoma was ordered to pay his lawyer a fixed amount of money each month until he had raised the fare.

I haven't been inside any courts this year, so my godson Michael is taking me. He is British-born, the son of one of my colleagues when I trained as a journalist, now an American citizen and a lawyer.

He picks me up at noon in his Mercedes and we drive to Newark. Here as elsewhere, he tells me, the post-World War 2 flight to the suburbs changed the demographics and led to a period when it was a dangerous place to be. Here as elsewhere the assassination of Martin Luther King led to a week of rioting.

'Newark has never really recovered. There have been efforts in terms of population but it's still a high-crime area,' says Michael. 'The city is trying to build itself up but it's very slow.'

We talk about the impact of changing technology. 'Our new generation of attorneys are people who grew up with the internet in school,' he says. 'They never had to go to a library to look things up. They always had their mobile phones so they could talk to their friends in informal social settings and were not used to having to talk with their parents' friends. So they've got used to having options. If they don't like something they will do something else.'

He takes me for lunch to Hobby's, a diner founded by a D-Day veteran in 1962. 'It looks like nowhere that anyone who cares for their personal safety would go,' says Michael, adding that judges regularly eat there. It is the kind of diner that I have come to expect, with the menu as it should be (I had a cup of chicken soup and half a corned beef sandwich), and the waitress is quite charming.

We walk over to the federal courthouse in an unseasonal 91 degrees (33°C). Security is much higher than I remember in 1969. Michael flashes his lawyer's credentials and is waved through, but I am searched thoroughly and warned not to use my phone in court.

Michael finds a court that is scheduled for hearings. A handful of people wait on the public benches, and a pair of lawyers talk earnestly. After about half an hour some US marshals come in (we can tell because they have the words emblazoned across their jackets). Then the judge appears, a white man of late middle age. A few moments later, and from a different door, come two more marshals, both white, flanking two African Americans dressed in violent yellow with their hands shackled.

The two men in custody are appealing for bail. The first, who has a long record of drug dealing and prison, was involved in a car chase during which he threw a gun out of his car. He does not get bail. 'Drug crimes have their victims,' says the judge. 'The weight of evidence here seems very strong.' The defence lawyer has not tried to rebut the prosecutor's arguments, Michael points out quietly.

The second man is a little older and has better luck. It seems that while we were waiting his lawyer and a court official have agreed that he can be released to go back to California where he will be electronically tagged. He will be subject to restrictions, including no alcohol, but will be able to drive his children to and from school, presumably to enable his partner to go to work.

And that's it – my up-to-date taste of US criminal justice – calm and relaxed. But it was a tiny part of what is clearly big business. Costs are hard to find but a few years ago a commonly agreed figure for incarceration was $80 billion a year.

Tuesday 24 September

It looks as if I'm going to make it.

My final planned activity is a visit to the Essex County Senior Wellness Day. Jim's wife, confusingly also called Barbara, is volunteering on a stand for the AARP (American Association of Retired Persons). I am curious to see the event, particularly because today's pensioners are the generation I mixed with so happily in 1969.

This is an annual event, now in its 14th year, held in the local ice rink and attracting 3,000 pensioners. Each is given breakfast, a lunch box (salads rolls, cookies, water and more), a bag of vegetables to take home, and free admission to the zoo next door. And entertainment is provided: we are waved into the hall by a senior citizen on stilts in red hat and green jacket. Inside, the East Orange Silver Steppers are performing a dance routine; they are dressed in white trousers, white gloves, red shirts and glittery silver caps.

Queues are everywhere: I ask one person what they are queuing for and they're not quite sure. Some 70 stalls are giving out pens and information: Rutgers University, free special phones for people with hearing loss, sheriff's office, colorectal screening and one under a banner reading 'Stop Prescription Price Gouging'.

I go up to an official who turns out to be a key organiser – Anthony Puglisi, Essex County Director of Public Information. 'We wanted to create an event for seniors where they could come out and have fun but also get information. So we came up with this event.'

I fail to draw out of him how much it all cost, though he said they always tried to attract sponsorship, and more than 200 county employees had volunteered to help. Notices of the event look down from many prime spots and are on the carrier bags filled with free food. At the top is the name of the Essex County Executive, Joseph N DiVincenzo Jr. It clearly won't do his re-election chances any harm.

After a while we take advantage of our free zoo admission. Jim says it was small and run-down when he was young, but now it is well equipped. We watch a lion strutting around his arena, and some monkeys hanging about on branches. I learn that the terms buffalo and bison are not interchangeable: the bison is American, the buffalo is an immigrant (and has no hump). I come face to face with an alligator (not a crocodile, though this has been another confusing area for me on this journey). He (or she) is huge and armoured, but thankfully the eyes are closed and not staring into mine. I think back to that wet night in Orlando when I scoured the bushes for the eyes of hungry alligators.

Then, on our way to the giraffe house, the good luck that has been with me on my trip finally runs out. I trip up over a grille (or possibly over my own feet) and execute a perfect forward fall onto my face.

Splat!

I am stunned. I spit out a bit of tooth and blood spills out of my chin onto my favourite turquoise polo shirt. My jaw feels unaligned. For a moment I can't get up.

Jim recommends against calling an ambulance because it will convey me to a hospital where I will be charged lots of money and miss my plane home. Instead he drives me to his local minor injuries unit.

I am used to the deal by now. I start by filling in a form and putting up a deposit – in this case $100. After a wait of about half an hour I am screened by a nurse, then wait some more. I am tended by Lorena, an ever-smiling physicians' assistant, and a student PA, Jessica, who feels my ribs, x-rays my jaw, sympathises about my tooth and sews up my chin. It needs seven stitches. They reassure me that it's not as bad as it could have been, and this time they don't slag off the National Health Service.

'You did amazing,' says Lorena as I leave. I agree. The bill comes to $185.

With the danger over, those around me turn out to be less than sympathetic. Jim tells me that I have just performed a 'face plant', and offers to make me a turkey tetrazzini smoothie. My wife points out sweetly: 'You said you wanted to end the book with a bang!'

So much for senior wellness days.

The trip is over: stitched up after the senior wellness day.

pack through the pain. The television is on and Nancy Pelosi, the Speaker of the House, comes on to announce that the Democrats are starting impeachment investigations of President Trump.

6. Back home: the reckoning

I fly home with my pain, my memories and five long-expired Greyhound e-tickets that I can't budge from Morris the mobile.

The man at the airport x-ray machine asks whether I am over 75. My trips – the long one around America and the short, sharp one in the zoo – must have taken their toll on my appearance. I am not that surprised: throughout my journey people kept asking me whether I was enjoying myself, but that wasn't the right question. It was an expedition, not a holiday – and it tested me. In many ways I was unsuited and under-equipped for the journey and knew it.

Yet I wouldn't have missed it for anything. It's pretty cool to realise that my 72-year-old self was able to do what my 22-year-old self had done, even though this time I had to ask others to put my bags in the overhead racks. It's good to have a confidence boost early in your eighth decade. It made me realise that I could still muddle through on my own. More importantly, it underscored what a privilege it has been to be part of a long-standing and happy relationship, and how much easier it is to face the world when you have a Barbara to be loved by and to love.

I never came to love Geoffrey and Morris, though, but we came to an understanding. I still find electronic devices annoying, unreliable and unforgivably unforgiving of errors. But I now realise how enriching they can be, particularly when they bring a world of information to the palm of your hand. I have extended my skills and knowledge – and had a timely reminder that learning should never stop.

My moments from the trip are now stacked up in my memory like the abandoned aeroplanes in the Mojave: stunning coach drives at sunset and sunrise; the Queen Mary restored from a rusting hulk to a holiday destination; the river at Covington still flowing gently; the history museums with their measured narratives; a real live mayor interviewed at the second attempt; pacing out a Saturn rocket in Houston; another soaking at Niagara Falls; and the sea of selfies on the top of a New York skyscraper.

One of my more vivid memories was coming face to face with a stripped-down Houston Astrodome standing abandoned in an empty car park, a stark reminder of how things change. In 1969 the Astrodome blew me away, and for half a century I have treasured its memory as representing the American qualities of flair, imagination, invention, confidence, capability, dottiness and extravagance. Then it was the future; now it's history.

I saw many more changes wrought in the last half-century, for good and ill: town centres denuded and their shopping centres knocked down; factories and family farms closed; food portions so big that small plates are back in fashion (though without small prices); men holding hands with men, and women holding hands with women – and everyone's hand holding a mobile phone. What hasn't seemed to have changed much, though, as I noticed from the GAP store golden anniversary window, is how we dress.

Changes to the national psyche were less easy to identify. What attracted me in 1969 was that despite divisions, assassinations, riots and war most people were positive. The main event that summer was man's first step on the moon: America was Great and you didn't need to wear a red MAGA cap to make the point. We disagreed on many things, but we talked to each other – and generally agreed that the world could be made a better place.

Nixon was unpopular then, as was the war he inherited. But I don't remember being conscious of two tribes facing each other so uncompromisingly, with two sets of certainties, as they do today. And with that division I sense that the mojo has gone. At the national level anger and criticism have replaced compromise and leadership. The slogan Make America Great Again is not a cry of hope but a cry of despair.

And there is plenty of fear. I can't remember immigration being a major issue in 1969 – but it certainly was in 2019. Everywhere I went the contribution of immigrants shone out, from Tesla's pioneering efforts with generating hydro-electric energy to the smiling people who served me my meals and drove the Ubers. Everywhere I saw signs that jobs were available, and the people I talked to – particularly in the hospitality industry – said they were desperate for more workers.

Yet the notion that the country is under siege has taken hold. Even the Uber drivers, many of them recent immigrants themselves, told me they didn't like how Trump was talking, and they didn't mind people coming to

America … but there were clearly dangerous characters trying to get into the country, and they needed to be stopped.

The gun culture makes life seem even more insecure. Before my 1969 trip, pretty much the only guns I'd seen in real life were in museums or carried by the guardsmen at Buckingham Palace. I was shocked when I got to America and saw them carried casually on the hips of policemen. But my 1969 diary has no mention of mass shootings, though half a century later they were taking place on a regular basis – 53 deaths alone in the month of August. Each time they were followed by a ferocious backlash against anyone who suggested that the problem might need addressing.

I kept asking those I met whether they felt optimistic about the future. There was always a pause. Then came a range of answers, from the student of political science who said, 'I think we're going to be the best,' to the caution from the Pasadena police chief: 'We want to make sure we're not living through the last days of the Roman Republic.'

And there I was going to end this story. But I realised that I needed – for my sake and for that of the book - to answer the question myself. After my two expeditions and the gap of 50 years, how do *I* see the future of the USA?

I went back to my 1969 writings and found my farewell article. It reminded me of all the things I loved then (and still do) about America – the outrageous landscapes, the can-do attitude, the erudition, the curiosity, the innovation, the creativity. What I would miss most of all, according to my article, would be 'the hospitality and kindness and humour'.

That set me thinking about all the good things I witnessed half a century later: the young shop assistant who nursed me through my first separation from Morris; children in the technology museum in San Jose totally at home with innovations that had me baffled; the energy and optimism of Boston schoolchildren demonstrating for their future in unseasonably hot weather with clever slogans and youthful passion; the succession of Uber drivers, many of them migrants from war-torn areas, swelling with pride for their children, now successful American citizens with good jobs; the gay pride event with ordinary people celebrating without fear what would have been criminal differences; the two ladies in Orlando who looked into their purses because they thought I needed some food, and in the same city the modest young woman buying a meal for a homeless man.

There's plenty there to give us hope for America's future.

Author's biography

After his American Grand Tour and an internship on the Pasadena Star-News in 1969, Tim Albert worked as a journalist on local, national and medical publications. He then spent nearly two decades trying to teach health professionals how to write effectively, and is the author of four books on medical writing and a memoir. He lives in Surrey with his selfless wife Barbara and a needy garden.

If you've enjoyed Two Summers, you might enjoy the back story.

MOSTLY WE HAD IT GOOD
— A BABY BOOMER'S JOURNEY —

When Prime Minister Harold Macmillan famously stated, 'You've never had it so good', the 10-year-old Tim Albert was being miserable, stuck on a hill in an all-boy school. But despite an at times unhappy start, some dreadful mistakes and a rather unpleasant illness, he came to realise that he had been born in a lucky place and at a lucky time – and was lucky to be still alive.

In this idiosyncratic and insightful look at the second half of the twentieth century, the author combines family material with his own recollections and writings as a journalist. He drops, albeit briefly, such names as Teddy Kennedy, EM Forster, Libby Purves, Jimmy Savile and Saddam Hussein. He also witnesses such historic milestones as the post-war recovery, the drive for fairer education – and the first attacks on the NHS.

'I was totally hooked, spending the rest of the day reading it until I had finished. It is beautifully written and full of enthralling facts... a rare good autobiography' - Dr Stephen Lock, former editor, BMJ

Available from www.timalbert.co.uk

Also from Elbow Publishing:

The Silver Thread: a journey through Balkan craftsmanship
By Elizabeth Gowing

From the mines in the cantos of Dante, to the prizes stolen in the wars of the 'nineties, follow the silver thread through Balkan history and culture to the new generation of craftswomen facing their uncertain future.

The Rubbish Picker's Wife: an unlikely friendship in Kosovo
By Elizabeth Gowing

How can you find the best rubbish pastures for scavenging? How can you free children to go to school rather than to go out begging? Can mayonnaise deal with headlice? An account of an extraordinary charity, and the challenges and delights of finding your community a long way from home.

Edith and I: on the trail of an Edwardian traveller in Kosovo
By Elizabeth Gowing

In 1900 Europe's last wilderness was explored by a stout, stubborn English-woman who travelled in her tam o'shanter across Albania's Accursed Mountains. One hundred years later, Elizabeth Gowing follows Edith Durham's trail into Kosovo, finding not only an Edwardian heroine but also a guide for today.

Also from Elbow Publishing:

Death and the Dreadnought
By Robert Wilton

A new hero. A new series of rollicking historical entertainments. Murder, mystery, melodrama, a couple of sentimental music hall numbers, significant incidents on battleships, thrilling chases in motor cars, desperate escapades on railway trains, fights to the death armed with only a duck sandwich, all in correct gentleman's attire.

Albania and The Balkans: essays in honour of Sir Reginald Hibbert
Edited by James Pettifer

A century of Albanian and Balkan history is seen from an unusual variety of perspectives in this collection of essays in honour of a man who parachuted into the country during the Second World War.

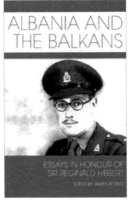

Printed in Poland
by Amazon Fulfillment
Poland Sp. z o.o., Wrocław

86744060R00148